FISHING ROUND THE WORLD

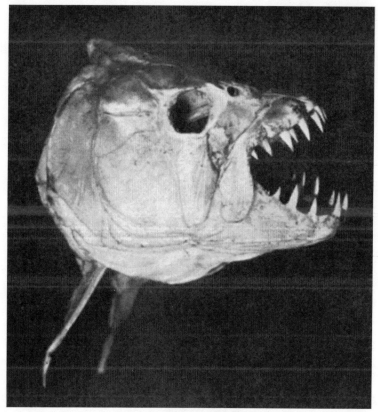

SKULL OF A TIGERFISH

BLUE WATER CLASSICS

FISHING ROUND THE WORLD

LEANDER J. McCORMICK

LYONS PRESS

Guilford, Connecticut

An imprint of Globe Pequot, the trade division of
The Rowman & Littlefield Publishing Group, Inc.
4501 Forbes Blvd., Ste. 200
Lanham, MD 20706
www.rowman.com

Distributed by NATIONAL BOOK NETWORK

First published in 1937 by Charles Scribner's Sons, New York

First Derrydale Press edition 2000

First Lyons Press edition 2022

British Library Cataloguing in Publication Information available

Library of Congress Cataloging-in-Publication Data available

ISBN 978-1-4930-6550-9 (paper : alk. paper)

♾™ The paper used in this publication meets the minimum requirements of American National
Standard for Information Sciences—Permanence of Paper for Printed Library Materials, ANSI/
NISO Z39.48-1992.

ACKNOWLEDGMENT

I wish to thank the *Sportsman* magazine and its editor, Richard E. Danielson, Esq., for kind permission to reprint in this book three articles which appeared in the magazine in abridged form.

I wish also to thank J. R. Norman, Esq., F.L.S., F.Z.S., Assistant Keeper, Department of Zoology at the British Museum (Natural History), for his very valuable help in identifying many of the fish mentioned herein, and for other scientific data he has kindly provided.

CONTENTS

LIST OF ILLUSTRATIONS

I

AN ANGLER EXPLAINS AND CONFESSES

FISHING is the oldest of all sports if one admits that when the first amœba absorbed another amœba in the simmering ooze of primeval time the fishing season may be said to have been officially opened. Ever since that remote instant fishing has steadily continued as the world's most popular and agreeable method of obtaining food and distraction.

We have gone a long way since the first cannibal amœba, and other pastimes have encroached on fishing, so that it no longer remains the universal sport. I would, however, venture to maintain that to this day no endeavour exerts over its subjects a more imperious dominion. Nevertheless it is curious that one must be born a fisherman, and that without the innate urge, a love of fishing cannot be acquired. The lack of this stimulus is a peculiarity which those who specialise in the study of human appetencies may be able to comprehend; but the angler is nonplussed when he discovers that his best friend, who adores shooting, has a dislike for fishing.

My brother, Edward, who is otherwise a fine fellow and a good sportsman, once spent an afternoon beside the Test, "greatest of Trout rivers," watching me as with bated breath I stalked superb fish. But I could not cajole him into wetting a line for any of them.

Man undoubtedly got his first taste for fish when he picked up and devoured those he discovered washed ashore after a storm. Later he speared them with a pointed stick or captured them in shallows and small bays, first with his bare hands, and then in primitive traps. Later he used crudely woven nets and learned to catch them on barbless hooks.

Without attempting to explore the psychology of early mankind, I presume that through all these stages in the art of fishing the purpose of man's endeavours was to catch fish and subsequently eat them.

Only in recent times has man put himself to considerable exertion to catch fish with the intention of returning them alive to the water. When this development occurred, fishing became a pure sport. Soon after this, however, man discovered that his genius enabled him to employ weapons which gave the fish very little chance of escape, and so we have reached the stage in which the sportsman handicaps himself by fishing with rod or line so fragile that unless great skill is employed success is problematical, since the fish can break the tackle. Man cannot go much further than this to obtain an equitable encounter unless he gives up fishing altogether.

To show how readily the desire to fish can be acquired, providing the individual has the innate urge, I would submit the following case history.

My first day's fishing was from a pier in Lake Michigan. We were a large party; we had bamboo poles, and, with red worms, in a couple of hours we caught 156 Perch. They were very good to eat and I think we disposed of every one of them. I was five years old, and after that I knew what I wanted to do in life. I was often down at the pier but never again did the Perch seem so numerous. Then came an interval of some years during which the opportunity to fish was lacking. My family moved to England. Once we went to Ullswater for the summer holidays. Now, in spite of the long lapse of time since the previous experience, without urging, without the example of another angler, and without any inducement except the personal desire to fish, I obtained some balls of string and a lot of hooks. I then began to put out night-lines for Eels. I used to spend the whole day rowing strenuously about the lake, tending my lines. Sometimes I caught two or three dozen Eels in a day. What I did with them I cannot remember.

There was again a long interval, and then came Amber Jack, Bagre, Barbel, Barracuda, Blue Shark, Bóga, Bonefish, Bonito, Brook Trout, Brown Trout, Catfish, Channel Bass, Chub, Codfish, Dolphin, Dorado, Gar Pike, Grayling, Great Northern Pike, Grouper, Hammerhead Shark, Jewfish, Kahawai, Karuka, Kingfish, Ladyfish, Lake Trout, Large Mouth Bass, Mackerel, Mako Shark, Mamba, Mojarrita, Mputa, Muskellunge, Needletooth, Ngassa, Ngege, Nile Perch, Pacú, Palometa, Paraná Salmón, Patí, Piper, Piraña, Piro Porá, Rainbow Trout, Red Snapper, Reremai Shark, Rock Bass, Sabalo, Sailfish, Salmon, Salmon Trout, Sand Shark, Sebago Salmon, Shovel Nose Shark, Skipjack, Small Mouth Bass, Snapper, Snook, Sole, Spanish Mackerel, Spanish Pompano, Stingray, Striped Bass, Striped Marlin, Steelhead Trout, Sunfish, Tarpon, Tigerfish, Trevalli, Trutta Criolla, Tuna, Wachone, Wahoo, Walleyed Pike, Weakfish, Whiting, Yellow Tail,[1] and many others of which I have long since forgotten the names, if I ever knew them.

Some of them, following prehistoric precedent, I have driven into shallows or small bays and caught with my bare hands or in nets. Some I have speared, others I have caught with heavy tackle to eat or mount or release alive. Others I have angled for with light tackle — too light to be sure of success.

Some were more sport to catch than others, but I assert that all fishing is good, though some is better.

---

1 The identity of all fish designated by popular or local names can be verified in the index.

Formerly the capture was important. I sought for good fishing conditions, and was annoyed when I had nothing to show for my angling, but now such considerations do not greatly affect me. If there are fish to be got, then, let the weather be good or bad, let the tides, temperature, and other portents come as they will, I am content so long as I am fishing. Nor will I distress myself too much if at the end of the day my creel is empty, my gaff unblooded.

This book tells of some of my fishing, but let none of my readers expect a catalogue of record fish successfully subdued after heroic encounters. I have no such stories to relate. My fishing has extended over four continents, but I have accomplished nothing that could not be done by the most commonplace angler if he had covered an equal mileage. I profess to enjoy angling as much as any man, and have had the opportunity to indulge it in many places, but I do not pretend to be a great fisherman, nor to be expert in the technique of angling for any single kind of fish.

Readers must, therefore, forgive me if I have made statements which in the light of their more exact knowledge are incorrect, or if I have offered opinions which are obviously based on insufficient experience.

2

ON THE ALTO PARANÁ

I ARRANGED to go to Paraguay chiefly because a boundary dispute between that country and Bolivia had forced some wretched newspaperman to look up South American history in an encyclopædia. From his labours emerged an article on Paraguay and its tragic career which so interested me that in the course of a round-the-world trip I decided to make a detour to that little-known land.

From Buenos Aires I was planning to voyage up the Paraná River to Asunción when I met Gustave Garcia, an Argentine friend, who volunteered to obtain for me the best accommodation available. A few days later he told me that he had secured the bridal suite at a small extra charge. In due course the little steamer cast off from the dock, and I went to examine my cabin. As I passed along the alleyway, I could see through some of the open doors that all the cabins appeared to be similar. Each within very small limits contained two berths, one above the other, with a narrow foot space opposite in which was located the wash-basin.

The *camarero* who accompanied me with my luggage enquired for *la señora*. He seemed quite depressed when I shook my head, but he opened the door of the bridal suite with a flourish. I saw at a glance that the interior designer who had planned this room was a thoroughly practical man. The cabin was the same size as all the others, but instead of two separate berths there had been somehow inserted a double bed which occupied the entire interior.

Apart from the disadvantage of having nowhere in which to stand up to shave, my trip to Asunción proved very agreeable. I spent a good part of the time playing chess with a number of young students on their way to Corrientes. We should have had still better games if they had possessed a slightly more extensive knowledge of the Queen's Pawn Opening.

After Corrientes the shore became less cultivated and more interesting. One thousand two hundred and sixty-five kilometres from Buenos Aires I saw the first alligator, and thereafter kept observing them. From time to time we passed troops of apparently wild horses, just as I had expected. The bird life, particularly the birds of prey, was fascinating, as was the foliage of the river-banks. Among other trees there were masses of paradise trees[1] in bloom with a brilliant magenta flower, which in bouquets covered the trees completely, so that not a leaf was visible.

At Asunción I put up at the Hotel del Paraguay, which will always remain, I believe, my favourite hotel. It consisted of a series of large rooms in a one-storey building surrounding a courtyard, at one end of which were the public rooms. In the courtyard grew most of the flora of Paraguay. I stayed in that country for several weeks, observing its inhabitants, perhaps the most courageous of all races. Occasionally I made shooting expeditions with the hotel proprietor which were astonishing from every point of view. I will digress for a moment, to tell of an experiment I made there with ants.

Paraguay seems alive with this the most populous visible creature in the world. There were many different varieties, and among them I discovered the leaf-cutter or parasol ant, which is of a delightful chocolate-red colour. As is well known, this ant has three sorts of workers: the minima, which are only about a quarter of an inch long, the media,

[1] A species of *Simaruba*.

about half an inch long, and the fighters, almost three-quarters of an inch long. These last are armed with enormous and formidable pincers. They act as guards for the busy lines of media, which spend their time cutting out little circular pieces of leaves and transporting these treasures to their nest, bearing them like small green parasols over their heads. The leaves are later chewed up very fine to produce a " soil " which is cultivated by the minima, and on which grows a species of fungus – the sole food of the ants. Besides mankind there is no creature except these ants and certain termites which has learnt how to raise crops for future consumption. I wished to ascertain whether the small workers had lost their fighting powers through being always protected by the warriors, and so I captured one of the media and put it under a glass on a sheet of paper. I then added an unwelcome neighbour in the form of a black tree ant, nearly twice the size of the leaf-cutter. For a time the two circled their enclosure in a snobbish manner, without paying attention to each other. Finally the black ant decided that one was company but two was a crowd, and attacked the red ant. He seized the leaf-cutter by a hind leg. No battle ensued. The red ant simply feigned death. The black ant held on for some time, and then, letting go, toddled away, apparently in a distressed condition. In a few moments they both seemed to recover, and shortly the black ant attacked again, with the same result; but the black ant now left the conflict even more upset. The third time the black ant attacked was still more tragic, for within a brief interval the red ant walked away intact, trailing after it the black ant, stone dead, a silent witness to an encounter in which the fighting had been one-sided, and in which the aggressor was the one who paid the penalty. Needless to say, the black ant had been poisoned by an emanation of formic acid from the red ant.

With regret I left Asunción and Paraguay and proceeded

to Posadas. As I have related elsewhere, my purpose in going to Posadas was to make from there a fishing expedition for Dorado up the Alto Paraná. Of Dorado (the Gold*en* Fish) I give an account later, and this chapter will be confined to the other fish captured during the voyage.

Through a friend I had been put in touch with James MacDonald, the local superintendent of the railway, and it was he who undertook the task of obtaining a suitable launch and crew for me. The launch *Iris*, which he found, belonged to Señor Alberto Engels, a Hungarian who had settled there. One may well ask, by the way, why anyone should settle in Posadas. Over a period of some weeks negotiations for chartering the launch proceeded. Some days the price would go up, and some days down. In the end I had a contract signed by Engels ; but when I got to Posadas to take over the launch, Engels concluded that he had not extorted enough out of me, and wanted to go back on his signature. MacDonald, with infinite tact, closed the deal by saying that I would pay extra after the trip if the launch proved all right. The amount was not specified, but Engels was satisfied with this.

The next two days were occupied in buying stores. It is astonishing how difficult it is to calculate what is needed for eight persons for twenty-one days. There are so many apparently unimportant necessities, the lack of which can spoil a trip. In the end, however, everything was procured. But I had not reckoned on meat. For one thing, our icebox had only a limited capacity, and I decided that we must catch fish to replace our stock of meat, or go without. Of course, we had to rely on canned vegetables and milk. The drink requirements, too, had to be carefully estimated and then doubled. At last, with two companions, Jock and Peter, whom I had discovered in the course of my wanderings, we started off. Half Posadas was at the dock to wish us *bon voyage*.

THE *IRIS* ON THE ALTO PARANÁ

As we proceeded north by east, the river began to unfold. We found that upstream the launch would do about six kilometres an hour ; not a great speed, but, in view of the current, reasonable enough. In a short time after leaving Posadas all cultivation along the river ceased, and the jungle closed down on us. The river-banks rose from forty to two hundred and forty feet above low water, and were hidden by the luxuriant tropical forest. As we progressed we saw in clumps the curious "Herring-bone" tree[1] which throws off its branches along two of its sides, like a fern, giving the effect of a giant Herring bone. Apart from this and bamboo, which was easily recognisable, the other growth was so confused as to be indistinguishable. At the water's edge the river was rocky, and it was on these rocks that we frequently saw alligators sunning themselves. From time to time a vivid yellow patch on the shore attracted our attention. We found out later that these spots of colour consisted of hundreds of blood-drinking butterflies which had found some carcase on which to feed.

At Isla Toroý, 1,583 kilometres above Buenos Aires, where we made our first stop, the river had already changed its character. From a broad and turgid stream with a fairly even flow, it had narrowed considerably. The current now seemed to seek certain channels according to the underlying rock formations. We anchored downstream from the island, and I then inaugurated a routine which proved most satisfactory throughout the trip. As soon as the launch was tied up for the night the crew came forward and were each given a ration of caña. This drink, which is a rum made from sugar-cane, was so fiery and potent that an ordinary man could scarcely taste it and survive. My crew, however, managed each one to lap up the best part of a tumbler every night *con mucho gusto*,[2] and without even

---

[1] It is curious that, though this is far the most noticeable tree along the river-banks, I have been unable to identify it either at the British Museum or Kew Gardens.

[2] With much appreciation.

becoming hilarious. Later, as we were preparing to retire, one of them came aft with his guitar and played us to sleep with the Gaucho music of the country.

The next day we continued north. The jungle gave a most grotesque appearance ; not that the individual trees were particularly unusual, but because they seemed to grow in every direction, thus presenting a wild and disorderly form. As we anchored that evening at Tabaý Alves we rigged up mosquito nets over the cabin windows, and this proved most necessary. The night was barely fallen when millions of Ephemeridæ descended on us. In spite of our precautions, masses of them, attracted by the light, somehow sifted through any crevice into the saloon. They filled my ears, my hair, and stuck to my fountain-pen. These insects, I found, are called *Bichos de Pulvo* (powder bugs), and it is claimed that their winged life cycle only lasts eight minutes. Their egg-sacs, of a pale mustard colour, dissolved when the insect died and left a heavy golden powder all over the launch, and it is from this peculiarity that they obtain their name. My friends, as they had no diary to write, went fishing, and it was not long before they had landed three Bagre,[1] huge and fearful-looking Catfish weighing from eight to ten pounds. These fish had long feelers, and were of a horrible purple colour with greatly distended paunches. Peter caught as well a Pacú of fifteen pounds. This fish put up a strong fight for a short time and subsequently proved very good to eat. It was of the shape of a Sunfish, being flat vertically, and had a firm, white flesh. It is noticeable that all fish with deeply compressed bodies make an excellent defence against the angler, the shape of their bodies affording them advantages in braking power denied fish of the more usual fusiform type. We discovered later that the best bait for these Pacú is wild oranges, and when we came to a wild orange tree

1 See Appendix Note, p. 295.

growing near the river-bank, we would stop, if we were in need of food, and bait our hooks with a whole orange. It was rarely that we failed thus to provide ourselves with a fish course. The Bagre came in useful, too, as we were able to exchange them for a dozen eggs and a litre of fresh warm milk at the tumbledown shanty of an Indian near by. Thus does commerce flourish by barter in a country where money has only a theoretical value. It was here, too, that we caught several small fish with large silvery scales, weighing about six ounces each, which are called Mojarritas. They have a very curious forward shape, as their back and head is all in one straight line, but they have deep, thin bodies curving up to their mouths, which are on the top of their heads. The outline of the fish, therefore, gives the profile of the small segment of a circle with a forked tail added at one end. These fish are cannibals.[1]

It was this day that I had a small adventure which had its comic aspects. The launch had tied up for the night in a still but deep backwater, and for some reason I wished to go forward. The central cabin being filled with our beds, I had progressed along a small projection of the hull which paralleled the superstructure. I had my rod in one hand and with the other kept catching hold at intervals to a brass rail along the cabin roof in order to maintain my balance. Without paying sufficient attention, by mistake I grasped a bamboo pole which was lying there, instead of the rail, and was at once precipitated into the river. I was fished out almost immediately by a sailor in the skiff, but was told by Peter that my face, when I emerged from the water, was a picture. It was the birthday of Carlito, the steward, and that evening, as I handed him a double ration of caña, Jock asked him what else he would like besides for his birthday. For a moment his expression was quite blank,

---

[1] I have tried to identify this fish, but have failed. I believe it is of the genus *Anacyrtus*, and it is certainly of the Characin family.

but then, breaking into a broad grin, he admitted that he would like to see *El Patrón* fall into the river again.

We continued our voyage the next day, and began to encounter the *correderas* and *remolinos*[1] which have given such a dread reputation to the river. The launch shivered and shook as our pilot, Captain Zarza, manœuvred to follow the true course upstream. This was by no means an easy task, and was complicated by the extraordinary illusion that in parts the river itself seemed to be flowing the wrong way. As we advanced the river became more wild in appearance, while on little spits and sandbars from time to time we saw the tracks of wild animals. Once the pugs of a jaguar showed plainly through my glasses, and in many places there were traces of *Carpincho*,[2] a kind of giant water rodent. At night we could often hear them grunting and splashing along the shore.

After a few days we found our food supply running low. One evening all the meat was gone except three small pieces which we saved for bait. The ice, too, was exhausted, and we had no more milk. As we anchored that night our lines were at once in the water ; we were hoping to catch our dinner, but failed, and had to content ourselves with bread and potatoes. This skimpy meal ended, we went out with landing-nets to try for some fish we heard jumping near the bank. Presently we had caught one. It was a silvery fish of about a pound, which looked something like a Florida Bonefish. It had a very small mouth, and was a mud-eating fish called Sabalo. We continued trying to net these fish, and finally with our torches located many in a small bayou. In a short time we found we had a greater number than we required, and counted up twenty-eight in the canoe. But they did not prove very good eating, even

[1] Rapids and whirlpools.
[2] This is the local name for the Capybara, largest rodent in the world. It resembles an immense guinea-pig, and its body is covered with stiff brown hairs. The hide of these animals makes into excellent leather for gloves and such purposes.

with hunger sauce. Again we tried bartering, and this time, in exchange for a dozen Sabalo, obtained a young goat. All my life I had heard how delicious kid tasted. Let no one be deceived by such tales. This kid, at any rate, was too tough to chew, and was quite tasteless even as a ragout into which we later tried to convert it.

We had now reached Puerto Aguirre, which is a short distance up the Iguazú River, and we went ashore to view the most beautiful of all the great falls in the world. We motored along a red earth track through the same jungle we had been observing from the river all these days. But now we could appreciate it much better. As we proceeded along the narrow road we passed many giant montbretias, some of them five feet high, with scarlet flowers. Among the trees were flowering cacti with rose-red blooms mingling with violet orchids. Everywhere huge lianas festooned the trees, while the trees themselves grew in such strange and fantastic shapes that they formed a leafy lacework of greenery, which, though exquisite, appeared somehow forbidding. Along the track scampered huge iguanas, four feet or more in length, and as they ran we took pot shots at them from the car with our revolvers. It was a kind of Wild West Show without danger to the iguanas. It was curious to see that these beasts appeared to run at full speed as if they have only two legs instead of four, the two on one side going forward and then the two on the other. They did not seem to have sense enough to turn off the road into the underbrush until we were almost on top of them. It is said that the flesh of these lizards is much esteemed as food, but owing to our poor marksmanship we were unable to verify the fact.

After a couple of hours of this rough riding we reached the falls of Iguazú, which are divided into a great number of subsidiary falls. There are thirty-nine of them altogether, and they are mostly of different shapes, heights, and volumes.

Some stream over a knife-edge cliff as symmetrically as a man-made weir; others fall in cascades large and small. The average drop is two hundred and ten feet, and the scenic effect is unbelievably beautiful. It was while wandering about there that I discovered the largest ants I have ever seen. They were one and a quarter inches long, jet black, and were called, unimaginatively, *Hormiga negra*.[1] We were told that they lived in pairs; at any rate they seemed to go about in pairs.

We got back to the launch and dropped down to Foz do Iguazú at the Brazilian frontier, and, after anchoring, caught a pretty silver fish called Salmón. We baited with oranges, which were taken readily. The Salmón, though having nothing to do with *Salmo salar*, proved delicious eating. After dinner we went up to the Brazilian customs bureau to obtain permits to proceed. There we discovered an exquisite gentleman in purple silk pyjamas, who informed us that he would have to put a guard on the launch for fear that we should be smugglers. When we discovered, after some argument, that this scented person was only the deputy inspector, we demanded to see his chief. He told us his chief had not been up all day because he did not feel like getting up, but, after some further discussion, we did meet the chief, and found him in full evening dress. He immediately granted us permission to proceed on our journey. On the way back from the customs we were astonished by the croaking of frogs, which was quite deafening, and before we got back I was almost run over by an immense toad the size of a grapefruit – a very batrachian evening altogether.[2]

We had set Puerto Sol de Mayo as our anchorage for the

[1] Black ant. This is the *Dinoponera grandis*. Of course, it lives in colonies like all ants. It is the largest ant in the world, though *Camponotus (Dinomyrmex) gigas*, from the Malay States, is fatter but shorter.

[2] I examined the toad with my torch and have identified it as a smallish example of the water-toad *Bufo marinus*. This toad is the largest in South America, and, except for *B. asper* of Borneo, the largest in the world, the body alone sometimes measuring over nine inches in length. Neither of these toads, however, approaches in size the giant frog *Rana goliath* of the Cameroons, which grows to twelve inches and is capable of eating rats and other small creatures.

next night, but we had not reckoned on our motors. They had lately been giving us some trouble, but this day they went even worse. Amid much coughing and spluttering we passed somehow the cataracts and whirlpools below Cancha Ytucú-Abá, and tied up above them to see if it would not be possible to get the engines going properly for the last two kilometres of our day's run. Alberto, the engineer, tinkered for a while and then told the captain he could cast off. We had, however, hardly reached mid-stream, when, with a last cough, the motors gave out. Alberto worked frantically to get them started again, without avail, and we suddenly found ourselves in the classical situation which has accounted for so many lives on this river. Our launch was completely out of control, and we were drifting at increasing speed into the *remolinos* and *correderas*. Below us we could see jagged rocks waiting for us. Our guide, Pedroso, at this moment let loose a despairing wail of terror, which did not encourage us. Luckily Peter did not lose his head, and he suggested sending Pedroso ashore in the skiff with a rope. The idea saved us, for Pedroso did somehow manage to get the rope snubbed round a rock, and the launch came gently to rest just above the rapids. Had we been in great danger? It looked like it, for the skiff could scarcely have survived the rapids, and swimming was out of the question. During the whole night Alberto worked, and after much labour got the engines in order to such effect that for the remainder of our trip they gave us no further trouble. It was just as well; for though we thought we had been through some rather difficult places, their dangers were trifling compared with the *remolinos* and *correderas* of Santa Teresa, and as nothing beside those of San Francisco. It was at the last that *El Capitán* made a mistake and we hit a *remolino* with a tremendous crash which seemed as if it would stave in the launch. These rapids continued for a long time, with the fierce water rushing apparently across stream or up, independently of the general direction of the river's flow. At times there would be a tide rip for two or three hundred yards, running a course parallel with the river, while the water flowed at right angles. It was very peculiar and alarming.

At last we got through this part of the river and arrived at Puerto Mendez, which was as far north as we voyaged. Our experiences there after Manguruyú are related elsewhere, so I will now continue our return trip. Before leaving, we accounted for many Dorado; a Pacú of thirty pounds, a very big fish for this variety; and a small silvery fish called Bóga which resembled a baby Tarpon with large staring eyes. The Bóga is highly regarded as a sporting fish and will give a good fight on either spoon or bait. Next to Dorado it is the fish most sought by anglers in this river, though its maximum weight does not exceed two or three pounds.

Our next strange fish was a Patí. This fish is built like a shark, but has a series of feelers projecting from its head which are said to be prehensile. The Patí was about twenty inches long and the feelers another ten inches. The same day we passed a large tree on which we had been told we should see some macaws, and to our delight we found a pair of them. They were of a beautiful deep blue all over, except for their breasts and the underparts of their wings, which were scarlet. As we approached, they flew away with a flight resembling that of wild duck, but their long tails destroyed the illusion, as these were quite unmistakable.

Fishing this day from the shore in an inch or two of water, I suddenly felt a fearful stabbing pain in my ankle. I thought it must be a snake, but, looking about carefully, could find none. Then I thought it was a bee or a wasp and so did not bother any more about it. But I still had to pass a painful night, and in the morning found my ankle terribly swollen. Fortunately the pain did not last long. On looking back now, I am under the impression that I had been stabbed by a kind of Ray which has the habit of lying concealed in the river mud, and which I did not see owing to its colour camouflage. The stinging spine had to penetrate my waders before reaching me, and so I was luckily saved from a nasty wound. I might say, in parenthesis, that I found the best footwear for this expedition consisted in *alpargatas*, which are canvas slippers with rope soles, and these I wore over wading socks when there was the necessity of stepping into the water. The rope soles of the *alpargatas* were practically slip-proof, even on slimy rocks.

Another creature there, from which it is quite impossible to protect oneself, is a tiny flying insect called *Mbaragui*.[1] It settles on one's face without buzzing and so gently that one cannot perceive it. A moment later it has thrust a poniard into one, and having thus announced its presence flies away happily. The subject of this unprovoked assault, apart from the moment of pain, thinks no more about it till the next day when a torturing itch sets up. Let him beware of scratching at this time, for it may involve all kinds of infections. After a day of itching there is no more annoyance, except for a pin-point of blood which lies just below the skin and which eventually turns black. One may see persons living in these regions whose hands and faces are covered with these small dots which, when they have turned black, can be safely removed with a razor. The night I was stung by the Ray my sleep was further disturbed by the cries of " howler " monkeys which made the night hideous, but though we looked for them the next day we were unable to discover them. It is curious that these monkeys had chosen the vicinity of a logging camp for their quarters. The trees which were being felled were called *Quebracho*. They are of the anacardiaceous family, the wood being extremely hard, and the bark much prized for tannin and as a dye.

[1] It is of the order Diptera and of the genus *Simulium*, of which there are many different species widely distributed over the world; but nowhere have I found them so infuriating as on the Alto Paraná.

Our next catch, apart from Dorado, was a Piro Porá, or Surubí: a Catfish weighing some thirty pounds, with a shovel nose, a white belly, and a back striped like a zebra. It had long tentacles on its head. We had it for dinner, and found it delicious. It had a close white flesh reminding me of Sturgeon. We also this day caught a Palometa, a fish of about the size and shape of a large Tench, which we also found excellent eating.

I must explain that our bathing arrangements had, up to now, consisted of soaping and pouring buckets over ourselves on the poop deck. We had refrained from swimming in the river on account of that world-famous man-eating fish, the Piraña – or Pirai,[1] to use the Guarani Indian name. At Porto Bertoni, however, the day was very warm, and we had anchored in a small bay of still water. Peter could no longer resist. He stripped, and said he was going in, " Piraña or no Piraña." He was on the point of diving when Jock (who almost always had a line in the water) pulled in a fish. Yes, it was a Piraña! The first we had seen the whole trip. I identified it immediately, and Peter decided, without further reflection, that he would take a bucket bath instead. This was one of the three miraculous occurrences we experienced on this trip. Another ten seconds and Peter would have been in the water. Quite possibly nothing might have happened to him ; it is also possible that in a fraction of time he might have been devoured alive. The Piraña is a small fish running to, perhaps, two pounds, and is shaped somewhat like a Pompano. Its teeth are of bear-trap form, and though not very long are frightfully sharp and powerful. The Piraña has a prognathous lower jaw but a comparatively small mouth, so it has to act on the theory that if it cannot take a large bite it must take a number of small ones. This, then, is its

---

[1] The blood-sucking Candirú, a tiny sliver of a Catfish, is equally dreaded by natives of the Amazon because of its instinctive habit of indecently forcing itself into the bladders of unprotected bathers, with possibly fatal consequences.

OUR CREW, JOCK, SOME DORADO, AND A PIRO PORÁ

method of attack on any creature, of no matter what size. Piraña are not really dangerous unless there are many of them together. If there are a couple of hundred of them (and they generally do swim in shoals), it can easily be realised that when each one is taking a bite the size of a nutmeg every two seconds, they can reduce any animal to skeletal proportions in a few minutes. It is, of course, the scent of blood which excites them to a frenzy, and thus even a wounded alligator would be quickly devoured if discovered by Piraña.

We continued our voyage downstream and caught many more Dorado. Of new varieties of fish there was only one, and that I caught at Isla Toroý, our first and last anchorage. This was a fish which weighed five and three-quarter ounces, but was ferocious enough to tackle my largest seven-inch spoon. The fish, in fact, was shorter than the spoon. It had enormous teeth for its size, and they were of a needle sharpness. Pedroso, on whom we relied for the names of our fish, did not know this one, whose savage courage was in keeping with that of most of the fish in this extraordinary river.[1] We had been very fortunate in catching a goodly number of different kinds, but there were, alas, many others besides, which we failed to account for.

We had completed twenty-one days of voyaging when we anchored once more in Posadas. My first job was to settle up for the boat with Engels, and I had been rather dreading an unpleasant interview ; but he appeared, I thought, to be very reasonable, and in the end was so delighted with our little transaction that he presented me, as a mark of esteem, with the following : (a) a slightly preserved alligator skin, (b) a pot of wild orchids, (c) a bottle of Teacher's " Highland Cream " whisky, and (d) a live snake, four and a half feet long. I in turn presented these to Peter, who, being an engaged man, presented them to his *fiancée*. I never heard to whom Aileen presented these treasures — after the wedding.

[1] See Appendix Note, p. 295, for this " Needletooth " fish.

3

THE GOLDEN FISH

THE average man grows up with many ambitions which are usually unfulfilled. Two of mine came off. I wanted to voyage up the great rivers of South America, and I wanted to fish. By a fortunate coincidence I was able to combine and fulfil both of these desires.

Some years ago I read a fine book[1] about angling for Dorado, or Golden Fish, on the Alto Paraná. This set me thinking. A long time later I found myself with no strings on my leisure in Paraguay. By chance I met two young Britishers, who also liked fishing, and I invited them to join my expedition in the launch *Iris* at Posadas.

We found it to be a dreary little town of some five hundred inhabitants on the Argentine side of the river. It is the terminus of a railway line to Buenos Aires, which connects up with the Paraguayan railway to Asunción on the other shore. There is a train ferry which takes the cars across, but it must be a losing proposition, since the two countries have decreed the usual high tariffs to cut off possible legal trade. Posadas, therefore, has to depend for its existence on bootlegging, and manages, indeed, to flourish satisfactorily on its orange smuggling business. The only other features of Posadas are the kapok trees from which life-jackets are made; the beautiful lapacho trees[2] in full bloom when we were there; and, most noticeable

[1] *The Golden River*, by Major J. W. Hills, M.P.
[2] The kapok is of the genus *Eriodendron* and the lapachos are a species of *Tecoma* bearing yellow flowers.

of all, thousands of humming-birds which covered the lapachos in multicoloured swarms.

Though Posadas is a thousand miles upstream from where the Rio de la Plata pours its yellow flood into the South Atlantic at Buenos Aires, the Alto Paraná, one of the three branches of the great Plate system, is scarcely a brook. At this point it is almost a mile wide; turbulent and treacherous, it flows through a rocky fault in the land. It is no child's play to navigate, but we had a first-class captain, Antonio Zarza. We had also: engineer Alberto, cook Estebán, steward Carlito, and guide Pedroso. They were all half-breeds (or pretended they were).

At Posadas we equipped ourselves with sacks of dried bread, potatoes, jam, gin, tonic water, and other stores. We had all the necessary fishing-tackle, and we started north. On our left lay Paraguay, a little fighting paradise, on our right Argentina and Gauchos.

It was a splendid day, the 24th of October, when we commenced our voyage. Beneath a balmy afternoon sun we stretched ourselves in camp chairs on the roof of the superstructure and sampled the gin and tonic. It was glorious. Of my companions, one, Peter, was English ; the other, Jock, came from Aberdeen. Peter had caught a three-quarter-pound Trout, once. Jock was an angler.

At intervals we discussed Dorado ; what a fine and sporting game fish it was to prove, possessing, as we found, the two important qualities which some authorities insist on for a true game fish — that is: active, intelligent resistance to the angler's wiles, and subsequent culinary satisfaction. The Dorado we sought (*Salminus maxillosus*)[1] is one of four varieties which are in no way related to *Salmo salar*. Its large scales are burnished brightly to a wonderful old gold tone, and, to add to its splendour, its fins are a brilliant

---

[1] The head of the great Characinidæ family of South America. The other varieties are *S. brevidens*, *S. hilarii*, and *S. affinis*.

scarlet-orange.   Across the caudal fin runs a black vertical
stripe providing a final note of elegance to the fish's powerful and robust body.   For colour there is no doubt that the
Dorado yields to no river fish, but its form does not quite
equal in design the stream-line of a Salmon.   It is this
stockiness of build, however, which accounts for its superior
strength.   The Dorado has an immense mouth considering
the fish's trim appearance, and one is always somewhat surprised to see its huge gape when opened.   Within there is
a series of short but powerful teeth, set like a rip-saw in a
single even row.   Dorado have been captured up to some
fifty pounds in weight, and it is probable that sixty pounds
is about their limit.

We anchored that night at Isla Toroý, a big granite rock
which boldly cut the current in two unequal parts.   Already
for a long time we had been preparing our tackle.   My
companions were not so well equipped as I.   Jock had an
eleven-and-a-half-foot Salmon spinning rod with a Silex
reel and some old Cuttyhunk line which turned out to be
unreliable.   Peter's outfit was a very hastily collected affair,
and consisted in a weird kind of twelve-foot rod of peculiar
action and a wooden Nottingham reel, both crude and
ungainly.   It is to his credit that he eventually mastered
this clumsy combination in an expert manner.   I had sundry
rods with me, including a Striped Bass rod, a " three-six "
outfit, and a Hardy Salmon spinning rod.   For reels I used
a Vom Hofe No. 2–0 and a Hardy Silex.   My lines were
twelve thread, white Cuttyhunk and dressed spinning
line.   I had also a large supply of piano-wire traces,[1]
anti-kink leads, tweezers, reel oil, and sundry other paraphernalia which became common property, and finally –
most important of all – a magnificent assortment of spoons.
I would add that after trying every kind of spoon we found

[1] In America the word " leader " is used to designate both the English words for
terminal tackle.   Thus leader signifies " trace " where spinning or trolling gut, wire, or
cable is employed, and it is also used for the gut " cast " when fly fishing is being discussed.

the Pfleuger " Record " No. 7 to be the most effective. This spoon is so constructed that the hook can be fixed to the spoon or allowed to swing loose. We preferred the hook in the fixed position.

That evening, though understanding nothing of the technique of a Nottingham reel, I knew enough to start Peter off casting, and then with my Striped Bass rod began putting out a reasonable line to what I considered likely spots. A frequent wail from Peter signalised a line snarl. After a short interval his despair brought me to his rescue. His spoon lay stranded about thirty feet upstream from the island – no place to cast for fish – while the line showed as a horrid mare's nest encircling the reel in inextricable confusion. I found that in spite of this the line could be wound in, and suggested reeling over the snarl for subsequent disentanglement. As he proceeded to do this, there was suddenly a fierce tug. For no reason a Dorado had chosen to take the spoon. Beginner's luck – call it what one will – but Peter, in a panic, was into the first fish. Jock and the whole crew came running, while the reel fell off the rod into the river, and then Peter fell in up to his hips after it, while the fish, a fighting fury, struggled desperately to carry him out and drown him. How the reel was replaced on the rod and the fish landed is still a mystery. There was practically no line to give, and Peter was almost out of his mind with excitement ; but land the fish he did. A fine eleven-pounder – rejoicings and congratulations.

That was the end of our sport for the evening, but we still anticipated eating the Dorado for dinner. We awaited with impatience the *coup d'essai* of our cook, Estebán, and thereafter we had no hesitation in proclaiming him *chef* and later " magician " as well. From the little galley forward which contained (besides the stove) the engine housing and the sleeping-quarters of five men, he produced a superb banquet. The main *plat* of this, our first meal, was, of

course, the Dorado. It proved delicious. The Dorado
was fried in slices, and we found the flesh to be firm
and flaky, not dry, and of an excellent flavour. It was
a pale pink in colour, and the choice titbit, most tasty of
all, was the head. Let me recommend to gourmets our
subsequent discovery – cold Dorado head with potato salad
mayonnaise.

We remained anchored at Isla Toroý for the night, and
early the next morning continued north. Dorado was
again the subject of discussion. We had already been shown
that the Dorado fights to the last ounce. It jumps well and
frequently, it shakes its head and tries to throw the spoon,
but it is fairly easy to hook as its mouth is not bony inside.
If the fish is hooked at all firmly it will probably be captured,
unless the tackle breaks. The Dorado is a predacious fish,
feeding on smaller fish which it catches by speed of swimming. It is, indeed, a noble game fish, stronger and more
ferocious than Salmon, and, as we later concluded, of about
the same average weight, though there is a greater proportion of big ones and small ones than one finds among
Salmon.

From our short experience of that first evening and the
suggestions of Pedroso, we decided that we must revise
our ideas of where to look for Dorado. A typical Salmon
pool, for instance, would contain no Dorado, since it
prefers much faster water. Why Peter's fish was where he
hooked it, we were never able to determine.

Our next stop was at Tabaý Alves, a journey of eighty-
four kilometres, during which at intervals we caught two
strange varieties of fish, but no Dorado. The following day
we voyaged through some of the *remolinos* and *correderas* of
the Alto Paraná. We had been warned that we should
encounter these conditions, but we were surprised to
find them so alarming. Owing to the rocky bed of the
river, the water in these parts followed strange courses.

PETER, A 9 lb. DORADO, AND ANTONIO ZARZA

Sometimes it seemed to be flowing upstream or straight across in vast, flat sheets against which our motors proved powerless. It was then necessary for Zarza to find the proper channel where the full force of the stream need not be met. At certain places submerged rocks caused the water to boil up as if from some huge cauldron, forming great eddies and tourbillons, which varied in size and position according to the height of the river. The Alto Paraná, it seems, changes its level as much as forty feet between the dry and rainy seasons. Navigation is thus both difficult and dangerous. Our captain told us that only seven years before a tug and barge had disappeared without trace, and this story gave point to the warnings which Pedroso gave us from time to time, to hold on to the rail when the little ship met the full strength of unavoidable disturbances. Then she would shake and tremble to regain her speed, and at last, in a zigzag course, struggle back into easier water. The river has been flattered with the name of " Golden," but a watery coffee with insufficient milk would better describe its usual colour.

As we plugged our way upstream there was much to entertain us. We saw occasionally a *Yacaré*, the South American alligator, sunning itself on an exposed rock. This naturally called for a shot with ball cartridge from my twelve-bore, though it was never sufficiently accurate. Along the banks green parrots of various species screamed as in flocks they flew from tree to tree. It was interesting to notice that, though there might be fifty of them together, they always flew in pairs. Indeed, there was usually some kind of bird life available for our field-glasses: several varieties of unfamiliar ducks, herons, kingfishers, and birds of prey kept us sufficiently alert when the sombre foliage of the river-banks grew tedious. As we proceeded we came, too, upon a stretch of the river fed by many small streams which tumbled down from the jungle floor, a drop of some forty feet, in charming cascades of graceful and varied form.

So we continued steering north by east till at Puerto Mendez in Brazil, almost beneath the Tropic of Capricorn, we had reached the destination we had set ourselves. It was our intention to do our serious fishing as we returned to Posadas, and fish we did. As soon as the launch was anchored there would be a line in the water. We captured no less than fourteen different species in this one river. The varieties unaccounted for must be many times that number.

Our method was to cast from the shore where it was practicable. But when this was impossible we used to take turns fishing from a skiff. Dorado is an extremely game fish and lies in swift water. Not for him the still pools. Upstream from a big rock where the water divides, or just in the eddy of a horse-tail below, he is found. Generally he prefers water three feet deep, where he can make a lightning dash for some small fish – his prey. Occasionally we found him in deeper water. Our largest fish, a hen of thirty pounds, I hooked at a depth of twenty feet, but she had just spawned and was in poor condition. She should have run much heavier.

My companions with inferior tackle suffered many smashes, but I never lost a fish through breakage. As we drifted downstream we had some glorious days. Our best was at the island of Parehá some way down from Toro Cuá, a famous place for Dorado, where we had had little luck.

At Parehá rocks and shallows encroach on the river from the Paraguayan side, forcing the main body of the stream through a deep and narrow channel. But on the shallow side there was sufficient water to form small cataracts. As we searched for likely fishing in this water, we found a narrow shelf of rock where the water curled over in a smooth glide for a drop of perhaps two feet. Above this little fall

OUR CATCH AT PAREHÁ

lay many Dorado. It took a longish cast to reach the good
water, and some skill to avoid letting the spoon spin over
the fall, where it would surely have been hung up. The
place seemed alive with fish. It only required a few casts
to get into one. We could see the fish rising occasionally
to the surface, and by casting a yard or two in front of the
rise we succeeded in securing four fish. This was a technique of which we had not heard. But it proved successful.

Though the majority of the fish we caught at Parehá
were hooked just above the fall, not one of them tried to
escape by plunging over it, but sought instead to fight it
out upstream. In this respect the Dorado does not seem
as resourceful as a Salmon. Otherwise one cannot complain of the Dorado's defensive qualities. Generally it
takes the spoon with a fierce and determined tug. So
strong are its jaws that, unless it has also taken the hook
in its mouth, it will often be found impossible to strike hard
enough to slide the barb into the fish. Until we added a
second hook near the head of the spoon, we thus lost many
fish. Once the Dorado has taken, it starts off with a splendid
run, both powerful and determined. After about fifty
yards it comes up to do some jumping, at the same time
trying to shake the hook out. Then there are more runs
interspersed with sulking and jagging deep down. Great
care must be exercised not to allow the fish to get too far
away, and very strong pressure must be applied to keep
contact. As long as the fish remains in fast water it is a
great fighter, but having lost the current its defence does
not continue long. Between 3.15 and 6 that afternoon we
landed eleven fish to two rods, and felt well satisfied with
our performance.

The next morning we went up to try again at the same
place, but the fish were no longer in evidence. I got one,
and then there was a long interval without the sign of a
fish or a rise. After about an hour I suggested that Peter

should take, for the cinema record of our trip, a picture of me casting. After measuring off the distance for focus, and making all preparations, I was about to cast when I saw a Dorado rise. I told Peter to start filming and made my cast, which by chance was perfect ; the fish, a beauty, took the spoon. It gave me a grand fight, with many jumps, and was duly gaffed and landed. The film turned out a complete success, showing every feature of Dorado fishing. I was informed that a few months before a film company had spent some time on the Alto Paraná trying to get a picture of precisely such a sequence; but, after lavishing much money, they had to give up the task, without obtaining what they sought.

From Parehá we drifted downstream, and when we reached Caraguataí called on an acquaintance named Benson, who was manager of a large Yerba Maté plantation there. As an old and expert Dorado angler he offered to take us out for a day's fishing. With joy we abandoned our own arrangements and joined him. His method included the use of a small dinghy, equipped with a gasoline engine, and to this was lashed a native, flat-bottomed skiff which served as an excellent casting platform. As the steering of this combination was difficult, he employed a *peón* to help direct the skiff with an oar, while a half-caste engineer controlled the motor and rudder of the dinghy. The two of them seemed to be able to muddle along as imperfectly as possible. That day I was to experience three incidents which I do not care to repeat. We had commenced with a little trolling and had then landed at a small island which we fished without success. We were getting aboard the boats again, and I was standing up in the dinghy, when the engineer stupidly ran it hard on to a rock. I fell down, and the palm of my left hand was badly cut on some metal portion of the engine, while my chest landed on the sparking-plug of the motor. It never occurred to the engineer to stop the motor, as I lay prone in the machinery, which was revolving madly. I was expecting to lose a few fingers at least, but managed to get out intact except for these two injuries. A little later Jock caught a Dorado. I was trying to release his fish, which was fairly firmly hooked, when the engineer, who was holding the fish down, suddenly let go his grasp. One of the hooks of the spoon stuck in my fingers as the fish jumped, and before I could get free I had been pierced in four places and was bleeding profusely.

They say that misfortunes always occur in threes, and the third one nearly finished all of us. We had been trolling for some time with moderate success, when Peter got his hook fouled on the bottom. The boats were pointed toward mid-stream, and I had succeeded with some difficulty in getting the hook loose, when, happening to look across the water as I was returning to my seat, I saw within twenty feet of us an enormous whirlpool. Benson noticed it at the same moment, and began giving directions to the engineer in a calm voice. His handling of the situation was excellent in this respect, but his method of getting us out of danger seemed strange. The whirlpool was about fifteen feet across, and from the lip to the vortex there was a whirling drop of four feet. It appeared certain that if the boats were sucked in they would be swamped, and our chances of reaching land quite hopeless. We were above and slightly to the right of the whirlpool, and it seemed simple enough to turn inshore, but Benson gave orders to the engineer to point the dinghy upstream. Not knowing anything of watermanship, he locked the rudder over so hard that the motor could not pull against the current, and thus threw the sterns of the boats still closer to the whirlpool, which was now only about twelve feet away. Benson then told his man not to put the rudder so far over, but, having got the boats pointed upstream to apparent safety, the engineer again locked his rudder and in doing so spun our cumbrous craft round so that in a moment we were headed in the opposite direction, and were drifting down on the whirlpool, bow first. Now it looked even worse for us, as we had only the reverse gear to pull us out, with no alternative but to back away. At last the little motor managed it, though once it coughed in an alarming manner, and by inches we crept upstream to the slack water of the bank. The episode reminded me of a nightmare in which for minutes on end one feels a terrible doom impending. It appears that this whirlpool was very famous and was named Mboy Mbosu. How Benson had failed to remember it I cannot imagine. He told me later that some years before two men had lost their lives in the Mboy Mbosu, and during the subsequent enquiry, as an experiment, an empty canoe was let down so as to pass over it. The canoe was sucked in by the whirlpool and only fragments of it returned to the surface some hundreds of yards lower down.

After this unlucky day we left Caraguataí and continued our voyage back to Posadas, fishing with varying fortune. Our record at the end of the trip was : 44 fish, total weight $626\frac{3}{4}$ lb. My ten biggest fish averaged $25\frac{1}{2}$ lb., but, as I have already pointed out, Dorado come in all sizes. I had, for instance, one of two pounds, and several such small fish brought down our average considerably.

By the time we returned to Posadas we had become expert Dorado anglers. We could tell Dorado water so exactly that on the last day, when making a long cast to a likely spot, my spoon actually hit a Dorado, which jumped out of the water with a great leap of surprised fright. This feat might be called luck or chance, but I prefer to call it skill.

4

THE MYSTERIOUS MANGURUYÚ

A Tale of Frustration

FOR ten days we had been chugging steadily north in our little launch *Iris* between the sinister banks of the Alto Paraná, and had finally reached Puerto Mendez in Brazil. Beyond, it was not possible to proceed, for the falls and cataracts of La Guayrá stop all further river traffic.

At Puerto Mendez we had anticipated a sizable village, but there were only two or three mean shanties at the top of the cliff which we could ascend by a crude funicular.

We were much looking forward to a view of the falls, which were said to be spectacular. This involved a trip to the town of Guayrá, which, like the railroad and hundreds of square miles in every direction, belonged to the Compania Empresa Maté Larangeira. We therefore got in touch with the manager of the company, who was a Quaker, and he graciously accorded us transportation in the maté train. For sixty kilometres we bumped through virgin jungle behind a miniature wood-burning engine, to find ourselves after four hours in a Quaker town transported to the tropics.

That afternoon a young Englishman was detailed to take us to the falls in a Ford truck. There was no road, but wheel tracks, mostly obliterated by the encroaching jungle, could be discerned from time to time. Accompanying us were several *peones* carrying their inevitable *machetes* with which to cut a way where tangled lianas barred our progress. The falls, already long ago described

as the future power centre of South America, at this point
reduce six kilometres breadth of river into a stony gorge a
hundred metres wide.

It was while we were contemplating this raging cataract
that I witnessed what I must always consider the greatest
fluke I have ever seen. A cormorant was flying along the
river from right to left at about sixty yards range, and when
Jock saw it he took out his .38 Colt and, firing in a non-
chalant manner, brought it down stone dead. The *peones*
were loud in proclaiming their admiration for this feat;
but one of our own crew loyally explained that it was
nothing. His señores, he continued, shot birds like that
every day from the launch. Needless to say, Jock's normal
marksmanship would hardly guarantee hitting a house at
ten paces. I won't call that shot a fluke. Call it a miracle
and have done with it.

Our English conductor told us there was fishing to be
had in a backwater below the falls, and the anglers' spirits,
depressed by the sinister brutality of the river, rose at once.
The next day we were there with tackle hastily purchased.
Our rods we had left in our launch, but we had obtained
lengths of blind-cord and some huge hooks from the company's stores. For bait we had several kilos of raw meat.
We were told our quarry was called Manguruyú. We
had already heard tell of this fish by our guide and boatman,
Pedroso. With bated breath he used to murmur " Manguruyú " at points where the turbulence of the river had occasion to gouge out of the confining cliffs a small bay or
remanso. An enormous fish, it appeared, was the Manguruyú,
" *muy grande*," and Pedroso would stretch out his arms and
his eyes would bulge slightly for emphasis.

We descended a rocky cliff and circled a tiny lagoon
bordered with golden sand. At the water's edge our
friend from the Larangeira pointed out the tracks of some
large beast, a *tigré*, the jaguar of South America, which had

THE MANGURUYÚ

come down the night before to drink. We climbed again some rocks and decided to fish near where the *remanso* joined the river.

In a short time my two companions had found suitable positions and prepared their tackle. I went on a little further. My blind-cord was about forty yards long, and, having attached a hook, I put on a piece of meat the size of an apple and heaved it in. I had just done so when I heard shouts from my friends. Quickly tying the end of my line to a rock, I ran back, to find them considerably excited. It appears that Jock had hardly got his bait in the water when he saw his line moving away. He thought it was the current, perhaps, which was carrying out the bait, but when he took hold of it he knew it was not the current. Though a powerful man, he perceived in a moment that he could not hold the fish and called Peter to help. Their position on the rocks was not, however, secure, and they soon realised that the fish was too strong for them. The line went out, cutting their hands, almost at once they had to let go, and the fish proceeded majestically away with bait, hook, and line. I told them they should have attached the line to a rock, and then hurriedly returned to my own position. I was too late. I found a yard of my line left, still firmly holding to its support; the rest was gone. I prepared some more tackle and was casting out when more cries from my friends brought me back to them. Peter this time had lost his line to a fish which had broken him when it had reached the full length. I hastened back, and once more found my line missing. This was no longer a joke. The whole *remanso* seemed alive with monsters. What made the proceedings so eerie was the smooth surface of the turbid water which gave no indication that anything stirred below.

This time I decided to try strategy. So far I had had no sport for my lost tackle. I found a large limb of a tree, and, attaching it crosswise fifteen feet from the hook, floated it out.   It swam beautifully and circled slowly round in the slight current of the *remanso*.   Suddenly it began to move the wrong way.   I put a strain on the line, but it had no effect.   The tree branch disappeared and out went the line just the same.   I braced myself against a boulder and hung on.   I had a handkerchief to save my hands, but still I had to give line gradually, and with only about forty yards I could not give very much.   I put on more pressure and finally, when only about ten feet were left, I decided not to yield any more.   I might as well have tried to hold the *Queen Mary*.   There was a sharp crack and the line parted above the tree limb.   I never saw it again.   I went to look for my friends and found that our sixth line was also broken. Having no more tackle we had to abandon our fishing.

That night we journeyed back to our launch.   Across the track scuttled iguanas.   Over our heads flew blue and red macaws; in the trees screeched monkeys and toucans; purple orchids gleamed bright in the dense foliage of the jungle.   It was all very fascinating, but I was thinking about Manguruyú.

When we reached the launch, we tested a piece of our blind-cord and found that it broke, dry, at ninety-one pounds.

We were not yet finished with Manguruyú, however.   I had with me some tackle for big game fish, so we decided that the next time we found suitable water we would go after Manguruyú in a manner befitting the creature.   Some time later we came upon a quiet bay and I got on my body harness and baited a Swordfish hook.   This time I had to wait about twenty minutes for a bite, but then I got one. As I had six hundred yards of line on my reel I could afford to let the Manguruyú have some of it.   When it had taken out about sixty yards I slapped on the brake.   But, in spite of the powerful drag, it did not make any difference; the

fish went straight on swimming.   Now the Alto Paraná is
a fierce and mighty river.   I soon saw I should not have
enough line.   I wanted to play the fish, but it would not
play.   At about five knots it simply went cruising along in
an unconcerned and exasperating manner.   I took to the
small boat and followed.   The current was so fast that it
was all we could do to row upstream; finally we did make
some progress.   The line came in slowly, and then I
realised that I was caught up.   Now we had become
experts at releasing a fouled hook, but this time after frantic
exertions we found that it was the line which was held, and
in the end we had to break and lose some fifty yards.

   That was our last experience with Manguruyú.   We had
lost seven lines and we had never even seen a fish.   We were
interested to find out just what we had been after, and discovered that the Manguruyú is a kind of giant Catfish with
an immense head and a comparatively small body.   Nobody
knows how big they grow, but they have been captured up
to two hundred pounds.   In a book written by a famous
angler he mentions the fish, and concludes that it " possesses no sporting value."   All I can say is that a fish
which can break six lines testing to ninety-one pounds
may not possess sporting value, but it must possess *something*.   My advice to those fortunate enough to voyage up
the Alto Paraná is to fish for Manguruyú, but use a rope.[1]

---

[1] The Manguruyú (*Pseudopimelodus zungaro*) is related distantly to the Sheat fish or Wels
(*Silurus glanis*) of the Danube.   Both of them belong to the sub-order Siluroidea.   The Sheat
fish has been reported to attain some seven hundred pounds in weight, but there is little data
on the size of Manguruyú, which may reach four hundred pounds.   It is, indeed, probable
that those we hooked must have surpassed two hundred pounds if only from the tremendous
power they showed in breaking our lines without the necessity of fast swimming or rapid
manœuvres.

5

"BUT YOU CAN'T BEAT A TARPON, CAN YOU?"

— WAKEFIELD

A FRIEND of mine once said to me, " Now tell me, Leander, isn't Tarpon the finest sporting fish in the world?"

I hemmed and hawed a bit before replying. I had just been round the world trying to make up my mind about this very question, and in the course of my travels had acquired a favourite fish. For answer I described to him at length some of the characteristics displayed by other fish, but, when I had finished, he returned doggedly to his thesis with, " But you can't beat a Tarpon, can you?"

I must confess that he had me there, and I replied, weakly enough, " Well, not by much, anyway."

His question had proved an excellent corrective for enthusiasms, justified indeed, but perhaps a little too recently experienced to have yet acquired their proper perspectives. I vow, and I am surely not alone in my madness, that for me it is always the last fish which is best of all; and, furthermore, it does not matter much whether the last fish was a Minnow or a Swordfish. It is perhaps pitiable to enjoy fishing to this extent, but it is also very pleasant. As a matter of fact I have never caught enough Tarpon, nor has my Tarpon fishing been sufficiently rounded out for me to describe it from all angles. I shall, however, always be grateful to that Tarpon, my first big game fish, for all the agonies and emotions he put me through at Boca Grande Pass.

It is such a long time ago that I cannot now remember by what pleas of ill health, urgent family affairs, or other subterfuges my friends John and Watson managed to justify obtaining a month's surcease from business and social engagements in order to go fishing with me; but they did. We were all of us utter novices at fishing, and were thus fair game for the salesman in the tackle shop we visited before leaving for Florida. It is probable that he was as ignorant as we, and it is possible that in all innocence he sold us equipment which he thought adequate. We were quite content with our purchases, and proceeded first to a fishing camp run by Mike Evans near Sarasota. My recollection of it only extends to four incidents. We were in full prohibition at the time, but as drinking was necessary for our health we obtained from one of the coloured boys at the camp some home-made gin. It was called " White Mule," and kicked like one. I recall that John and I were deathly ill after partaking, while Watson, who had imbibed more than either of us, woke perfectly fresh next morning. It was that night, too, that in unloading a Colt automatic I just managed to avoid shooting off my foot, to the alarm of the whole camp. The other two episodes concerned Watson's shooting. With a revolver he took off the head of a rattle-snake at fifteen feet, and with a Winchester brought down a flying pelican at eighty yards. I have always considered these as genuine feats of marksmanship, for he was, indeed, an excellent shot.

We went fishing, of course, while at the camp, but soon discovered that we were in the wrong place for Tarpon, and moved on to Tarpon Inn, Useppa Island, which we reached on the 26th of April. By good fortune we obtained Johansen, one of the best guides; but he told us with some regret that we would have no success till the 1st of

May. Our confidence was unbounded, however, and despite his pessimism we started fishing at once. As is usual with novices, we imagined that fishing required extra excitements to make it interesting, and thus devised an elaborate sweepstake with various prizes for the most fish, the largest fish, the greatest variety of fish, and so on. What a delusion ! Surely if fishing is worth doing it requires no additional inducements, but we were young then.

For four days we caught all kinds of fish: Spanish Pompano, Kingfish, Grouper, Sea Trout, Jewfish, and many other varieties. We also speared Gar Pike and tried to harpoon a giant Manta which fortunately escaped ; but of Tarpon we had never a sign. On the 1st of May, however, we were awakened with the news that the Tarpon had arrived. At midnight they had begun to take, and several stretched on the dock that morning witnessed the accuracy of Johansen's prognostication. We could hardly wait to get to Boca Grande Pass.

It was Watson who had the first fish on, and it was a good one. We were fishing with live crabs sunk to some fifty feet with lead sinkers which could be easily shaken off. Watson had hardly let his line down when his rod was almost pulled out of his hands; the reel screamed, and sixty yards off a magnificent Tarpon jumped clear. It gave one shake of its head, and the hook came out. Next it was John's turn with a smaller fish and the same result. I waited with impatience, but nothing happened for a long time. The sun was burning down on us, and our enthusiasm had begun to melt somewhat when my crab received attention. The violence with which a Tarpon strikes is extraordinary, and this one was no exception. In an instant he was off in a splendid rush, and then began a beautiful leaping display. Seven times he jumped while I hung on as best I could. Those who have not had the opportunity to observe the jumping of a Tarpon, and have only perhaps seen the aerial acrobatics of a Trout or Salmon, can form no appreciation of a Tarpon's exhibition. The Florida Tarpon, whose form and colour give the impression of a Herring magnified two hundred times, is, apart from the Oxeye (*Megalops cyprinoides*), a unique fish without other immediate relatives, the genus itself being a rare terrestrial survival from prehistoric times. Among several peculiar characteristics, the most noticeable is the immense size of the Tarpon's scales, which measure some three inches across and, except on the back, are resplendent with a coating as brilliant as pure silver.[1]

The Tarpon jumps like no other fish; it seems to fling itself in the air, sometimes to a height of eight feet or so, with a lateral and twisting motion giving occasionally the appearance of one of those modern high jumpers. The Tarpon does not attempt to re-enter the water head first as do Mako Shark or Kingfish, but instead it falls back somehow, anyhow, with a colossal splash. In an instant it comes out again, with each jump seeming to attempt to break the angler's line by falling on it. In the jump there is an added handicap for the angler, as the fish takes advantage of this moment to shake its head violently in an effort to throw the hook.

I imagine I made all the mistakes a beginner can make in this fishing; but, unexpectedly, the hook remained fast, and, though I was already exhausted, it looked as if I would get the fish in. As so often happens, however, misfortune

[1] Another peculiarity of the Tarpon is the curious whip-like attachment it possesses at the rear of the dorsal fin which is also observable in the Thread Herring and other fish of that family. It has been claimed that this whip is of assistance to the Tarpon in enabling it to control the direction of its jumps.

The Tarpon is actually of the same sub-order (Clupeoidea) as the kippered Herring of our breakfast-table, and is also connected with that rare and astounding fish, the Pirarucú or Arapaima of the Amazon, which is, as everyone knows, the largest fresh-water fish in the world, attaining sometimes a weight of four hundred pounds and a length of fifteen feet. To add to the surprise of these scientific relationships, I would say that besides the Arapaima, the Tarpon also belongs to the same order (Isospondyli) as our own very prosaic Salmon and Trout.

was biding its time. Suddenly I discovered my reel was jammed. Though the line would still pay out a little I could not take it in. The fish was very tired now, or he would have quickly broken me, but my guide found he could hand-line the Tarpon. I tried this too, and got my hands cut for my trouble. At last it was only a matter of slipping the releasing hook into the fish's mouth. Johansen attempted to do so, but the Tarpon gave one last jerk and the hook came out. The fish slowly sank from sight through the translucent water. Needless to say John and Watson were loud in their complaints that I had wasted a valuable hour of their fishing time without anything to show for it, but I at any rate had enjoyed many thrills. I cursed my reel and found later that it had completely seized from friction. When Watson's reel also jammed on a second fish, we decided to borrow some proper tackle. It was obvious that the reels we had been sold may have been adequate for small fish, but were worse than useless for Tarpon. This mistake which we had made is one which must often have been duplicated by beginners. They do not understand that a Tarpon is a fish of outstanding strength and resource. It is not, indeed, necessary to purchase an expensive Vom Hofe or Cox reel, with exquisite and complicated mechanical brakes, in order to catch Tarpon. In fact any straightforward reel which carries enough line and a thumb pad will perhaps provide better and more exciting sport. If, however, a mechanical brake is used, then the reel must be of first-class quality, or it will surely break down under the strain.

We paid heavily for our ignorance, as five days passed without another strike. John by this time could no longer spin out his vacation, and departed. As if he had been a veritable hoodoo, the next day brought us magnificent sport. First Watson made no errors in landing a small but active fifty-pound fish, and then I was lucky enough to get into a larger one. I shall never forget this struggle. The fish, a hen, was perhaps not quite returned to condition, but she was still strong enough and very heavy. The fight was a plugging one, with only two jumps, but her determination to get away was magnificent. As before, I made all the possible mistakes. I tried to take in line when I should have let her have it. I worked far too hard; I tightened for the jumps instead of slackening,[1] and I used my arms instead of my weight for pumping. I should perhaps explain for those unacquainted with big game fishing that the only method of recovering line from a large fish is by " pumping." This consists in raising the rod tip when a lessened strain from the fish permits, and then winding in the line as the rod point is lowered. Thus with every " pump " a yard or so of line is regained. At the end of an hour I was completely worn out, while the fish still appeared quite fresh. I begged Watson to take the rod, for I was ready to give up, but he fortunately refused. Then, to my horror, the line looked as if it were fraying; and there was a moment, as the fish surged up to the surface, when I imagined that the hook was only holding by the merest filament of skin to the fish's lip. What a nightmare of apprehension I went through as I tried to ease the pressure, expecting each instant to see the fish get off ! My Tarpon was, however, more tired than she seemed, and in another fifteen minutes I had her alongside. My guide used the releasing hook skilfully, and thus it was that I became a Tarpon fisherman. I can remember well my exhaustion combined with the exhilaration of my triumph. I lay back in the boat and murmured that I needed something to revive me. It was, as I thought, but a hopeless wish, for we had brought nothing with us, but to my

[1] The usual practice in America is to keep a strain on the line when the Tarpon jumps. The theory is that the fish cannot thus fall on the line. Whether this is correct, or whether the line should be kept slack at this moment, is a point on which I am not quite clear. Naturally, in Trout and Salmon fishing the rod point is dropped so as to avoid the danger of a sudden strain on the fragile gut cast.

surprise our guide produced a large demijohn and asked if I could use some of it. I have seldom tasted anything more potent than what Johansen later explained was Cuban cognac. It had the required effect, however, and I was soon restored and ready for another fish. We got two more that day, but my first was the best; and it scaled eighty-six pounds.

Watson and I fished together for another week with varying fortunes. We graduated out of the beginners' class and began using lighter rods and eighteen-thread line. We caught several more Tarpon, including a hundred-pounder which earned me a gold button from the Tarpon Club. It was only just a hundred pounds, the minimum weight for a gold-button fish caught on eighteen-thread line, so I considered myself extremely lucky.

Our last morning came, but we were determined to fish to the ultimate minute. With all our bags and equipment on board, we took the launch once more for Boca Grande. Our train was leaving at 2.32 that afternoon, so we had not much time. I must remark that our sweepstake pool had mounted by now to a considerable sum, and I was placed in the comfortable situation of being entitled to the major part of it, but the pool was so devised that if Watson could obtain a larger fish than my hundred-pounder, then the positions would be reversed and I should be paying instead of receiving. The day looked perfect, and we soon each of us released small Tarpon which had no bearing on the sweep. It was almost two o'clock, and I had suggested going for the train, when Watson got into an apparently immense fish. It seemed to play somewhat like my largest fish which never came to the surface before it was brought to gaff. Watson was in a frenzy. He swore that it was a world record, and that he would land it if it took him all day. I kept looking at my watch as the minutes sped by, and began mentally composing a telegram for my office

BUCK McCANN AND TWO TARPON

which would explain my delayed arrival. Then, when all hope of catching the train seemed gone, the fish suddenly came quite gently to the surface. One glance at its flapping fins revealed a large Jewfish. We released it and did just manage to get our luggage on the train as it was moving out.

Some years later I returned to Useppa, with my first wife. The fishing had, for some reason, become more difficult, and it was considered of little use to try during the day for Tarpon. We had Buck McCann for guide, and we spent two weeks at the mercy of the tides. Whatever time of night the tide was on the slack, then were we at the pass. We got up at unearthly hours and slept during the day when best we could. Very often we would sleep on the boat between tides, thus managing to work in two chances of fishing during the night. It was exhausting, but also very fascinating. We allowed ourselves very little respite throughout our " holiday," and if the tides permitted we even put in some extra time during the day at Captiva Pass fishing for Channel Bass. These fish were not always to be taken, but during the flood of the tide they could often be obtained at Captiva. Our method was to go out to the edge of the pass and then let the launch drift in with the fast flowing tide. Every such drift would account for several Channel Bass. They were fine fish which we captured, running up to twenty pounds or so, and possessed of sufficient power for a short, vigorous defence.

If Tarpon give a fine display during the day, at night, like all fish, they go quite mad. Some of their jumping was magnificent and, as can be imagined, the difficulties of the angler were multiplied, for it was hard to determine just where the fish had got to in pitch darkness. There was one unusual incident. One evening Alice had hooked a big fish, but did not keep sufficient pressure to avoid a very long run.   The fish eventually got out far enough to foul the line of another angler, and when this was at last disentangled it managed to twist the line round the propeller of another launch, and eventually broke it and escaped. We calculated the fish had taken away some sixty yards of line.   Judge of our astonishment when the next morning a fellow angler told us that he had caught this same fish during the night, still with the hook and sixty yards of line attached to it.   The fish weighed over a hundred pounds as it turned out.

My next and last experience with Tarpon was quite different.   I had been travelling up the west coast of South America with the intention of changing ships at Colon for a voyage to New Zealand.   On reaching Panama City I discovered that I would have several days before my ship arrived.   It was an excellent opportunity to do some fishing, and I went to the Gatun locks, where, through the courtesy of Mr. Atwood, and after making a small payment, I became a member of the Panama Canal Tarpon Club.   I was then introduced to Lorenzo, the coloured man-of-all-work at the club.

I had with me a light fourteen-foot Salmon rod of split cane and a standard Salmon reel and casting line.   It was not long before I was fishing.   Below the Gatun locks there is a concrete apron which forms the spillway for the overflow from the locks.   The water pours over this spillway a foot deep, and then with a slight drop rejoins the river which continues out to the Atlantic.   Below the spillway masses of Tarpon congregate.   I have never seen more anywhere, though the majority of them were not large.   It is reported that General Pershing, after hooking and landing a Tarpon at this point, remarked : "*War* was never like this."   I would like very much to believe that he made the statement.

Actually I had prepared almost a year previously for this

very fishing, and had brought with me a number of Tarpon flies made specially in Scotland for the purpose. There were only two patterns: one was of white cock feathers with dyed scarlet trimmings, the other was a beautiful thing in blue and silver composed mostly from the neck feathers of the Lady Amherst pheasant. The flies were of various sizes, but there was one size, four inches long, which appeared the most suitable. For cast I was using a synthetic gut called Telarana Nova which I had tested to sixteen pounds. The concrete apron of the spillway was slippery with slimy weeds, and in order to obtain a footing I bought some baseball shoes with steel cleats. This was a necessary precaution, as a year previously an angler had skidded off the apron and his body was never recovered. There were many anglers at the lock, but most of them were only interested in edible fish. Along the apron they were lined up in numbers and with short rods were bobbing their lures in the fast water in the hope of catching Snook, which have a delicious flesh. I must have appeared very strange to them, with my peculiar tackle. Lorenzo, that knowing expert, told me with conviction that I would have no success at Tarpon without a brown fly, of which he sold me a couple. I was soon busy casting out into the river, but early decided that my Lady Amherst fly was ideal; in fact during my fishing at Gatun I never got a strike on any other, and I also seemed to surpass the results of all the other anglers, catching more and bigger Snook, which I did not want, and one Ladyfish, equally undesired. The Tarpon, however, considering how many there were of them, did not appear to take much interest in any fly at all. I put in several days of very hard work, but without a capture. Occasionally I had a heavy strike from a Tarpon, hungrier than the others, but found my cast missing when I brought it in. I could not make out why the cast was gone, and thought it must be that my knot where the line and cast were joined was a poor one. I changed the knot, with the same result; but at last I was broken again in a manner which revealed unmistakably from its mangled condition that the synthetic gut was not strong enough for Tarpon, even though these fish possess no teeth. I then changed my gut cast to a short piece of piano wire, with a swivel between the trace and the line. This made an ungainly rig for casting, but I still managed somehow to get it out.

Shortly after this change I was working the rocks of the left bank just below the apron, when I saw a Tarpon following my fly. The water below me was deep and crystal clear, but I was just making my retrieve and, though I tried, I could not slow up the action. The Tarpon, however, was fast enough to catch up with the fly. At the last moment he sheered off, having no doubt seen me, but too late to avoid the fly, which foul-hooked him. In an instant he was away in a magnificent run. I may say that with this same tackle I had already played many Salmon, but this was a very different affair. Sixty yards he ran while I fumbled with the reel and managed to burn my fingers on the line and rap my knuckles painfully with the reel handle. There was, of course, no mechanical brake on this reel, and it was a wonder that I did not get an over-run, but at this moment the Tarpon made a splendid jump which gave me time to find an effective way to check the reel; a problem which, through lack of similar speed and power, no Salmon had ever set me. I then clamped down on the outside disc of the reel and applied all the pressure I was able. The Tarpon continued his run, and gave another leap, without paying much attention to what I was doing. All my casting line had gone and most of the backing, though I had one hundred and ten yards on the reel, as the Tarpon tore across and slightly downstream. I could see already the barrel of the reel, and thought I had lost him, when at last it occurred to me to release all pressure. This time-old tactic succeeded perfectly, and the Tarpon only went a few yards further, at which point I doubt if I had four yards of backing left. With infinite precaution I played him back, abandoning all pressure if he resisted and taking in line when he permitted me. Thus at last I got him under control and beached him on a small sandbar. When he gave his first jump I said, " He's a fifty-pounder," when I got him ashore I thought, " Twenty-five," but on the scales he showed an even twelve pounds. He had been foul-hooked in the snout, between the eye and the lip, and was far the smallest Tarpon I had ever taken, and also the one which gave me the biggest thrills. Let others who fancy themselves as Salmon fishermen try Tarpon on the same tackle, but look out for squalls.

This was my last day at Panama, and though I tried hard enough I failed to get another strike. Thus my experience of fly fishing for Tarpon is limited to this single fish. I have never tried trolling for Tarpon, nor had success with any of several other methods frequently employed. I am convinced, however, that fly fishing with a brakeless reel is the ideal method, and that it will furnish any angler with the maximum sport possible. Tarpon, in fact, possess only the one defect: that they are not good to eat; and this alone disqualifies them from being considered the finest all-round game fish in the world. Though a Tarpon does not grow as big as do Swordfish and other of the great game fish, it is big enough to test the strength of any man. As a jumping fish it, naturally, puts out of court all game fish which do not jump, and its exquisite armour of silver scales cannot be surpassed for brilliance. The Tarpon has heart, strength, finesse, and beauty. It was therefore after reflecting on these matters that I was forced to reply to my friend's question that, though it might be possible to find a better sporting fish than a Tarpon, no fish could beat it by much, anyway.

6

CAPTAIN FINE

IT was March in Miami, and, after a certain amount
of sea-bathing and sun-tanning had been done, there
did not appear to be any good reason to put off going fishing.
A friend recommended to me Captain Clarence Fine as an
excellent guide, and I accordingly went down and saw him
and his boat *Amron II*. The weather was very unsettled
that year, and the sea did not seem ever to have a chance
to compose itself. As I had plenty of time I left my arrangements with the captain open, and decided to go fishing
only when conditions were pleasant. It is delightful when
neither time-tables nor the end of a holiday necessitates
strenuous fishing on days when one would rather rest, and
I took things easily, sometimes not going out to the Gulf
Stream for two days running.

The captain was a first-class fisherman and thoroughly
understood his job. It was he who, during a previous season,
enabled President Hoover to make a respectable catch after
a succession of blank days with another guide. Indeed,
according to the papers, the President's fishing had then
reached such a pass that unless he caught something
soon it was feared the Administration and the Republican
party would be disrupted.

After some delay occasioned by bad weather, a day arrived which seemed to me auspicious, and we went out to
the fishing-grounds. The sea was a deep blue, and fairly
smooth. I caught several Kingfish on a light rod, but

CAPTAIN FINE, WITH SAILFISH, MARLIN, WAHOO, AND DOLPHINS

was really looking for Sailfish. After a while a breeze got up, and shortly there were some small waves slapping us from time to time. The captain had an assistant who steered the boat for him, while he himself gave me personal attention in the matter of fishing. I admired particularly his method of cutting bait, which would have done credit to the most expensive surgeons. Before long the wind was strong enough just to flip off the tops of the waves in little splatters of foam. Our trolling was parallel with the waves, so that we were rolling, though not unpleasantly. I caught another Kingfish and was contemplating returning to port when, through a wave and across the trough of the next, darted something which missed my bait by a fraction and kept on going straight through the following wave before disappearing. It was an extraordinary impression I received; an impression that I had not seen anything moving but had only seen the resultant commotion. I looked at Captain Fine, who merely opened his mouth enough to say " Wahoo." I happened to know there was a fish with this peculiar name, otherwise I should have been still more astonished at the remark.

I said, " Let's try for him."

We made a big circle and turned back over a course some hundred yards further out. It was like looking for a needle in a haystack, but most anglers are willing to take such odds. Either there was another Wahoo, or the laws of chance were out of gear, because a moment or two later I saw the same strange phenomenon. This time the Wahoo took my bait with a force which almost left me rodless. The reel screamed with the impetus of that lightning strike, and then with my reflex tug the line whizzed out at redoubled speed. I must say I was astonished. I had heard that Wahoo were quick, but this one seemed much quicker. Alas, Wahoo do not jump. If they did they would surely be acclaimed the most sporting fish of the

seas.   This one continued a short distance and then turned
towards the launch and dived.   It was a complicated tactic,
and quite confusing.   I reeled in for a moment and thought
the fish was off, only to realise that he was not so far away
as I expected, and then the reel screamed again as the line
went out to starboard and lifted to the surface.   The
Wahoo next turned left-handed, and we had to steer the
launch round to get him astern.   After all this high-speed
swimming, the Wahoo decided to go down again and fight
it out.   He did a lot of rapid short runs quite deep, and I
had the opportunity to recover a little line.   The fish
obviously did not like my pumping, however, and whirled
off to starboard once more.   No fish could long continue
such fast fighting without tiring, and in about ten minutes
I felt he was weakening.   I was getting tired myself when
at last I had a sight of him.   He was a fine fish of about
thirty pounds and he did not mean to come in yet.   My
rod, however, was too much for him, and after one more
short run I reeled him to the boat.   Alas, I had counted my
first Wahoo too soon; he gave one last tug and the hook
came out.   The fish was right at the boat, and almost dead,
but, in spite of a great effort to gaff him by the captain, he
slowly moved away and disappeared from view.   We put
back for Miami, quite disheartened.

Another day I went out when the sea was very calm and
very blue.   In the morning we saw a large Hammerhead
Shark. The captain had put on a whole Mullet for bait.
It was interesting to see how skilfully the bait was cut open,
the hook inserted, and the fish sewn up again; as neat an
operation as one could wish; in fact I told the captain that
he had missed his real profession.   The Hammerhead
swam about on the surface exposing its dorsal fin, as is the
manner of these fish.   It is always most fascinating to
watch this kind of Shark following the emanation of the bait
exactly in the way a good gun dog follows the trail of a

wounded bird, but with even more accuracy. Three times the Hammerhead took my offering and three times I failed to hook it, chiefly, I think, because I did not give it time to gorge the bait. My rod, however, was a very light one, and I am sure it was just as well that it got off. A little later another smaller one came up, and this time I made no mistake. It probably weighed eighty pounds. The captain, who was a very powerful man, had an unusual way of taking the fish aboard. He simply caught hold of it by the two ends of the Hammer and lifted it up out of the sea. As he did so, the Shark gave one flip with the long lobe of its tail and caught the captain across his body. Even this small fish was so strong that the blow almost broke a rib. The captain, with justified profanity, stripped off his shirt and exposed a great blue weal where the tail had flogged him.

We saw a Sailfish that day, but could not entice it to our lures. It was not till my third day out that fortune smiled. This time we had trolled north instead of south as we had done hitherto. When we were about opposite the Pancoast Hotel and some four miles to sea, I observed a Marlin following my bait. I do not think there are any fish so interesting as Swordfish when it comes to trolling. With every other fish almost the first indication an angler has is the strike, but in the Swordfish family one generally sees the fish first. It may be that the tail fin is out of water, or that one simply sees the purple shadow of the fish in close attendance on the bait. In any case it is a thrilling sight, and calls for good timing and quick judgment. This fish first came to my cut bait and then changed over to the captain's. Several times we thought he was going to tap the bait with his spear, but in the end he decided that there must be something unusual about the curious little fish he saw ever swimming before him, and instead of trying to kill it he sheered off, in spite of all the captain's wiles, and left us disappointed.

Lunch-time arrived, and I was in the midst of a banana. Let me broadcast to the world, and particularly to novice anglers, that there is no time in the fishing calendar so productive of fish as the lunch-hour, when one is engaged with a banana or a meat *pâté*. Having had much experience of this crucial moment, I was quite prepared, in an exceedingly awkward manner, for a strike, and was scarcely surprised when my bait was hit hard by a Sailfish. I quickly let the bait drop but the fish, instead of taking it, went over and struck the captain's bait. He decided, apparently, that he liked mine better, and hurrying back this time managed to hook himself. I was fishing with light tackle and was able to enjoy a really splendid fight. The " Sail " is different from all other Swordfish, inasmuch as it is very long and slender. The convolutions and contortions that my fish went through on the surface were extraordinary, and required a meticulous finesse to circumvent. The fish was, however, well hooked, and after ten minutes began to tire quickly. I gave it all the pressure I dared, and shortly it came quite gently to the launch. Captain Fine seized the spear and lifted it aboard. Like all Swordfish this one was practically dead from its exertions and needed no finishing blow to kill it. I was very happy, as a Sailfish was one of the world's great game fish which had hitherto eluded me. It weighed only thirty-four pounds, but it was a good example of its species, and luckily on account of its small size it gave me the distinctive and unusually twisting fight characteristic of these fish, which in those of larger girth is modified and not so clearly exhibited. Indeed, one has the impression when hooked to a small " Sail " that one is playing an immense Eel which, unnaturally, has chosen to display its defences above water. This fish had a Remora attached to it, and thus two fish were landed at the same time.

During the morning I had caught several Dolphin

HOW A MARLIN IS LANDED

(*Coryphæna*) of various sizes, none of them very large. The Dolphin is one of the most beautiful fish of the seas, not because of its shape, indeed, as it has an exaggerated square head, but for its colour.   There is scarcely a fish which shows such extraordinary chameleon shades. Generally it appears at first in brilliant metallic yellows and golds alternated with violent and unnatural greens.   When landed it goes through a series of rainbow tones which are astonishing and marvellous.   The fish, too, from a fighting standpoint, is quite remarkable for its size, so that the angler believes he must have something quite important on his hook till he sees the peculiar conformation of a Dolphin near the boat.   But this excellent fishing day was not yet ended.   I had barely disposed of the Sailfish when I saw another and larger fish following my bait.   It was the typical sickle tail of a White Marlin which announced its presence and consequent anticipatory thrills.   I had my hook baited with a small fish, a " Ballyhoo," and the Marlin attacked it with vigour.   Twice I made the drop, and twice I failed to hook the fish with my light rod.   A third time it came, and this time I discovered, after the strike had failed, that the Marlin had bitten off all but the head of the Ballyhoo.   This Marlin must have been very well brought up, and apparently had been taught that it was bad manners to leave anything on its plate, for it continued following the head alone, which went skipping along the surface in a ridiculous way.   It appeared likely that if the fish again tapped the bait, the obvious incongruity of a head swimming along at five knots by itself might occur to the fish, so I handed my rod to the captain while I let out the bait on the other rod, and after a little trouble substituted it successfully for the first bait.   A moment or two later the Marlin decided it was time to exert itself if it was ever to finish lunch, and it tapped the new bait.   The captain's rod was much stronger than mine, and when I struck I felt

the hook was well set.   The fight that followed was one of
the finest I have ever experienced.   The fish gave a magnificent display.   I estimated that it jumped at least twenty
times, and between jumps was careering all over the ocean,
sometimes deep down, but mostly on the surface.   In the
end the rod had its say, and the fish came in quite dead after
forty-five minutes.   When the captain saw it in the launch
he suggested that we should take it right back to the pier.
He explained that one of the civic bodies of Miami offered
prizes for the best fish caught each year, and that he thought
this one was worth entering.   On the scales it registered
ninety-eight and a half pounds.   The largest caught that
year up till then weighed a hundred and thirteen pounds,
but the captain thought mine might qualify for second
prize.   As it turned out his opinion was well founded, for
some months later I was awarded a Heddon bait rod to
celebrate the capture.

I was informed of a peculiar fact in regard to these White
Marlin, and their big cousins, the Blue Marlin.   It appears
that these fish had rarely been observed in Florida waters
until some seven years previously, and that it is only recently
that anglers have been landing them.   These Swordfish
look to be the same fish in a half-grown stage which appear
mature off the coasts of New Zealand some years later, and
are there known as Striped and Black Marlin ; but
this is not actually the case.   However, to compare the fish,
I would point out that whereas the record White Marlin
for the year 1931 at Miami weighed a hundred and thirteen
pounds, I do not believe so small a Striped Marlin has ever
been caught in New Zealand, the average weight there being
over two hundred and sixty pounds.   The same observation applies also in comparing the Blue and Black Marlins,
with an even greater relative disproportion between the two
fish.[1]

[1] See Appendix Note, p. 296.

I would say, however, that my Marlin at Miami gave me a more active, though, of course, less impressive display, than many of the fish I caught in New Zealand. As usual, the smaller fish is more agile, and requires sometimes quicker decisions to frustrate its manœuvres. This is, one might say, a universal rule. The three-quarter-pound Trout is livelier than the three-pounder, the twelve-pound Salmon is more active than the thirty-pounder, and so on.

In fact, to vary slightly a modern saw which I have heard disrespectfully applied to lovely woman, " Catch 'em young, treat 'em rough, and they'll make you like it."

7

THE ALL HIGH GEAR FISH

THE secrecy, the obscurity, the mystery which surrounded, only a short time ago as years are numbered, the then esoteric art of Bonefishing has departed. With small thanks to the movies and a too revealing Press, we, if not the pioneers, at any rate their successors, must realise that the joy which we once experienced when we landed a fine Bonefish is now an incident of everyday angling occurrence.

How tragic to have our illusions, no matter how fragile their foundations, thus swept away by the commonplace practice of the average man. All things pass. No longer now, for instance, could the impossible escapes of Houdini enthral us. We know that it was with him simply a question of flexing certain muscles, of the constant repetition of manœuvres not apparent which enabled him once to straighten out our back hairs at an unusual angle. There was a time when we used to swoon at the eyelashes of our most admired actress; now we know that they are stuck on by the coiffeur.

I am thankful that as far as Bonefishing is concerned I was able to squeeze every ounce of thrill out of it, and that my illusions were only fractured later when other pleasures of the angle could supply compensation. But I must at once make it clear that Bonefishing itself possesses no disappointments. It is only the secrecy which is ruined.

Not many years have rolled by since my friend B. and I

found ourselves still wintering in Chicago, though it was already half-way through March. The cold, the sleet, and the snow were gradually getting the better of us, and yet we could find no excuse to justify an escape from the climate till one afternoon we wandered into a tackle shop. B. had been with me on many a fishing trip, and a nicer companion or one more altruistic I do not expect to find. We fingered through the tackle, groaning that the Bass season was still so far distant. I cannot remember whether either of us thought of it first; I think the idea must have come to us simultaneously. "Why not go somewhere else and fish?" We adjourned to the Club and began to consider. Tarpon? Sailfish? Yes, we had already done that and it was good, but could not we do something different? Then one of us thought of Bonefish. Ah! That's the thing, Bonefish! And we went to look for various friends who could give us some information. Now we discovered something strange. None of our angling acquaintances knew anything about Bonefish. They had heard of them, of course, but that was all. We made a more extensive search, and visited several tackle shops, but could find out nothing definite. However, a short paragraph in a book confirmed our impression that Bonefish could be captured in shallow water along the Florida Keys and satisfied us that the season was already on. We found too, at last, a friend who was the friend of a great fisherman in New York. Mr. A., he said, would tell us all about Bonefish.

Two days later we were on the *Century* and on arriving hastened to look up Mr. A. He was a short, nervous-looking fellow, but he took our eager questioning in a pawky and guarded manner. We could not make out whether he really wanted to give us information and did not know how, or whether he had no information to give, or whether he had the information but did not want to give it. The conversation kept getting off the subject, and we constantly had to bring him back from Tarpon to Bonefish. The plot thickened, as it seemed, to prevent us from catching Bonefish.

We went to a famous tackle shop and there at last we began to obtain some disclosures. We were shown rods and reels suitable for the purpose, and before long we were completely equipped. We were also given the names of several places along the Keys where Bonefishing could be obtained, but beyond the mere names there was nothing authoritative to guide us. After some discussion we decided to try Matacumbe, seventy-six miles south of Miami, chiefly because it was the headquarters of a well-known fishing club. Two days later we got off the train there and discovered a small hotel on the American plan. A quarter of a mile east lay the Atlantic; fifty yards west, Florida Bay and the Gulf of Mexico. The hotel proprietor said he could get us a first-class guide, and after lunch we met Captain Edney Parker, who gave us great confidence as he admitted at once that he was the best Bonefisher in all Florida. The tide was not right for Bonefishing, and the wind from the west was the worst possible, so we took a run out in the captain's launch to the Gulf Stream, four and a half miles distant. We trolled for a while, but our only catch was a tern which dropped down on our cut bait and was hooked miraculously through the nostrils. It flew away quite happily when released.

The next morning we went out with the captain's brother-in-law, Captain Henry Pinder – they are all captains down there. We steered north along the shallow coral shore in a small skiff, but in spite of diligent search no Bonefish could be found. We had had a good tide too, just beginning to go out. That afternoon we put in after Snapper, and very excellent they proved later, split open and fried. Two days and no Bonefish. We were becoming worried in spite of some jovial hospitality offered us by

Mr. Johnson at the Matacumbe club. There was, however, always to-morrow, and the third day things looked better. Though the wind was still from the west it was moderate and the sea calm. We had both our captains with us and in two skiffs they sculled us further north than the day before. I had Captain Parker as guide to start with, and once arrived at the fishing-grounds he manœuvred the boat expertly with a single oar along the coral flats. The water seldom reached two feet in depth and was of a milky greenish tinge. As usual, he was full of confidence and claimed that the water was alive with Bonefish. He said he could see them " mudding." It appears that Bonefish move in with the tide and can be found on the flats both before, during, and immediately after the flow, but when the tide has ebbed they move out to deeper water. My eyesight, of which I could scarcely complain, failed to confirm the mudding. I could see no signs of it even when they were pointed out to me. I took it all with a grain of salt and more than ever decided that Bonefishing was a recondite art. Our method of fishing was simple enough. When the captain had observed some mudding he anchored fifteen yards or so inshore and baited my hook with the mangled shell and contents of a hermit crab. I then cast out with a special Bonefish rod to the edge of the mudding. There was a lead some two feet above the hook. The lead was so devised with a hole through it that though the line could be pulled out freely through it, the lead itself could not in turn travel down to the hook – an ingenious arrangement, obviously. Once the lead had reached bottom, the tide could take the baited hook either inshore or out, but tension between the bait and rod was always established so long as there was any current to move the bait. For reel I had purchased a No. 2 Vom Hofe, a sturdy, beautifully made little winch with a thumb pad and check, but without an automatic brake; on the reel was wound three hundred yards of six-thread Cuttyhunk line. The captain now explained to me that, as Bonefish generally move up-tide, my first warning of a bite would be the momentary slackening of the line. How different from most other forms of fishing! The Bonefish has no prehensile teeth, but takes its food in with its lips and then proceeds to chew it up with its back molars. The fish is in no special hurry, and thus it happens that when it has taken the angler's bait it continues gently on its way. Sometimes if the water is shallow enough the tail fin projects from the water as the fish advances, nose down, feeding. In these circumstances the angler can take good notice of what is happening, but a little more depth and no warning is provided. There is one very necessary precaution: no noise in the boat, no tapping of empty pipes or shifting of feet, for in such circumstances then surely also no Bonefish.

We continued thus for three hours with never a sign of a Bonefish except the hundreds which the captain constantly observed. At noon we were anchored for the dozenth time. The captain had also a line out connected with a clumsy rod and reel. I admit that I was half asleep when with infinite precautions he handed me his rod. The line was slack, all right, and when he nodded I struck hard. And what an answer I received! Instantly, without the slightest pause, that Bonefish started out for England. And at what speed it travelled! It seemed to be in high gear right from the start, and supercharged besides. It looked as if the fish would get there much too soon, and so after a moment to collect my wits I decided to check it. As this was my first introduction to the captain's reel I did not see the brake pad which had turned underneath the drum. So I simply clamped down my thumb on the revolving spool. I let go quickly enough as in an instant my thumb was burnt by the line, and then at last I found the leather pad. The Bone-fish was by this time eighty yards away, and even with

strong pressure it kept on going. At last it decided to be
more reasonable and began in a wide circle to surround the
boat. I reeled in when I could. When I had it half-way
back, again it made a fine run. But now the heavy rod
began to tell. I brought the fish closer. And then it gave
another run and then another; its strength was astonishing.
Even after I had it quite near in, it would not surrender, but
tried to run under the boat or foul the line with the anchor
rope. A curious feature of all these runs was that they all
seemed to be made at full speed. The fish did not seem to
know what it was to take it easy, nor how to vary the defence
with other methods. All good things come to an end, however, and this splendid fish ran out of strength at last. The
captain netted it without difficulty. I was astonished to
find the fish so small – only five pounds; it was built like
a destroyer, all engine and no hull. Quickly despatching
it, I took leisure to admire it. What a lovely fish! It was
covered with large scales of brilliant silver which on its back
toned to a wonderful olive shade. Its body, firm and
streamlined, terminated in a huge tail, forked like that of
all fast-swimming fish. Only its snout betrayed the fact
that the fish was not predatory, but that is just as well, for,
if it were, with that speed it would soon have all the seas
cleaned out of other fish.

I turned to shake the captain's hand, and as I did saw
B. struggling desperately with another fish. He got it in
finally – a seven-pounder. I found out soon that I badly
needed my sore thumb for casting, but still managed to get
out enough line. We continued fishing and eventually B.
and I secured one more each. My second seemed even
stronger than the first, but proved to weigh slightly less.
This is a peculiarity of Bonefishing; each fish appears
stronger than the last, the reason being that they are *all* so
strong. On taking an inventory, B. and I discovered that
we had had seven strikes that day and all but one of them

(which failed to hook the fish) were on the rods of our captains. We were elated with our good luck. At last we had become Bonefishermen and had entered through the mystic portals with those others who had been initiated into the secret brotherhood.

The next, another fine day, saw us out early, but this time we steered south. We also changed captains so as to equalise our chances. Soon I had a heavy bite, and as usual the fish seemed stronger than ever. It gave me a wonderful fight, with many runs. I had it on my own lighter rod, which gave it more advantage. After twenty minutes, however, it had at last to admit defeat — eight and a half pounds. A little later I had another fish on. Again it seemed the biggest yet, and it did, indeed, give me the longest run of all — perhaps a hundred and fifty yards — before I could check it. At this point, to my horror, I discovered my line was badly frayed forty feet from the rod. In an agony of apprehension I played the fish, expecting each moment to see the line part, but somehow the weak spot lasted out long enough for me to weigh the fish — seven and three-quarter pounds. B. had by this time also collected two fish, and even Captain Parker admitted that he could no longer see any mudding. It was strange that of the six Bonefish strikes this day, not one of them had been on either of the captains' rods, a curious reversal from the day before. We then decided to put in the rest of the afternoon chugging about the Gulf Stream for less sporting fish. That night we sampled fried Bonefish and, though B. managed to obtain some nourishment, I gave up early on account of the bones (for which this fish is aptly named), not to speak of the rather dull and tasteless flavour of the flesh.

The following day, our last, in spite of a favourable south wind, turned out a total blank. It proved an anticlimax to our expedition, but we were well satisfied. We had spent

B. AND BONEFISH

two glorious days Bonefishing, we had collected eight splendid fish, and we were convinced that the mystery which surrounded Bonefishing, though justified, was simply a camouflage erected by those fortunate but selfish ones who, having already had the experience, wished to keep the sport for themselves.

We had discovered that Bonefish, finding themselves hooked in shallow water, were forced to expend their efforts to escape horizontally instead of vertically, as do most fish, and that in doing so they swim quicker and further than any other fish of their size. We appreciated that the circular swim they make after their first run is admirably adapted, if not expressly intended, for cutting the angler's line on sharp coral projections, and finally that the only criticism which could properly be levelled against Bonefish is that they do not jump. If they did – heaven help the poor angler.[1]

[1] See Appendix Note, p. 297.

8

" WHAT ? NO SWORDFISH ? "

In which Consideration is had of a Strange Ineptitude

THE swivel chair in my office, though designed to afford as much relaxation as is consistent with business, had begun to irk me enough to put me in mind of those other revolving chairs one finds in the cockpits of sea-going launches. Thus it was not surprising that a few days later I found myself in Miami and the fishing season just starting.

There, driven south by the rigours of a delayed Chicago spring, I discovered three fellow citizens : Laurance, Earle, and Vin. Over lunch and illicit Bacardís we discussed prohibition, the depression, the regrettable dissensions of formerly well-mated couples, and finally got down to a topic more worthy of consideration.

Why not forget all this and go fishing ? The idea took. With the second Bacardí, it was only a question of how, where, and when. With the third, the problem was solved. A mutual friend had a Sikorsky amphibian, lapsing into obsolescence through lack of use. We would ask for the loan of it and fly to Bimini the day after to-morrow. There were a few details to settle. We had, for instance, to obtain two fishing-launches, tackle, and stores; but in an after-noon of intensive concentration there remained nothing of importance to do, except for those thus blessed to bid good-bye to their respective spouses.

Two days later we took off from the Miami aerodrome

and went up a thousand feet. Below us the purple waters
of the Gulf Stream turned to deep indigo and seemed to
flatten out from a moderate sea to a slight ripple. In thirty-
five minutes Bimini, that small British outlier, was in view.
Shortly the Gulf Stream channel shoaled, the dark indigo
turned to viridian, then old gold, and finally to palest pink.
In the shallows far below we could see small flotillas of
Bonefish slowly searching, tails in air, for hermit crabs and
molluscs. The plane circled once and swooped to a perfect
landing in a little bay. Very soon we had joined our
launches – Laurance and I in the *Jolly Roger*, the others in
the *Caliph* – and proceeded to fish. We trolled with cut
bait and with little success all day. In the end Laurance
and the captain had each a Barracuda, while my sport was
purely Barmecidal. Our companions had collected a
Sailfish of forty-one pounds and two Tunas weighing
twenty pounds each.

That evening we went ashore to watch negroes dance to
wonderful music, and to fraternise in the local saloon with
the rum-runners who composed the aristocracy of the
island. We found them charming, alert, earnest young
men, keen on their jobs, and some of them already rich
enough to retire. When we had returned to our launches
for the night, we could hear the runners going to work.
Without a star to guide them they roared their 500 horse-
power racing-boats out of that tiny harbour into which our
captains had crept with such precautions in broad daylight.
In two hours cutting through the steep seas of the Gulf
Stream, the runners would reach one of the many small
inlets of the Florida Keys, where they would dump their
cargo and collect the $600 fee for their services. In six
trips the boats would be paid for, and the rest was all
" velvet."

For the next day's fishing we changed boats. The sea
was rougher and the launch smaller. We had good sport,

however, and accounted for twenty-one fish. My seven were all Barracuda, but Laurance had, in addition: Dolphin (*Coryphæna*), Bonito, Spanish Mackerel, Jack, Muttonfish, Tuna, and a few jumps out of a Sailfish. The Dolphin was hooked through the smart guide work of our captain. He had noticed a man-of-war bird hovering over a patch of sea, and, turning quickly, trolled us there. The man-of-war bird was not mistaken, but the Dolphin mistook Laurance's cut bait for one of the small fish he was chasing. There was, however, still another witness to our angling, a Shark, which in the end benefited by all save the head of what would have proved an almost record Dolphin. I was a little piqued by my performance that day. After all, when sitting side by side in the same launch and using the same bait as a companion, fortune alone decides who shall have the most strikes, but fortune had been quite impartial. Why had so many of my fish become unstuck, and why were those I captured all so small ? Laurance thought that I was not striking correctly, but I felt that was not the answer to my problem. The other boat had enjoyed good luck too, their most interesting fish being a twenty-four-pound Wahoo.

The next day was to be our last. We had returned to the *Jolly Roger* and in a moderating sea steered out for the big game fish grounds. I was hoping with this new day for better success. That feeling of competition so foreign to the proper spirit of the true angler had taken possession of me. It is all very well to be philosophical, but it is none the less annoying to keep failing, without obvious reason, to hook fish which should, normally, be landed when, after all, no outstanding skill is required. I had, besides, a certain confidence this day, for not long previously I had fished successfully in New Zealand for Swordfish – the grandfathers of what we were now after. Among the expert guides out there I had even earned a sobriquet of an

unparlour-like description denoting how fortunate I had
been with those fish.

In a short half-hour we were on the fishing-grounds.
Laurance had soon landed a Barracuda, and then, to our
joy, we saw a White Marlin evidently interested in our
lures. He hit first the captain's bait (for there was a third
line out) and then turned to Laurance's, which he did not
quit till he was safely in the launch; a fine sixty-two-
pounder he proved. We continued trolling, but for three
hours nothing showed. Then at last a Blue Marlin
appeared. He was a nice fish, and he sampled all three
baits. He chose mine in the end, so I struck hard and had
him on for fifty feet. Then he got loose. He must have
been very hungry, this fish, for, not content with one taste
of steel, he came back for more, and this time selected my
companion's bait. The fight was a good one, and very
interesting. In a short time, however, Laurance had him
up to the boat. In the crystal water we could see the fish,
broad and strong, not ten feet below us. His pectoral fins,
stretched wide, strained to carry him down and away to
freedom. Still, in spite of all his efforts, after forty minutes
he began to weaken, and had, at last, to acknowledge defeat
when his one hundred and thirty-five pounds were lashed
aboard.

We continued cruising, but it was only after a longish
interval that another White Marlin came up. By chance
at this moment the other two lines had become entangled.
If the fish was interested in cut bait, he must, therefore,
devote his attention to mine. And was he devoted! I
have never heard of a fish as anxious to be hooked as this
one. The usual procedure which these fish adopt is to tap
the bait with their spears; the fisherman then " makes the
drop " – that is, he releases all pressure, so that the bait,
which simulates a small fish, will appear to have been
killed. The Swordfish then seizes the bait, and, after a

suitable interval to allow the fish to swallow it, the angler slaps on the brake and strikes hard, thus hooking the fish. This one tapped my bait, and I made the normal " drop," but to my surprise there was no response to my strike. The Swordfish was still there, however, and came again. Not once did he come, but *nine times*, without my once driving the hook home. I tried every kind of drop and strike I could think of, including two or three invented for the occasion, but nothing succeeded. During this interval Laurance was working frantically on his tangled line, and at last he was able to put on a new leader and bait. The moment this new bait came down to him, the Swordfish deserted mine, which had by this time become rather frazzled, and took my companion's hook without apparently the slightest intention of ever relinquishing it. Nor did he, till it was prised from his mouth on the poop. He was another sixty-two-pounder.

This concluded our fishing and we had to return, though we learnt that the other boat had not seen a fish the whole day. In a short time the Sikorsky ferried us back to Miami. Naturally as we flew we discussed the events of the expedition. One of my companions evolved the theory that Laurance's hands had been attuned by constant horseback riding to delicate response in contact with other creatures, and that this accounted for his success. But I have captured many varieties of fish without ever having shone as an equestrian. In the back of my mind I was considering two explanations for my own poor showing, which I will now expound. The first is psychological, and has to do with trying too hard. How many times have I netted, with little difficulty, five fish, and then experienced a perfect inferno of trouble to complete my three brace, when that was all I was seeking. If, on the other hand, it is the twelfth fish which I particularly want, then it is that one which inexplicably becomes elusive. This strange inhibition, which prevents the capture of a particular fish, may be caused by

LAURANCE AND HIS CATCH OF MARLIN

nervous tension which again produces bad timing. When I have used the expression " pressing," even non-golfers will understand the idea I am trying to convey. In very delicate angling, such as dry-fly fishing, where micrometric timing makes all the difference, this is undoubtedly the elucidation of many failures which most anglers must have suffered. But in the case of the last Swordfish that explanation would hardly hold. On that occasion there was no other bait offered; I had all the time necessary to experiment coolly and scientifically with many different techniques. I will reject this answer to the question.

My second reason has to do with tackle. Throughout these three days I was fishing with a rod tip weighing six ounces, and rather soft besides, whereas the rods of my fellow anglers were considerably stronger. Consequently, though I could hook the lighter Barracuda, it was not possible to put sufficient force into my strikes to be certain of the heavier fish. To confirm this with a specific example: when I caught a ninety-eight-and-a-half-pound Marlin a week previously, it was with the heavy rod of my captain, after two failures to strike the hook home with my own six-ounce tip. But I could offer instances where it was not I who had the softer rod, and where under such circumstances abnormal success has crowned my own endeavours. I therefore suggest to anglers whose vacations are too limited to permit the luxury of a lost fish that they employ strong, stiff rods, and I think it can be demonstrated that the stiffer the rod the more likelihood that the fish will stay on. It has occurred to me since that, if there is no choice but a light rod, a fairly firm strike could be given by holding the rod pointed towards the fish and then striking with the full strain of the brake.

When we landed that afternoon at Miami, we took a car to join some friends who were expecting us. There was, of course, keen interest shown in the results of our fishing.

Each of my companions was questioned and congratulated. Finally it came to my turn to describe my catch. I explained that I had captured seven small Barracuda. The loveliest of the ladies with some surprise interjected, " What? No Swordfish?" To which I could only reply, " No, no Swordfish."

9

BLACK BASS

" Inch for inch and pound for pound the gamest fish that swims." — HENSHALL.

ONE must, of course, pardon an advocate, and Dr. Henshall was one, if he is carried away by the claims of his client. Nor will I reflect on his judgment of things piscatorial in this chapter. In fact I will not challenge his assertion set forth above, and will instead for my own pet fish seek other honours. The American Black Bass can swim on its own fins without the authority of great anglers to buoy it up, for it has many qualities that are unique.

I must acknowledge a great debt to Black Bass, the fish which convinced me that my childhood enthusiasm for fishing was not ill-founded. As I have recounted elsewhere, my first angling experience had to do with lake Perch; later came other coarse fish; but it was not till my friend Bill asked me to spend a week with him at the Island Club, Wisconsin, that I had the privilege of being introduced to a game fish.

The invitation I accepted with glee, but Bill was going to make sure that I would obtain the full benefit. As he knew I was a complete neophyte, his forethought included valuable assistance in the choice of equipment. With him I invaded the tackle shops, from which I emerged with all that was necessary for the expedition. At this date I would question his judgment in selecting an automatic reel for me.

What an abomination, with its spring tension so neatly devised for shattering the rod tip. But of the other items he chose there could be no criticism. It was he who helped me obtain a nine-foot-three-inch fly rod at a reasonable price, together with a line, fly box, casts and Bass " bugs " of sufficient variety for the purpose in hand. I purchased, too, a six-foot casting-rod and several spoons and " plugs " which I was informed would take care of Muskellunge as well. I could hardly wait to board the train for Lac du Flambeau.

It was a large, mixed party which descended from the train and proceeded in cars some fifteen miles through second-growth timber to the lake. The club was on an island, which we reached in row-boats. It consisted of a series of log cabins, of various sizes for sleeping-quarters, and two larger ones served as dining and club rooms.

Bill soon had us out on the front lawn taking preliminary lessons in casting. First it was the plug and then the fly. It proved a difficult programme to start on for most of us. Bill's cries of " One – hold it – two! " boomed out as we tried to propel ungainly Bass bugs with some semblance of a line. It was not long before we had all had enough of this and the party divided up into boats. Where possible a novice accompanied one who possessed a little knowledge of fishing, but, as there were not enough knowledgeable ones to go round, this was only an optimum arrangement.

Of those days, now long past, my recollection is rather vague. I can remember a fierce sun beating down as my companion or I rowed in shifts round the weed beds where the big "Muskies" lay. There were crowds of them, but our lures did not attract as they were intended. Occasionally one of them, less lethargic than the others, would make a sudden lunge (how well named, the Muskellunge), and then intense excitement reigned. I remember one of my friends trying to remove a spoon from a Muskie before it was quite

A 12 lb. MUSKELLUNGE AT THE ISLAND CLUB

dead, and the painful and alarming wounds he received. Our Bass fishing did not amount to much. Those cork-bodied bugs were far too big for our casting powers, and we did not know enough about Bass haunts to bring much success. I did, however, manage to secure one, and he " sold me " on Bass for life.

I think this was the extent of my fishing that year, but my interest was now thoroughly awakened. I spent almost every evening the rest of that summer fly casting on the golf-course. My golfing friends must have formed the opinion that I was queer. In the winter I moved to the city and joined a casting club. It was a splendidly managed association. We had a corner of one of the lagoons in the park allotted to us. Here there were piers erected for casting, and all the necessary paraphernalia. I have never seen a more friendly and helpful spirit among men than that we enjoyed.

Most of the casting was with the plug. In those days there were three recognised tournament weights for the plug: the quarter ounce, half ounce, and five-eighths ounce. This last was made of wood; the other two were streamlined teardrops of aluminium. I soon discovered that it was necessary to have three rods for the different plugs, and purchased a "matched set" made by Thomas. I was lucky, I think, for I have never seen three finer Bass rods. They were each of them six feet long over all and weighed respectively four and one-eighth ounces, four and five-eighth ounces, and five ounces, but the rather heavy metal mountings of the reel and handle fitting accounted for a good part of the weight, the actual bamboo being very delicate and fine.

For reels I used the No. 3 M. J. Meek. This reel had jewelled pivot bearings; it was an exquisite little instrument of precision, and was provided with a cork arbour to aid a rapid retrieve. It had no mechanical arrangements of any sort, except a light click which could be employed when required. These reels were fixed above the hand grip on top of the rod and controlled by pressure of the thumb on the arbour. For line I used one of braided silk with a four-pound breaking strain.

The art of tournament plug casting was at that time a comparatively recent pursuit, but the technique was already standardised. Each competitor would take his place in turn on a casting platform and would then cast in rotation, once each, at targets anchored in the lagoon at distances of sixty, seventy, eighty, ninety, and a hundred feet. He would then reverse the process, starting again with the hundred-foot target. The targets were circular, with a diameter of thirty inches. If the target was hit, the competitor scored ten points, but a point was deducted for each foot or fraction of a foot by which he missed the target. It was astonishing how accurate the casting could be. The theory of this system of casting is that the spring of the rod should give the whole impetus to the cast. By experts, therefore, for distances of up to a hundred and fifty feet the rod is brought from a horizontal position in front of the caster to the vertical *and not beyond*, by the movement of the wrist alone. This movement is very rapid; then, without the slightest pause, the rod is returned. The plug, which is usually suspended about a foot from the end of the rod tip, continues, of course, beyond the vertical by its own momentum and then leaps forward in a magical manner as the caster releases all but the faintest pressure on the reel drum. Thereafter, at the moment when the plug is above the target, pressure on the drum causes the plug to fall gracefully to the spot intended. I give these details in order that those unacquainted with the art can appreciate that American bait casting can approximate in its development of delicacy and finesse to the highest angling standards.

THE FIRST BLACK BASS

The next season I was ready to do some real fishing. I had joined the club in the meantime. Even Bill, my friend and mentor, was astonished by my transformation. There was no longer necessity for lessons, and, in fact, it was only how to catch fish which still baffled me; but I had the delight of knowing that if my judgment was correct as to where the fish lay I could at least present them with a lure to sample. It was not long before I had abandoned Muskellunge fishing entirely, though it took some time before I could convince my friend Bernard, with whom I usually arranged my expeditions to the club, that Muskellunge as a sporting fish was very inferior. It is a large and ferocious-looking beast, but possesses little fighting heart. I think Bernard came round to my way of thinking the day he landed a fourteen-pounder with scarcely any trouble on a four-and-three-quarter-ounce, nine-foot Trout rod. I dare say, for I am always ready to give the devil his due, that Muskellunge in fast water might be fairly amusing, but in a lake they proved of faint interest. Another fish often pursued and well considered at the Island Club was the Walleyed Pike. This fish, which makes delightful eating, is of small value from a sporting point of view. It is closely related to the Fogosh of Austria and Hungary, which is considered the most delicious of all edible fish in those countries.

Bernard and I spent some glorious days after Bass at the Island Club. We would usually go out in a canoe and take turns paddling. In the front of the canoe the angler sat facing forward and casting to the left of him. Sometimes we fished the plug, sometimes the fly. Black Bass, as I have said, possess some attributes which are unique. They have for instance the unusual quality of maternal and paternal solicitude for their eggs and young. From the moment the eggs are laid at the edge of a lake, or in some retired spot, the parents guard them with a courage which can only be described as suicidal. It is due to this instinct that it is possible to fish for Black Bass with plugs of immense size, considering the fish. No sooner does a plug approach the nest than one or other of the parents dashes out to defend the home. They won't stand any interference with their domestic arrangements, and who can blame them for that ? The plugs used are generally wooden cylinders painted in various colours. It does not seem to matter much what is the colour or form of the plug, nor how it performs in the water. Some of them dive or wallow on the surface or wiggle; the Bass pays no attention to these details. Out he comes at a " dead swim " and attacks the intruder viciously. But the plug possesses from two to five triangles of hooks prepared specially for such an emergency, and soon the Bass finds himself pierced in several places by the barbs. He would like to get away, but he has little chance. He jumps, he dives, he tries to swim under tree-stumps or twist himself free among the lily pads. His possibilities of escape are few, and soon the angler has netted him. It is a pity no plugs seem to be on the market which allow the Bass a fair defence. If single hooks could be attached to the plug on the principle of the " automatic striker-spoon baits " it would be much less cruel to the Bass and provide more sport for the angler. With such an arrangement, if the fish seized a hook it could be so contrived as to slide out of its slot in the plug on a short length of chain, enabling the fish to make his display without danger from other hooks, and without the handicap of the plug to bother him in his fight. Some such device would also afford the Bass a better chance of escape. I expect there is something impractical in the idea or it would long ago have been developed. If it were not for this disadvantage in the plug, bait casting for Bass would be ideal sport. The delicacy and accuracy required in making casts of thirty to fifty yards just to the edge of a lily pad or the protruding stump of a half-submerged log, rivals in every way, and in fact almost surpasses, the beauty of a perfect dry-fly cast.

I must say Bernard and I preferred the fly rod. We went through the usual stages commencing with cork-bodied Bass bugs and naturally found them wretched things to cast, being both ungainly in the air and difficult to retrieve from the water. We then began to experiment with various flies. One day Andy, another friend of mine, produced a " Hair Basser " with which he had enjoyed phenomenal sport. I tried it and liked it, though it was a fearful-looking thing. In the water, however, it swam beauti-fully, giving the motion and appearance of a Minnow. This fly was made of buck tail instead of feathers, and was dyed in various colours. It was not long before we changed the hook on which it was mounted from 1 /o to No. 6, and had some specially made up for us. When we had thus evolved a lure which cast and retrieved well, we tried it on the Bass. It worked beautifully, and we sought no further. With these small Hair Bassers of various colours we could obtain all the sport we wanted. It is possible, though it requires proving, that Bass do not go for these small flies as well as they do for larger ones, but the additional accuracy and ease in casting more than compensated us. At any rate, our catches compared favourably with those of other anglers at the club. By this time we began to feel a certain confidence in our fishing, and engaged a delightful character named Beaver, who worked like one, and with him took excursions through the forest to different lakes. I confess that Beaver did most of the portaging, though we sometimes assisted when we felt in need of exercise. When we came to a lake we launched our canoe and fished. We were rarely disappointed by the Bass. At lunch and at five we would build a fire, and Beaver, who had the accomplishment of being a superb Black Bass chef, would split our catch in half and fry it. I would claim Brillat-Savarin never concocted a more savoury dish.

This, then, was the usual type of Bass fishing I enjoyed, except for one curious experience. My friend Paul, a very extraordinary person, apprised me one day that there was some fine Bass fishing in Lake Geneva, Wisconsin. This lake lay hundreds of miles south of where I had fished previously. In a short time we had arranged with two other friends to go and try it. We motored there early one morning. Paul, who was always a mine of information, had engaged two guides beforehand. Applegreen, he told me, was the best guide on the lake, and when we got there I found myself with Paul in Applegreen's launch. Everything was ready except the motor of the launch, which coughed and spluttered. Our two companions were off like a flash in the launch of the second-best guide. When they had got a start of a hundred yards, our launch came to life. Applegreen (who, by the way, Paul always called " Applesauce," much to his annoyance) turned to us dolefully and announced that we should catch no fish. We asked why, and he said that the others would get there first. We did not understand this cryptic answer, but at his suggestion we prepared our tackle. This expedition, I must explain, was designed simply to catch Black Bass. I would pause for a moment to remark that I had long passed the stage when the mere catching of fish was my sole pleasure in fishing. I protest that though this is a very agreeable termination to a day's sport, for me the main gratification results from the intelligent application of sporting angling to the purpose in hand. If the fish has proved worthy of my art or guile, and has succeeded in circumventing my stratagems, then I have still had a splendid day.

On this occasion, however, I was carried away by Paul's primitive desire to catch fish. I found that we were going to fish the bottom with crawfish as bait. Applegreen forced his motor to the limit, but he could make no impression on the other launch. Suddenly I saw it come to an abrupt anchorage. Applegreen took a couple of sights, and remarked that the other guide had found it. We still understood nothing when our boat slewed round and anchored within fifteen yards of our friends. By the time we had stopped, one of them was already pulling in a fine fish. For an hour Paul and I fished as hard as we could from the starboard side of the launch. Applegreen had assured us that the port side was no good. As for our friends, they captured fish after fish, while we never had a bite. Applegreen kept looking at his watch, and suddenly hissed " Reel in." We did, and in an instant we had up-anchored and were off.

" We got 'em this time," vouchsafed Applegreen. We traversed a mile of lake and then our guide, after taking several sights, anchored again. Behind us we could see the other launch pounding along. We did have them too, and in half an hour landed six splendid fish, while our friends sat twenty yards off in their launch waiting vainly for something to chase monotony. Paul had just netted a good one when Applegreen snapped his watch to and remarked that we might as well go back to lunch. Paul said he wanted to stay on longer, but in twenty minutes we had no further sign of a fish and gave it up. I have recounted this story as it occurred. What was the explanation? Did all the Bass in the lake go to a certain rendezvous till a certain hour and then move to another at a fixed time? I do not know, but if any of my readers will go to see Mr. Applegreen at Lake Geneva he will, perhaps, be able to inform himself on the subject.

It will be noted that I have not hitherto differentiated between Small Mouth and Big Mouth Bass, nor will I, for, though I have captured both, the process has proved similar. So far this chapter will no doubt have been

accepted without comment.   It is now time, however (as
is probably expected), for me to put my head in the lion's
mouth and compare Black Bass with Trout.   I will protect
myself as best I can by remarking that, though some people
like beefsteak, others prefer lamb chops.   I have not told
of all the fishing I have done for Black Bass, but I confess
that I have never had the pleasure of trying for them in
rivers.   My judgment is limited to still-water Black Bass.
I am further uncertain as to my competence to judge between these two fish, owing to a sentence written by a very
well-known angler which stated: " Compared to the
proper handling of fly-rod tackle in fishing for Bass, the
casting of a dry-fly for Trout is a fairly simple matter."   I
am so confused by this dictum that it makes me wonder
whether any of those fish I caught with the fly *were* Black
Bass, or were they Perch or what ?   The author goes on
to speak of the big Bass of the Delaware River, and it is
undoubtedly to the difficulty of capturing them that he
is referring.   Now these fish would have to be a
lot different from the Bass which I caught (assuming I did
catch Bass) before I could agree with his thesis.   The
method which I found satisfactory was as follows: First,
I would locate from a boat or from the shore a spot which
looked like a probable Bass lie, and would put out a reason-
ably long and straight line to it.   I would then make the
retrieve in various manners according to whether the lure
was being fished floating or submerged.   If the fish was
seen before the cast was made, it would be necessary, of
course, to place the lure with a certain accuracy to bring it
into the range of vision of the Bass.   That, as far as my
experience goes, is about all there is to it.   Naturally the
angler must be either sufficiently far away or sufficiently unobtrusive in his movements not to alarm the fish.   As for
the manner in which the lure alighted, the Bass seemed to
take little stock in such.   If it was hungry or angry, out it

would rush with the speed of a torpedo and seize the fly in no uncertain manner. The rod point was then lifted and the Bass was hooked.

The angler I have quoted expands his ideas of the difficulty of handling fly tackle for Bass by enumerating how on one occasion he instinctively made five successive and different kinds of casts to search a likely spot for a Bass, and that these different casts were varied so as to loop the line and flick the lure to right, left, and centre of the small space he was fishing without getting hung up in the surrounding foliage. Undoubtedly, to be able to employ such finesse with the clumsy lures necessary for Bass denotes a mastership to which few can attain; and I dare say that in such circumstances the difficulties he claims are demonstrated. I maintain, however, that the occasions for such complications will occur less frequently in Bass fishing than in dry-fly Trout work.

I do not believe that a wily old Trout would wait for the five casts. How often has the big moment in a Trout day depended on one single cast to a well-known Trout, with the knowledge that only perfection will produce the desired response. My favourite author on Bass has cast reflections on the difficulties of Trout fishing. It is, perhaps, presumptuous of me to question his opinion without having ever experienced his famous Delaware Bass; but it is possible that he has never tried his skill on an English chalk stream and we may, therefore, both of us be arguing at cross purposes without sufficient background to justify our claims. There is a neat saying which may reconcile us: "What do they know of England who only England know?"

Fly tackle for Bass fishing is, as I have said, of the bludgeon type, but against the ungainly Bass bug, so exasperating to cast at all, I would place the gossamer lightness of the small dry-fly which is deflected by the slightest air current from its intended destination. The successful Bass fisherman must know and practise a score of different methods in retrieving his lure, but he does not have to deal with " drag " (that terror of the dry-fly angler), nor with the necessity of keeping undisturbed contact with the approaching fly.

There are many other points of comparison which could be made, but perhaps the main difference between angling for Bass and Trout lies in the attitudes of the two fish towards the lure. Whereas it is possible that the Black Bass seizes the bug with the intention of eating it, the fury of the attack gives the impression that the fish is making a warlike assault on an enemy, and the angler has not much difficulty under such circumstances in setting the hook. There is no doubt, however, that the different techniques which a Trout employs in taking a fly are all concerned with the idea of eating it, and are varied by many considerations, depending on the hunger, confidence, temperament, and other characteristics of the Trout at that moment. The response of the fishermen to the rise, and the correct timing of his rod, will then make for success or failure; but the delicacy and judgment required at this climax of the hooking exists scarcely at all in Black Bass fishing. This additional and fascinating problem which Trout afford the angler decides me that I must certainly score *one* for Trout up to the hooking.

Once the fish are on, I think perhaps the Bass is a little better than the Trout. He is stronger for his weight, though not quicker; he jumps more, shakes his head more, and battles a little more desperately. Further, he generally has some horrible submerged tree limb round which to snarl the line. If he can get a purchase somewhere he will more likely manage to pull the hook out than will a Trout. Against this is the smaller hook employed for Trout, which stays in less easily than a Bass hook.

Finally, having landed both the fish, one must consider the eating. Well, I have eaten Trout cooked in more different ways than I can count. How good they are *au bleu, meunière, bonne femme, béchamel, genevoise*! Still, Beaver could certainly fry Bass. It makes my mouth water now. No, I won't decide that problem. To sum up: if there were no Trout to go for, then I would go for Bass. On the other hand, if there were no Bass then I would go for Trout. If there were both Trout and Bass available, then I would probably go crazy.

IO

THE FISH COURSE

IN 1928 we were enduring in America — who can ever forget it? — the noble experiment imposed on us by Andrew Volstead and F. Scott McBride which succeeded so admirably in debauching the nation.

That summer I spent in Southampton, Long Island. The presidential campaign was on with a violence not observed since the days of McKinley and Bryan. At every dinner-table, discussion, so fierce as to be no longer funny, took place between elderly dowagers who should have been minding their knitting, and their table partners who knew only that whisky was costing too much. Naturally the dowagers won every argument, martialling factory statistics, no matter where they got them, to which one had only to bow in defeat.

It was noticeable that, at the show of hands after dinner, Smith had a great majority but Hoover pulled off the election.

In those days the " National " was playing beautifully, though MacDonald still refused to have the rough sufficiently mown; tennis was booming, and the sea-bathing was excellent.

Between these various diversions I managed to squeeze in a little fishing. With Lawrence I went Black Bass fishing in a near-by lake; the fish came to the fly almost as well as the mosquitoes to our exposed portions. Then there was good sport after Weakfish in Peconic Bay, using fine gut casts.

A little later we sailed in Brooks's yacht to Block Island and caught pound-and-a-half Skipjack on fly rods, chumming them to the yacht with minced Mackerel. For this fishing I used 3x wet-fly casts and sometimes had three fish on at once, though I never landed more than two of them together. To vary the sport we occasionally pursued small Tuna, using stronger tackle.

It was all very amusing, but we did not reach any great heights of enthusiasm till we drove with Van Ingen to Montauk Point. It was there we encountered a coastguard who told us about Striped Bass.

None of us knew anything about this fish, but the more we heard the more we wanted to know. The coastguard showed us the casting piers erected by the Montauk Striped Bass Club and gave us some general information. The next day I was in New York buying a Striped Bass rod, lead squids, and other requisites. I found that the type of rod used may be as much as eleven feet long, with a diameter above the reel of an inch, the whole casting top being of split cane. From the butt to the centre of the reel seat measures about three feet, the long handle being held at the end with the left hand, while the thumb of the right hand controls the free running reel. The leverage thus obtained enables the angler to make extremely long casts when he has mastered the art. While in New York I also took care to absorb all that the tackle-maker could tell me as to the method of catching these fish. After another expedition to Montauk, where we obtained further details, we were ready to begin operations. We had been told that the fishing was only good on the slack of the tide and that it was best when this moment occurred at an early hour. By this time Ellsworth was also of the party and, though new to the idea, made up with his *brio* for what we possessed of knowledge as theoretical old Striped Bass fishermen.

A few days later, conditions promised to be perfect and

we motored to Montauk, arriving at five in the morning. It was the fifteenth of September, too early for Striped Bass, but we thought the ideal conditions might have brought in the fish. At this stage our proceedings became scarcely gentlemanly. Hastily assembling our rods, and without paying any dues or even submitting our candidatures for membership, we took possession of the casting piers of the Montauk Striped Bass Club. To this day I regret this lapse from becoming behaviour, but at the time we were seized with a frenzy to fish for Striped Bass, and no social considerations could restrain us.

The piers were handily constructed. They consisted of two parallel boards running some ten yards out to sea and terminating in a small platform, the whole supported on piles which stood about twelve feet above high tide. From these we could obtain a perfect stance for casting.

The method of fishing for Striped Bass is simple enough. Having attached a lead squid weighing about four ounces to the end of the line, one casts out to sea as far as possible and then retrieves the lure. The Striped Bass come in on the slack to feed at the point where the waves break on the rocky shore. At any moment until the squid is drawn up out of the water one may hope for a fish.

With my special rod I could cast about sixty yards, but I found it hard work. After about ten minutes of casting, Lawrence was pessimistic enough to announce that we should catch nothing. At this moment a vision appeared on the last remaining pier. It was a genuine member of the Montauk Club. At a time when shorts were only worn by Englishmen in tropic lands he was already thus arrayed. He wore also, if I remember rightly, an Eden Rock blue and white barred jersey. His tackle was superb, and the way he handled it was beyond compare. He was soon shooting out his squid like a bullet a hundred yards or so. He made us all look very amateurish.

The slack of the tide was already waning when suddenly I got a strong strike. These fish are certainly game. Though I exerted considerable pressure, the battle which ensued was fierce and protracted. At last after a good struggle I beached a fine ten-pounder.

We continued to cast, but conditions were becoming less favourable. We were about ready to depart when the club member also hooked a fish and had it ashore in jig time. As we returned to our car we asked the member – without apologising for our trespass – what luck he had had. He told us this was the first fish he had captured that season, though he had been fishing for fourteen days. We congratulated ourselves on our good fortune and returned to Southampton.

That night we had arranged for a dinner-party, and, as there was a fresh Striped Bass available, we cancelled the lobsters. After consultation with the cook it was decided to serve the fish whole, *poché*, with *sauce mousseline*. There is no better eating fish than Striped Bass. This one was to be the main feature of the repast.

I must explain that our domestic arrangements included an English butler of impeccable character as far as his references were concerned. He did seem to have one slight failing, however, which had probably been accentuated by the zeal of Messrs. Volstead and McBride previously referred to. That season there was a trend towards rum cocktails. The stuff used to arrive at my house in five-gallon jars direct from Jamaica (Long Island). I had had to speak to the butler about his failing, and we had reached an understanding that one more slip and he was *out*.

After cocktails the party settled down to dinner. The creamed-mushroom soup was served by the maids. Everyone was on the alert for the Striped Bass, for I alone had already modestly recited the tale of its capture a dozen times.

At last the butler appeared bearing the fish, which looked silvery and magnificent on a large dish.

I noted a slight stagger as the butler advanced; then, majestically, as the *Queen Mary* being launched, the fish gently slid off the plate. There was a muffled explosion. Now the flesh of Striped Bass is extremely flaky and, when we looked for the fish, there remained naught save the head, tail, and backbone. The rest was scattered like snow over the carpet. Murmuring a confused " Sorry, sir," the butler stumbled from the room.

I never saw him again.

IN DARKEST AFRICA

MY friend Reggie and I made a compact that if I would accompany him to Capetown and other places in South Africa where he could sell his oils and by-products, he would accompany me where fishing could be obtained as we journeyed north to Cairo. It seemed a reasonable proposition, and it worked very well.

A few days later we left England, and arrived at Capetown just in time for the New Year celebrations, which must be unique, I imagine, the world over. Here the Cape boys – rather pale-coloured negroes they are – on New Year's Day form into bands of a hundred or so. Each band dresses up in fancy costume to represent some idea with a predominating colour scheme, and thus arrayed they parade through the streets with great gaiety all the morning. It is a quaint and amusing spectacle which makes one think of a *mardi gras* in black face, with ten times the animation that phlegmatic Latin decorum usually displays. In the afternoon the exercises continue and the different bands compete for prizes which are awarded for singing, dancing, and costumes.

A few days later, while Reggie attended to business, I drove out to Hermanus Bay, the best-known fishing-ground of South Africa, which has become famous through the energy, ingenuity, and persistence of W. R. Selkirk. I went at once to his store, where I looked over the finest collection of fishing trophies it has ever been my fortune to inspect. I do not suppose there is a shop like his in the world. All the walls from floor to ceiling bear witness to his prowess. The jaws of scores of Sharks grin out with gruesome horror, strange fish, mounted in different ways, display their former proportions, while over all gapes the colossal denture of the greatest fish ever caught on rod and line. I met Selkirk, of course, and he gave me an account of his historic struggle with the celebrated 2,176 lb. monster which he captured. This, which he called simply a man-eater, was really a Great White Shark (*Carcharodon rondeletii*), and measured thirteen feet three inches, with a girth of eight feet nine inches. Selkirk used a ten-foot rod and a Hardy Sea Silex reel with only a standard brake. The line, two hundred and fifty yards long, was of eighteen cord, with a breaking strain of fifty-four pounds. A regulation Swordfish hook was used for the fight, and this was connected to the line by a six-foot wire trace. Where the line and trace met, two empty petrol tins of four gallons capacity were attached, to act as floats and help exhaust the fish. Selkirk told me that he had caught ten other man-eaters which weighed over a thousand pounds each, and all of them were landed from the shore without a boat. He said that many of them attacked the floats and punctured them with their teeth, thus showing that Sharks are not so stupid as one might think.

He had in his shop the jaws of what appeared to be a Mako (*Isurus glaucus*) and many other Sharks, including several Sand Sharks (*Odontaspis taurus*), also the skin of a seal he had caught with quite a small hook. In addition he pointed out to me mounted specimens of the various game fish most sought in those waters, particularly Steenbras, Leerfish, Snoek, and Kabeljou, which last is a kind of White Sea Bass, greatly prized on account of its fighting and eating qualities.

I was keen to have a combat with a big Shark, and had

brought with me, for the purpose, my New Zealand big game fish tackle, and a special rod made up for me by Hardy Bros. I was hoping, indeed, to try conclusions with one of these Sharks without the petrol-tin floats, for I had six hundred yards of line and a Vom Hofe reel with a powerful brake which would have given me a great advantage, and might have compensated me for the omission of the floats. I found out, however, that the big Sharks only come into Hermanus Bay from time to time when the wind is exactly in the right quarter, and that lately none had appeared. I had thus to content myself with an attempt on lesser fish, which, as it turned out, was not successful. I fished near the hotel where other anglers were also casting out from the rocks, into a roughish surf which broke over a rugged shore. I saw a Kabeljou hooked; and a Sea Snake, a horrid, poisonous beast with long feelers in its mouth, was landed.

The next day I fished in Still Bay, which was better sheltered against the " black south-easter " then blowing. I managed to account for nothing, however, though I had two strikes, and a Sea Snake also attempted to take my bait. I had to return to Capetown the following day, and thus was unable to test my tackle on one of the big Sharks. There is, all the same, no doubt that with proper big game tackle extraordinary sport could be had with these Sharks if rubber balloons tied to the line with fine thread were used instead of petrol tins to carry the bait out to the fish. When submerged by the Shark the balloons would burst or come loose, and the angler might, if lucky, be enabled to break all records for shore fishing without the aid of a float.

After visiting Johannesburg, Bulawayo, Salisbury, and other cities, Reggie and I took steamer from Beira for Mombasa. We stopped at Mozambique, Dar-es-Salaam, and Zanzibar, and then found ourselves early one morning just arriving at our destination. As we steamed up to the town we could see, lining the banks of the estuary, the strangest trees I have ever laid eyes on. They were baobab trees, and were remarkable for the fact that they had huge trunks and limbs but their height suddenly seemed to have stopped before they had grown up. They gave the impression of having started as forest giants, but ended up as immensely fat dwarfs.

We took train that day for Nairobi, and passed through our first locust swarm two hours later. Without straining our eyes we could see a field of maize melting before this insect attack. As we travelled north we began to enter the game country. For those who have not visited Africa before, it is an extraordinary experience to sit comfortably in the train without any safari work, and observe creatures in a wild state of which they have seen hitherto only the mounted heads at Rowland Ward's. We saw nothing very rare, but we passed Grant's and Thompson's gazelles, kongonis, gnus, ostriches, a secretary bird, zebras, a duicker, and in one place water-buck, while birds of prey, eagles and vultures, circled overhead on slow wings.

I had an introduction to the chief of the railway systems at Nairobi, and, when we arrived, went at once to see him about chartering a ship to take me up to Murchison Falls. In a surprisingly short time I had at my disposal the *Livingstone*, a sixty-foot steamboat completely outfitted and ready for the trip I was contemplating. Having made these arrangements we took advantage of several opportunities to view a spectacle which must be unique within such close range of a large town. I refer to the astonishing numbers and varieties of game that can be seen near Nairobi by simply taking a taxi to the Masai reserve (where, for instance, we were surrounded by a herd of fifty giraffes), or, still nearer, within twenty minutes of the town centre, at the aviation field, which seems to be a favourite rendezvous for most of the common fauna of the continent. This sight alone is worth a trip to Africa.

We left Nairobi after a few days and took train for Tororo. That afternoon we reached the Rift Valley, that extraordinary hole in the earth which is one of the wonders of the world and certainly does not belie its reputation. During the night our train crossed and recrossed the equator many times, and, in fact, passed a small town called Equator which is appropriately situated. At Tororo we took a motor for Jinja, a trip of ninety-seven miles. On the way we noticed that the old and ugly native women wore nothing above the waist, while the young and pretty ones were well covered up — surely a characteristic observable among women in different ways the world over. There was one exception to this rule, for we encountered on this trip a young woman walking along the road completely naked except for one very small string of beads. Her body, after the custom of some tribes, had been anointed with rancid butter and then powdered with red earth. In the warm sun the butter had absorbed the powder, so that her figure glistened like a statue of terra-cotta, moulded in the most exquisite proportions.

I had arranged to go to Jinja to try for a fish of which I had heard when in New Zealand. It is a kind of Barbel (*Barbus radclyffei*), resembling somewhat, and closely related to, the Mahseer of India. Jinja is situated on Lake Victoria, and the best fishing was to be had at the Ripon Falls just below the town. These falls, discovered by Speke in 1862, form the source of the White Nile, for this reason being of interest to the traveller, though as a spectacle they are not outstanding, the drop only amounting to about thirteen feet. On arriving at Jinja we quickly got out our tackle, and, after obtaining the services of an old native named Juana to carry our gear, we repaired to the falls.

The water issues from Victoria Nyanza in a very considerable volume, curling over the rock shelf of the lake in a smooth and deep but narrow glide, which spreads out at once over a wide expanse of slow-flowing water. Below the falls there are rocks which form a good platform for fishing, so, after rigging my Striped Bass rod, I began to cast with a Pfleuger spoon. As we had not much time to fish, Reggie decided to postpone his attempt till the next day. We could see the fish I was after lying in great numbers just below the white water of the falls, but I was afraid of getting caught up and so preferred to cast further downstream and let the spoon swing round in the current. With my fifth cast there came a heavy tug, and I was on to a nice fish. It splashed and floundered about with some energy, but did not display any great resource, though as long as it was in the fast water it afforded considerable resistance. Once I had worked it into slower water it gave up quickly enough. I only had nine more casts and obtained another fish which was smaller but proffered a better fight. These fish weighed nine and a quarter and eight and a half pounds respectively; they were a dark olive-green on top, shading to pale greenish yellow on the belly, and had large scales on their bodies, which were of the shape of a Salmon but with a forked tail. They were adorned with the small barbels hanging from their mouths which most of this family possess. As we returned to the Ibis Hotel we saw many hippos in the lake, and one of them came up quite close to us and opened its huge mouth for us to inspect. During the night some of them came ashore to feed and we could hear them grunting like immense pigs around the hotel. It appears that it is almost impossible to keep a garden there on account of the hippos – a quaint circumstance.

This place is quite bad for malaria, and also for various biting flies and midges which required all the resources of our Flit guns.

We continued to fish at Jinja for several days, trying again at the Ripon Falls and lower down the river at the Owen Falls, and again at some rapids below there. At the Owen

BARBUS RADCLYFFEI AT JINJA

THE *LIVINGSTONE* AND THE 70 lb. NILE PERCH

Falls I was amused watching an old native catching fish in a very simple but effective manner. He had an empty five-gallon petrol tin, open at the top, and with a sieve at the bottom. He merely held the tin below the falls so that any fish trying to jump up and failing to do so fell back into the tin. In this way during the morning he caught eight fish of a small variety of the Nile Perch tribe. Our own fishing was successful enough, and we accounted for about a dozen Barbel between us, of which the largest weighed eleven and a quarter pounds. We found, after experimenting with various spoons, that the Pfleuger " Record " No. 5 was the best; in fact we never caught a fish on any other. The last day I fished alone, and experienced a curious reversal of luck. Up till then we had neither of us lost a single fish after a strike, as these Barbel have no defences of teeth or bone to prevent the hook holding. On this day, however, though I had two strong strikes, both fish departed. Was it that they were striking at my anti-kink lead, or were they taking the spoon too high up ? At any rate this remained a minor and unsolved mystery.

Though these fish would hardly justify a trip to Africa, anyone in the vicinity might well put in a few days of good sport with *Barbus radclyffei*. I warn the angler, however, not to attempt to eat them, as at some seasons of the year they are considered poisonous for Europeans, and even the natives accept them as gifts, with gratitude indeed, but also with a certain reserve.

We left Jinja the following day, and journeyed by car to Kampala, where we went to see, on Reggie's business, the local medical officer. He showed us the two varieties of tsetse fly: *morsitans* is fatal to cattle but does not hurt man; it is a small fly; *palpalis* is larger, and gives sleeping sickness to man but is not dangerous to cattle. I realised then that I had killed one of these last on the train to Tororo. Entebbe we visited, and there tried to summon up from the lake the famous tame crocodile " Tembe," but he had been too much fed recently and would not come. Finally we drove on to Butiaba on Lake Albert. On the way we saw Colobus monkeys, whose white and black fur is so popular as trimming for ladies' cloaks, and also a mongoose, quite a large animal; and we passed through a district which contained a big herd of elephant without seeing them. I believe the herd numbered about four hundred, but they are protected from hunters and are left free to wander about in a country which is cultivated and inhabited in parts.

At Butiaba we went on board the *Livingstone*. I found that we had fourteen natives as crew, and Vaz, an Indian who spoke their language, for captain. I never did discover to what tribe my crew belonged, but I have rarely seen a finer lot of men. They were all about six feet tall and of splendid physique. Their uniform consisted of red fezzes, thick and itchy-looking navy blue sweaters, and white shorts. Whenever they rowed or exerted themselves they would sing continuously a refrain which, though monotonous, was very stirring.

All the free space of the *Livingstone* was covered with cords of wood, this being the fuel employed; thus there was only the cabin and the roof of the superstructure for our use, and after once entering the cabin we decided to live on the roof instead. That afternoon I went out with my Trout rod in a dinghy which was towed behind the *Livingstone* and began casting for small Tigerfish. I managed to catch several, some with a small spoon and others with various wet-flies. These little fish, called " Ngassa," of a pound or less, were extraordinarily game. They were quite as fierce as their parents, and combined the activity and shape of a Trout with the pugnacity and strength of a Black Bass. While we were engaged in this fishing, a hippo rose from the lake within short range but luckily did not see fit to pursue us.

We slept under mosquito nets on the boat that night, and before retiring put out a night line baited with a small Tigerfish in the hope of catching a Nile Perch. I woke up in the morning at six o'clock, while it was still dark, and, observing dimly something moving near the boat, thought it was a hippo. In another half-hour it was light, and to my surprise I discovered that the supposed hippo was a Nile Perch caught on the night line. It was still alive, but cannot have put up much of a fight, as by some oversight the line was not attached to the boat, and all the fish need have done to free itself was simply to unwind a small ball of line. I went out in the dinghy to try to get some movies of the fish, while Reggie attempted to stir it up a bit, but the wretched thing had no energy at all and we had to pull it in and kill it. This fish weighed seventy pounds, and confirmed an opinion formed long before that Nile Perch, in spite of its reputation, cannot be considered a game fish. Nile Perch have huge mouths and are covered with large scales; in colour and shape they resemble Codfish. An unusual feature which I do not remember seeing in other fish concerns their eyes, which even in daylight gleam out like burning coals with a yellow-orange incandescence. The only other fish in which I have noticed this peculiarity is the Tarpon, but that was at night when reflecting back the light of my electric torch. There is one thing to be said for Nile Perch: they make delicious eating. This one was enough for ourselves and our crew — even with their appetites. I did some other fishing in Lake Albert for small fish, and caught several kinds, including Mamba, Ngege, and Wachone; at least those were the names as far as I could make them out. The Nile Perch is here called " Mputa " and the large Tigerfish " Wagassa." A fish resembling those I caught at Jinja is called " Karuka." This makes a complete list of the varieties of fish I accounted for in Africa, but, of course, there are hundreds which must well deserve attention, and, indeed, the untried denizens of the waters of this vast continent still require extensive cataloguing.

While I was engaged in this small fishing, I heard shouts from the *Livingstone*, and, hurrying there, discovered that Reggie had hooked another Nile Perch. This fish had displayed enough ingenuity to get the line twisted round the anchor chains, and I found it necessary to pass the rod under the chains to get it free. The fish was being held on twelve-thread line with a breaking strain of only twenty-four pounds, and I thought to get some kind of fight out of it with a lightish rod, but it could show me no sport, so I reeled it in and found it weighed sixty pounds. It proved in excellent condition. I was astonished and discouraged to find that this large fish possessed such wretched game qualities that it could not even break the line, and yet in a famous publication on world fishing I have noticed this comment in regard to Nile Perch: " Probably Africa's finest fish." Later on I caught several other Nile Perch, all equally unenterprising, notably one at Sennar. This fish, weighing only twenty-four pounds, was captured in a peculiar way. I had been casting into a veritable cataract of water coming from the spillway of the Sennar dam. In casting I had failed to allow for the large limb of a submerged tree below me, and, on the retrieve, my line caught in a splintered portion of the branch. To my annoyance I thought it would be necessary to break my line, which was the same twelve-thread mentioned above, but as I wished to lose as little as possible, I began to pull it in by hand through the splintered wood, until there remained only about six feet suspended beyond the branch. The line then became stuck, and the spoon hung dancing and bouncing in the racing water, presenting an enticing lure for any fish. I was just preparing to break the line off when a Nile Perch seized the spoon. To my surprise the fish was able to pull the line back through the splinter about fifteen yards before it again stuck. The fish now had every opportunity to break me. It had plenty of line to work with, and a terrific current to help, and yet with these advantages, and the line held unyieldingly in the branch, it had not the power. My Sudanese boy, to my alarm and against my orders, waded in and freed the line, after which the fish was at my mercy. It is to me a mystery how Nile Perch has acquired its reputation, and I can only surmise that, owing to the huge size it sometimes attains, it has been over-praised by anglers who have not previously had any-thing to do with large fish.

That morning we left Butiaba and steamed north to the embouchure of the Victoria Nile. There is a vast and shallow passage, through which we had to sound our way as we proceeded upstream towards the Murchison Falls. I can recommend this voyage to big game experts, no matter how familiar they may be with ordinary safaris, not indeed for shooting but for the large quantity of game observable. All this country is a preserve which has in addition been placed out of bounds for natives on account of sleeping sickness. Thus, undisturbed by mankind, all sorts of animals can be found there gathered together in masses.

When we had proceeded about an hour through the shallows, the river-banks began to draw in and the water became deeper and faster-flowing. On the left the banks were hidden by papyrus, while on the right the jungle came down in a gentle slope to the water. Beyond we could see a typical African forest, not dense at the edge, but seeming to grow thicker further away. The usual thorny trees with flat tops which one has seen in so many cinema pictures were always the most noticeable feature, but it must be admitted that, at any rate in this country, the jungle was both gloomy and uninteresting. We now began to observe hippos in pairs, and then saw the sky almost black with great clouds of soaring birds. These turned out to be storks, which had arrived from Europe just in time for a gargantuan feast on a swarm of locusts which we had shortly to traverse. It is impossible to estimate the locusts in this swarm, but I should say there were about three to every cubic yard of the air in which we found them. It took us several minutes' (perhaps two hundred yards) steaming to get through the swarm, which extended up into the air some two hundred yards if one could judge by the storks, and longitudinally the swarm appeared about a mile long. I therefore calculate that it contained some two hundred and ten million locusts. But this is only a tiny fraction – an insignificant sample – of the numbers to which these insects can congregate. I have been told by some South African friends that they have witnessed swarms of locusts flying over their farms ceaselessly for several days on end. The locusts were so closely packed that the sun was almost blotted out, while, from reports, my friends heard that the swarms extended over a front of ten or twenty miles. I have since had the curiosity to attempt to discover whether my approximation was anywhere near accurate, but a world authority said he could give me no assurance that my total was correct within hundreds of millions. In fact he explained that the only figures on locusts which have been verified hitherto, were the millions of pounds different Governments have expended in trying to curb these pests.

After having got through the locusts, we came upon more and more hippos; in one small bay, no larger than a ballroom floor, we counted fifty of them together. Some of those which were in shallow water when we approached would go galloping along with mighty splashings to submerge in deeper places. One on land lumbered downhill at a great pace and took a vast plunge into the river which we could hear at a range of half a mile. Then we passed two on shore at twenty yards' distance which were so exhausted that they made no attempt to move off. They had been fighting, and were dripping with blood and covered with huge scarlet wounds.

To starboard the river was shallow, and we were thus unable to approach the bank, but on that side we began to see water-buck and antelopes, and then at last elephants, first in pairs or singly, some of them bathing, but most of them leaving the river in a dignified retreat from our presence. The elephants became more numerous, appearing in small herds of twenty or so. We watched them through our field-glasses and noticed many with fine tusks. The hippos were now scarcer, but they were replaced by immense crocodiles. On every sandy spit, wherever the bank afforded a resting-place, we saw these fearsome beasts. As we came near, waking from their slumbers, they would rise high on their legs and make sneakishly for the water.

At last at a turn of the river we came in view of the falls. They form a magnificent picture. The water rushes in one deep but narrow sheet through a gap in some high cliffs. Above I believe there are two other separate drops, but to get to see these required an expedition on foot.[1] The *Livingstone* was now anchored in mid-stream about three miles below the falls. At this point the river had broadened and had had time to slow its first mad turbulence. The jungle, much more luxuriant than further down, crowded the river-banks on both sides, with a dense and sombre screen. At the water's edge gleamed short strips of yellow sand from which, as the little ship stopped abreast, there slithered further numbers of loathsome crocodiles.

We decided to go ashore on the left bank in order to get close to the falls for some photographs. We were accompanied by Vaz and two " boys." There were great numbers of tsetse flies about, and they kept us busy swishing them

1 The whole fall totals 118 feet.

away with our handkerchiefs. The usual method of attack which these insects adopt is to settle silently underneath the brim at the back of one's topi helmet, and then they take this platform as an easy jumping-off place for injecting their insanitary *piqûres* in one's neck. Vaz had informed us that we stood a good chance of seeing elephants, and in a few moments we came on traces of them, which as we advanced became more and more mephitic. The two " boys " had been sent on ahead, and they shortly came running back very excitedly to explain that there were elephants just in front of us. Reggie and I at once lost all sense of precaution. Though our only arms were the handkerchiefs we were waving, we rushed ahead as if to inspect the animals in a zoo. Later we were able to reflect on our folly, but at the time our only idea was to get some close-ups of wild elephants. We came upon them in a moment. There were an old tusker and a female at the water's edge. They were not more than twenty-five yards away, and were occupied in breaking off and eating the topmost foliage of some small trees. We got our cinema cameras into action, and obtained some splendid pictures. In the midst of this my film ran out; I had to change it, and then continued taking more footage. It was remarkable that though for fifteen minutes we were within twenty-five yards of the beasts, and in plain view, as they were facing us, they did not see us. We were talking and making considerable noise, yet they did not hear us. As for their sense of smell — we were, luckily, down-wind.

When we had secured all the photographs we wanted we continued on our way to the falls, but after a little consideration we decided that to climb the cliffs and see the upper drops would be too fatiguing. It was only when we wished to return that we began to think about passing the elephants a second time. Fortunately they had moved off, and we had no difficulties in reaching the boat. Near the falls, which thundered in the approved manner of such phenomena, we had noticed thousands of the Mamba fish, as well as many other varieties I could not identify, so when I got back to the *Livingstone* I started fishing. I tried all sorts of different lures and baits, but failed to get a strike. Reggie, in the meantime, occupied himself by observing the crocodiles through his field-glasses. On one small sandy spit he counted forty-eight lying all together, some on top of others, while on another low bank, which he reckoned less than fifty yards long, he estimated that there were over a hundred. Nor were these "crocs" the little babies of the reptile house in a zoo, but immense creatures, most of them twelve feet or more in length. Readers who had the opportunity of seeing the film *Trader Horn* will be interested to know that this was the scene of the filming of the crocodile section of the picture, and that there was no Hollywood faking in regard to the crocodiles.

As the sun began to set we abandoned our pursuits and stretched ourselves on deck-chairs to discuss the happenings of the day. With the approach of darkness we were startled to hear a great splash of water within a few feet of the boat. We thought it must be a hippo, but this splash was simply the prelude to thrashings and heavings of water all round us. We soon realised that all this commotion was caused by the crocodiles, which at dark swim out into the river to catch fish for their evening meal. The method they employ is the same old gambit which has always proved so successful for them. At dusk they paddle out into the stream to a suitable place and, pretending to be floating logs, drift down with the current until they find a fish within range. It then only requires a lash of their tails or a bite of their teeth, and dinner is served. This gruesome orgy lasted but a short half-hour, and thereafter nothing more was heard from the crocs except the occasional snapping of their mighty jaws,

The next day we put in taking photographs of the falls, and trying to get movies of the crocodiles. Our plans were frustrated. By ill chance this almost unknown niche of darkest Africa became that day a sort of meeting-place, as it seemed, for half the white population of the continent. First arrived a survey ship loaded with gentlemen bearing geometric instruments; second came two prospectors for gold, with geologic instruments; and thirdly paddled up a tourist ship full of trippers, with photographic instruments. We decided to leave early the next morning, and thus at any rate obtain an undisturbed view of the wild life on our way downstream.

That evening we were witnessing again the night fishing of the crocodiles, when it occurred to me: why not try for one of them with my big game fish rod ? Vaz was summoned and told to kill a chicken in such a manner as to produce much blood, while I frantically unpacked my tackle. After some delay, the chicken was duly attached to a Marlin hook and fifty yards of line paid out. Alas, my idea had come too late. The crocodiles were already sated with fish, nor do I know whether they would have cared for chicken; at any rate none came to the bait, though we kept it out for an hour in the current.

It was only later that, thinking it over, I began to wonder whether, in a country where firearms are forbidden, it would be permissible even to catch crocodiles, the horrid co-habitants with nobler game of this preserved jungle. It is possible that I was attempting to do something extremely illegal. I do not know about this, but of one thing I am certain, that catching a twelve-foot crocodile on big game fish tackle would prove a most interesting and exciting experience for even the most *blasé* of anglers.[1]

---

[1] It is very difficult to estimate how large these crocodiles (*Crocodilus niloticus*) were, as we could seldom approach them except when they were making quickly for the river; but this species has been obtained up to 19½ feet and reported up to 10 metres, or about 32½ feet long.

12

THE FIERCEST FISH THAT SWIMS

AFRICA! The mere word conjures up visions of tanned, sweaty gentlemen in khaki shorts, long lines of natives bearing immense burdens, and lions; above all lions.

My own expedition lacked all these. I had been lured to Africa in pursuit of Nile Perch; a fish of which I had observed much had been written, though, even before starting, I had already formed some misgivings as to its sporting possibilities. Nor was my lack of confidence unwarranted, for Nile Perch proved after all to possess only the one quality of making up into the finest *filet de sole* obtainable south of Dover – a consolation, obviously.

But I had another object in mind, namely, Tigerfish of the genus *Hydrocyon*,[1] which has *every* quality except that one can hardly eat it at all.

Some time before planning my African adventure I had seen at Hardy's, in Pall Mall, the skull of a fish. It was not a large fish – about eight pounds, I judged – but I had never seen such an armament of diabolic teeth. I was curious to know what fish could require these weapons, and was told it was a Tigerfish from Africa. I mentally filed this information. After all, other fish such as Barracuda and various Sharks possess fine dentition, but prove lacking in imagination against a stiff rod.

As I worked up north from Capetown I gathered further

1 See Appendix Note, p. 298.

details. At Johannesburg I was told that if I could hook a Tigerfish it would give me a very sporting fight. I got out my Striped Bass and " three-six " tackle and went over it rather carefully. I found out that Tigerfish frequent most of the rivers of the east coast such as the Limpopo, Zambesi, and even the upper Niles. Another amusing item was that they only flourish well in hippo and crocodile waters.

In spite of a couple of washouts, caused by storms, the train finally got me to Victoria Falls one morning. I had several days to put in there, and, having interviewed the hall porter, was informed that I could go Tigerfishing in the afternoon. Having collected my tackle, I made a rendez-vous about half a mile above the falls with a crew of four natives in a dug-out canoe. Rhythmically they paddled upstream; the smell of their warm bodies tainted the air. The pull of the falls was not very strong inshore, but I could not help wondering what would happen if the canoe upset. I soon saw several crocodiles lying on some rocky islets. I rigged a six-inch fish (a Gillieminkie) on to some gang hooks, and let it troll. Nothing happened. I under-stood from the steersman that we must go into faster water. I did not like the idea, but we were soon cruising further out. The natives, paddling steadily, held the canoe stationary, and I made a few casts. About the fifth, on the retrieve, something seemed to stop my line dead and then, with my strike, came a vicious jerk. My line came in freely, minus the bait. This happened several times; generally the bait was gone or badly mangled. I wired a bait on, so that it could not come off, and then had the humiliation of counting six strikes and failing every time to hook a fish. At the seventh I was on. There was a considerable battle. I could feel the fish was a small one; but what a fighter! At last I got him to the canoe. He was a Tigerfish all right, and, though he had a whole triangle of hooks in his mouth, I did not fancy him too much in the boat with those teeth. The steersman knew what to do and killed him with a large club.

The Tigerfish is different from most fish, inasmuch as it has long, fearfully sharp teeth fixed like a bear trap on the *outside* of its mouth, there being slots in the lips to allow the teeth, when the mouth is closed, to remain on the exterior in a glittering menace. This gives to its face a devilish expression, which can be well appreciated at close range. Apart from this, it is one of the most beautiful of fish. Made like a very stocky Salmon, it is covered with large, bright scales. In this fish they were a pale lemon colour. Along the body ran darker scales in stripes, and it is from this circumstance, no doubt, that it has received its English name. The fins were all a brilliant orange. The colour of these fish in the Zambesi is yellow, but in other rivers the body may be an electric blue. My Tigerfish only weighed two and a half pounds, but he was full value. I continued to fish, but only caught two more, both of them smaller. At six o'clock I hurried back to the hotel and its mosquito screens, for this is a grand place to acquire malaria.

The next day I went on a picnic upstream in a launch to Kandahar island. They do things well there, and I lunched off silver plate. When the sun had become a little more reasonable, I tried for Tigerfish again. After a while I got a small one. Then there was a long pause. We were in very swift water. Suddenly I got a really strong strike; the line ran out at astonishing speed, and then I saw a splendid fish jump sixty yards away. These fish jump like Tarpon, with a wiggle and a twist and then the well-known head-shake which has thrown so many hooks. It happened that way this time, and the fish was off. However, I had had my first experience of a larger one; a ten-pounder, I estimated. I was beginning to get very much excited over this prelude when the steersman also showed some excitement and pointed out a hippo not far off.

Now hippo are peculiar animals. They are extremely timid on occasion. On the other hand, they seem to be strangely attracted by boats. For no particular reason they seem to delight in upsetting small craft. In the circumstances I could visualise a rather rapid swim over the falls — always supposing, of course, that the crocodiles did not catch me first. If the crocodiles got me and anything was left over, the Tigerfish would have the rest. This, it seems, is the reason Tigerfish thrive best in hippo and crocodile waters. I said I was thirsty and we paddled back to the launch. The natives did not seem averse to this.

When I got back to the hotel I asked whether one could not fish casting from the shore, and was told that, though it was quite feasible, it was not considered advisable on account of the snakes.

I continued my trip north and, on reaching Butiaba on Lake Albert, tried again for small Tigerfish with a Trout rod. With twelve inches of fine wire for a trace I used various wet-flies with great success. I caught many weighing up to a pound or so and was looking forward to a fish dinner, only to discover that they were practically inedible on account of their numerous bones and rather tasteless flesh. Though already arrayed with formidable teeth, these babies had not yet acquired the solid interior to their mouths which made hooking the large ones so difficult. But could they fight!

Dr. Henshall must have overlooked Tigerfish when he made his famous claim for Black Bass. But since he has already pre-empted the title of " gamest " I will cast my vote for Tigerfish as the world's " fiercest." Later on during my trip I saw a Tigerfish jump four feet out of water into the engine-room of a paddle-steamer. He seemed anxious to devour the machinery and, given time, might have succeeded. He was only subdued with a crowbar after a great struggle. It is undoubtedly curious that Tigerfish have failed to get due recognition from most of the great anglers. Holder, for instance, in his *Game Fishes of the World* (1913), omits all mention. Even South Africans themselves do not realise what swims in their rivers. " Oh, Tigerfish," they murmur vaguely, when one remarks on their good fortune. The Tigerfish has, however, one defect for anglers. It is so fierce and powerful in the swift waters it prefers that one is almost obliged to try for it with stronger tackle than its weight justifies. I can imagine no angling more thrilling than Tigerfishing on light tackle.

We continued our travels, and on the way to Murchison Falls I landed a twenty-two-and-a-half-pound Tigerfish trolling with a hand line. But that is no way to judge a fish. As we steamed up this placid and savage river we passed herds of hippos. Though the steamboat I had chartered displaced at least sixty tons it was charged several times by these beasts. One could feel them bumping their heads on the iron keel with quite a formidable jar. After our excursion to the falls, I steamed down the White Nile to Kosti and crossed to Sennar on the Blue Nile, where a great dam impounds and regulates the snow waters of the Abyssinian mountains and of Lake Tana. The British staff at the dam knew all about Tigerfish, and, the first morning there, one of them acted as my escort. We crossed by car along the top of the dam, and then recrossed by boat to a small island in midstream. From the dam to the island there is a masonry wall, forty feet high, which serves to confine the water from the spillway in a channel. I was told to climb this wall and cast into the tumbling waters. There were some giant steps up which I could go, but the top of the wall was only a yard

wide, with a rough stone surface.   On one side were some
jagged rocks, on the other a raging flood.   It speaks for
the vigorous qualities of Tigerfish that they should choose
to swim in such a current.   I put on a No. 6 Pfleuger
" Record " and cast out with my Striped Bass rod.   As
the spoon hit the water there was a ferocious strike.   I was
scarcely expecting it and was nearly pulled into the flood.
The hook came out with a jerk and I nearly crashed backwards on to the rocks below me.   It was not an agreeable
sensation, I must say; and, further, this fish appeared later
to have been the biggest I hooked during my stay at Sennar,
but I lost the brute, of course.   The Britisher called out
" Tight lines," and departed.   I went down to the rocks where
my gear had been deposited and took a pull from my flask,
which did not contain water.   Back on the wall I tried again,
and continued thus all the morning, alternating between the
flask and this sort of premeditated suicide from the wall top.
But what seemed to me, unaccustomed to such matters, a
kind of perilous tight-rope act with angling variations, was
regarded by the engineers of the dam as normal fishing
procedure.   I watched two of them one day galloping up
and down the wall, while they played Nile Perch with complete sang-froid.   I regretted that they were missing
my thrills.   At noon I returned to my rest hut, where it
was 108 degrees in the shade, and did not venture out to
fish again till five o'clock.

I caught some Tigerfish, but my best was only eighteen
and a half pounds.   I counted once sixteen strikes before
the hook stayed in, and this was by no means an abnormal
ratio.   Generally the fish would clamp down so firmly
on the spoon that with all my strength I could not drive
the hook home, while deep scratches were scored on the
tough metal by their teeth.   Reflecting on the hooking
of Tigerfish, I am disposed to think that, apart from their
extraordinary array of teeth and the impenetrable interior

MY GHILLIE WITH 18½ lb. TIGERFISH

of their mouths, they seem to have stronger jaws for their size than any fish I know. The Dorado, which is a similarly predacious fish, and occurs at once to mind in this respect, appears to have only a feeble grip in comparison. I tried every kind of hook and bait, but a Pfleuger 5 or 6 was best, chiefly because Gillieminkies were hard to come by. At the head of the spoon I later added a triangle hook, so that if a Tigerfish took hold at all it must get a barb in its mouth. The eighteen-and-a-half-pounder was caught with this new armament; in fact it was obtained with my first cast after I had gone to all the trouble of wiring on the extra hook in that blistering heat. I had lost so many fish by that time that I felt sure this one would get off too, but he did not. He was in marvellous condition and was in such a hurry to go downstream that it was all I could do to stop him. In the excitement I almost lost my topi hat and my balance as well. The fish did not quite know whether it was better to shake the hook out in the air or to pull me in and swallow me. I have never seen a finer exhibition of jumping, nor experienced a fiercer strain on my line for so small a fish. I fought him as best I could, slowly giving way and creeping gingerly along the wall in the direction he seemed anxious to go. To land this fish was quite difficult. Having played him for a while in the swirl of the spillway, I let him drag me downstream. The wall became lower and lower; finally, at the bottom end, I could descend. There was a small recess of still water. I had to steer him into it, and it was very important not to let him swim below the backwater, where the current would be too fast to bring him up again. I think we were equally tired when I got him as far as that; but once I had drawn him into the little pool my Sudanese ghillie gaffed him with evident delight.

I thought I had solved the problem of hooking Tigerfish, and as soon as I was recovered I returned to the wall, expecting that my extra hook would guarantee me a fish with every cast. I was quickly disillusioned, and soon found out that there was more to Tigerfishing than a couple of hooks. I did catch several others before I left, but nothing to equal this, my first fish. Sennar is the best place I know of for Tigerfish, though they must miss their playmates, the crocodiles, of which the year previously an Englishman had shot a hundred and thirty-nine below the dam.

The largest Tigerfish to the present accounted for at Sennar weighed thirty-three pounds, and was caught by the Duchess of Westminster. I am told she was assisted to maintain a footing on the wall by one of the staff at the dam, and this, I must admit, is a far better method than the one I adopted.

I do not know if I have made out a case to justify the heading of this chapter. What convinced me of the fierce qualities of Tigerfish was the reply of one of the engineers to a question I had asked him about the *principal* food of Tigerfish. He said: " Well, when a croc sees a nigger baby on the bank he sweeps it into the water with his tail and seizes it by the middle; then the Tigerfish swims up and bites off the baby's feet."

THE DUCHESS OF WESTMINSTER AND HER RECORD TIGERFISH (33 lb).

13

CHRISTEN THE FISH

SOME time ago I had an unusual experience. It was the third of June when I got an invitation from my friend Pelham for a fortnight's Trout fishing at Bad Aussee in Austria. He had fished there the season before, and told me that he and another rod had caught some three thousand Trout (though he added that, of course, most of them had been put back). What a delightful prospect. Having hastily sorted out my tackle, I did not delay my departure. The next day I had joined him and, though there was a slight drizzle, he took me out at once to sample the Koppen Traun.

This river is a part of the Traun system which wanders for a hundred miles through Upper Austria, connecting several charming lakes. This particular stretch is not very wide, varying from ten to twenty-five yards across. It is a typical mountain stream on the large size, which can be shallow and crystal clear and can change, with snow or rain, to a cocoa-coloured flood in a few minutes. Its course lies through a picturesque and narrow gorge, above which tower minor pine-clad alps.

At Pelham's suggestion I put a couple of wet-flies on a stoutish cast, and, wading out to a suitable run, I had a nice three-quarter-pounder in a jiffy. I released him and had his brother after the next cast. In half an hour quite a number had been similarly returned, all from the same spot. It was exciting and very pleasant. We continued

downstream to a large rock.   There the river was less
rapid, and in a small back current I could work my flies
and see them clearly.   I missed a small fish without wanting
him very much, and then, just as I was lifting the line from
the water, a much larger one came lazily for the end fly.
I could not slow up the retrieve enough, and he just failed
to reach the hook, which was practically snatched out of his
mouth.   I tried several times more for him, but he thought
better of it.   How annoying! was my first reaction.   Then
I reflected that I could come back for him another day;
on the whole I was glad he had refused me.   When I
wanted to enter my catch in the fishing-book that evening
I could not recall how many fish I had released, nor could
I remember any one of them except the first, though each
one of them had fought like tigers.   The last fish, the one
that got away, I remembered well, however, and christened
him " Henry " for no special reason except for the stolidity
he exhibited.

The next day I was told about a pool some further
distance down the Traun where it was suggested I should
try with large wet-flies for some bigger fish.   It was hinted
that there might be something very big in the pool.   To
my surprise and delight I discovered this water was slow
enough for the dry-fly, and that in a very small space there
were numbers of fish rising steadily.   To get to them was
difficult, and therefore interesting.   The fish had to be
attacked from an awkward position on the left bank which
was overhung with foliage.   In a few minutes, however,
I had several, slightly under a pound.   Unfortunately I
had nothing with which to oil my fly, and, as it was drizzling,
after every fish I had to change it.   Soon I had no more
which were dry enough to offer, but with my last one I did
manage to get a very nice one-and-a-quarter-pounder.   I
had had my eye on him for some time, but had been unable
to offer the fly to him before a smaller fish had snatched it.

Just as I was leaving I saw a workman passing with a bicycle, so I asked him if he had by any chance some bicycle oil. He had none and offered me some butter instead. I tried it, but by now all my flies were so water-logged that it did not help much.

On my way up the bank I saw at last the fish I had been searching for all this time. He lay under the overhang of the far bank, a beautifully coloured fish, and the best of all for size. I considered his position and decided that I would have to cross to the other bank and cast round a corner to the fish. A successful attack would further require someone on the opposite side to tell me when to strike. It would be a very nice little problem which I would have to postpone solving. On account of his elegance I christened the fish " Alphonse." Again I could not remember how many fish I had released, though the one-and-a-quarter-pounder tasted delicious.

I went out fishing every day thereafter, but for seven days there was rain or snow up in the mountains which so discoloured the water that I had to content myself with fishing in the Grundlsee. One afternoon I wasted looking for Alphonse and Henry, but they were invisible in the flood water. Another day at the Grundlsee I tried dry-fly for an unknown kind of fish called *Eitel* in German which I discovered later was Chub. Not a sporting fish, of course, but shy enough to be amusing. Here, too, I released a great many Trout of about a pound each, which I caught on the wet-fly in the two main streams which feed the lake. Later Pelham ran me over to the Salza, near Mitterndorf. The Salza is one of the tributaries of the River Enns, and is a charming little stream which flows through a valley justly renowned for its beautiful mountains and difficult chamois shooting. Here I found, amid much fast water, all of it alive with fish, a slow stretch above a weir. There was only about two hundred yards of it, but what a charming piece! It possessed plenty of obstacles to conquer before one could get at the fish. For one thing most of the right bank was so overgrown that one could scarcely get a fly out, yet all the best fish lay on that side. It required, therefore, a left-handed cast from the left bank across the stream before one could cover anything good. It was curious that in half an hour I got out the two best fish I ever saw there, though I fished it again many times.

Below the weir there was a sawmill, and the river-banks were strictly controlled against flooding. At one point there was a little wooden buttress built out to deflect the water from a bend in the bank. Thinking there would be a fish in the backwater downstream from the buttress, I took a very quiet look. There was one, of course, right in the corner. He was dark and long, but his nose was pointed downstream, which made casting upstream to him very difficult. Taking great care in my stalk, I put a medium olive dry-fly to him. He paid no attention to it, though I repeated the cast several times. Thinking the fish must be blind to be so neglectful of my fly, I took an incautious step forward. He had been watching me all the time, and darted away to safety. I came back for him some time later, but he was still not at home. I decided to call him "Herbert."

From then on I stuck pretty faithfully to the Salza. This is the kind of Trout fishing I prefer. I like a short stretch of dry-fly water where there are enough fish so that I can find something always to occupy me, and then I keep going over it trying to locate a specially good or difficult fish. Herbert I interviewed regularly. Considering the fact that this was almost virgin water, he was a very educated fish indeed. The second day I tried for him, but he saw me at once, and it was not till the third day that I realised that my head showed against the skyline if I approached him as I had been doing. On this occasion I avoided my mistake, and put on a small Tupp. In the little backwater there were several bubbles floating, and whether it was that the fly was invisible in the bubbles, or for some other reason, he took no notice of it at all. The casting was difficult, too, as there was some overhanging grass just above where he lay. I found, however, that if I cast in a certain spot, the current would swing the fly to him. After several tries I changed the Tupp for a large brown sedge. I dropped the fly as planned, and was expecting it to drift over to him in a few moments, but Herbert did not wait for that. He was at the fly in a second, and took it so hard I did not have to tighten. I said to myself: " I've got him." This is a fatal remark which I must surely remove from my fishing phrases. Herbert rushed out into midstream and then dived to the bottom. I thought he had got beneath a stone as there was no movement of the line, but in a moment I was aware that the fly had caught in some obstruction, and Herbert was free. The score stood " three up " for Herbert. He was thoroughly frightened now, and did not return that day at all. The next day he was back, however, and I tried him with a very small iron blue. This did not interest him, so I put on the largest mayfly I had, with huge fan wings. I made a mistake with my cast, and the fly, instead of alighting as planned, got hung up over the grass, where it dangled in the slight breeze, three or four inches out of water. Herbert had his eye on it, I could see, so I gave the line a slight twitch which dislodged the fly. Herbert took it in a great gulp almost before it had settled. Thus did fortune favour me, and this time I made no mistake in netting Herbert. He was thinner than I had expected, and only went slightly over the pound, though he should have weighed much more. I released him in the dry-fly water for another occasion.

The next day I went down the Koppen Traun to look for my two remaining Trout friends. Alphonse I could

not find.   I do not know if he had been poached, or whether
the snow water had washed him out of his retreat.   It was
a pity, for he was a really good Trout.   I did, however,
observe three smaller fish which seemed to be sharing his
vacant home.   On looking over the position again, I decided
that a right-handed steeple cast almost straight across stream
would just get into the little overhang.   Why I had worked
out such a complicated method before I cannot think.   This
is a common mistake.   It happens so often that the simplest
approach is the best, and it is always worth trying first
anyway.   I revenged myself on Alphonse by removing
his three boy friends without too much trouble.   It was
a moral victory anyway.   There only remained Henry.
When I got to the rock behind which he sheltered, I
took considerable pains not to be seen, and then dropped
a black gnat where he should be.   Henry, as a matter of
fact, was a disappointment.   He turned out too easy for
fun, and only weighed one and a quarter pounds in the
net, but he was not in good condition.

I had to leave Bad Aussee the next day, but I was very
satisfied.   I had caught perhaps a hundred and fifty fish,
of which I had kept eight, but if I had really tried for
numbers I could have had many more.   I had never before
been on a water where Trout fishing was so simple, where
the fish were so numerous and so uneducated that almost
any kind of cast was good enough.   I had found the
remedy for this strange state of affairs by naming the
shy and difficult fish, and then concentrating on them.
Alphonse, Henry, and Herbert I shall remember for a long
time, but the other hundred and forty-seven are already
only a dim memory.   Let me recommend the system.

It was not till the end of August that I again went fishing
at Bad Aussee.   Pelham's invitation had this time included
my stepson, Toto, aged fourteen, and in preparation for
this glorious wind-up to his holidays I had been preparing

TOTO ON THE SALZA

him for some time with daily casting instruction. This was, in fact, to be his first attempt at Trout fishing in a river.

I must say that my first glance at the Salza astonished me. I had been expecting low and clear water, but the changed conditions still surprised me. The Salza in June had remained moderately transparent even during the week of rain we had experienced at that time, and thereafter in a short interval appeared as bright as one could wish; but on this second visit even in the deepest pools I could see every pebble on the bottom. As for the shallows, it was as if they had been newly glazed with plate glass. Indeed, it became quickly evident that Toto would have little success with the wet-fly, as the trout could see him at too long a range. For three days, therefore, I became a dry-fly nurse to Toto. I showed him the easy places and fish, and advised him until I was satisfied by the contents of his *Lagl* that his technique was sufficient for him to succeed by himself. It was now my turn to put up a rod.

This chapter so far has been intended to show a method of extracting pleasure from Trout fishing when the Trout are too easy. My August visit proved in a striking manner how quickly uneducated fish become wary when they have a little knowledge of what a man in waders is after.

During my June visit I had found shallows where I could stand without moving a step and net a dozen nice three-quarter-pounders with practically successive casts. I now returned to these same shallows. There was but little water left, perhaps a foot, and the Trout were scarcer too, but still sufficient remained, and to compensate they were much easier to see. I stepped in at the bottom of one of these flats, disturbing as I did so several fish, and, after giving a few moments for things to settle down, advanced a short distance with caution till I was in range of a nice fish. The sun was shining brightly on the water, which was smooth as a mirror, and without a single ripple from wind or current. I was using a nine-foot cast tapered to 5x and, getting some line out, I made my first false cast. To my astonishment the fish did not wait a moment but was off at full speed. I was a little to the side of this fish and thought he must have seen the flash of my rod. I advanced a little further and found an even better fish. When I was directly behind him I got out line again. This time I shot my line, but as the fly was falling beyond him, and before it had even settled on the water, the Trout was away. This happened more than once, and I was wondering what was wrong till I realised that my 5x gut was throwing a shadow on the water as noticeable as a telephone wire; yet this gut was unstained and as nearly transparent as one can hope to find it. I next cast with the left hand, and managed to curl the fly round from the left towards another fish. I was thus able to avoid bringing the shadow of the gut across him, but, after inspecting it for a moment, this fish decided there was something wrong about the fly and let it go past him. I tried this system several times, and found that if occasionally a Trout would take, he still would not do so with sufficient decision, and I was as like as not to lose him. As though to confirm my theory that these Trout had all become gut shy, my next cast into a ripple resulted in my netting a fish without trouble. I have fished in recent years on many clear-water streams, but have never had such a lesson as to the opaque qualities of 5x gut. Nor have I appreciated before the advantage, in the conditions described, of breaking its tell-tale shadow by casting into disturbed water, or, failing that, fishing in shady sections of the river.

Some days later I returned to the same flats. It was a dull day without a trace of sunshine. No longer could I see the sharp outline of my cast etched black against the pebble bottom of the stream, and once again, as in the June fishing, I found the Trout came gaily to my medium olives, with their former confident abandon. Reflecting on this discovery, I have decided that if the Trout were thus advised of even a transparent gut by its shadow, how much more so would a stained gut warn them of danger in the fly? After this experience I will logically avoid any gut dyed to no matter what colour for no matter what theoretic reason.

I read some time ago in a famous sporting magazine the bitter complaints of fishermen who protested that during the unprecedented drought of an English summer the Trout were coming short in an inexplicable and infuriating manner. I am wondering whether the gut revelations on the Salza in early September do not furnish one excuse for the bad manners of the Trout, and also a little balm for the vanity of the disgruntled anglers.

14

" ONE AND A HALF POUNDS ? THROW IT BACK, PILZ ! "

I PRESUME that a great many anglers are like me, and that when they have done a certain amount of fishing for a particular kind of fish they consider that, except for inexhaustible details, there is not much more to learn on the subject. My own complacency was rudely disturbed at Gmunden, where my guide, Pilz, showed me entirely new techniques for big Trout and Grayling.

Gmunden is a small town in the Salzkammergut district of Upper Austria, which has become justly celebrated for its Trout and Grayling fishing. It lies at the north end of the Traunsee, a very beautiful lake, some twenty miles long, surrounded by mountains. In the town itself a large weir regulates the outflow of the lake into the River Traun, which is a tributary of the Danube. As that part of the river which affords the fishing is practically entirely lake fed, it is not discoloured by snow water and, except when there is a heavy local rain, can be fished without interruption throughout the season; for Trout, from May 15th to October 1st; for Grayling, from June 1st to March 1st.

Some time ago the fishing was let by the local authorities to an Englishman, Dr. F. S. Duncan, who proceeded to organise it on a systematic basis. This stretch of the river has a length of about fifteen and a half kilometres to the Traunfall, which forms the north boundary. The waterfall is very important to the fishing, as it effectively blocks the access of Huchen to the Traunsee and thus

preserves the Trout from their voracious cousins. Dr.
Duncan's fishing is divided into nineteen beats, so that
nineteen anglers can fish it at the same time. During the
height of the season the different beats are allotted to anglers
in strict rotation, but when there are fewer rods on the water
a more elastic arrangement is permitted.

I arrived at Gmunden on the twenty-first of June and at
once went to see Dr. Duncan. He informed me that the
river was in good condition, and that several fine Trout
had been taken recently. Then he began to tell me all
sorts of strange things. I was expecting (such are the
inaccurate reports one gets from friends) that I was going
to find an extremely slow-flowing river in which one fished
upstream with a dry-fly for very large Trout. Under these
conditions I had brought casts tapered to 3x and some
2x points in case I discovered something very large to try
for. Dr. Duncan told me they used x points, or even
ox. He further told me that the fishing was dry-fly,
indeed, but from a boat and downstream!

" Downstream ? " I questioned in surprise.

" Yes, downstream – that is, across and down," he replied.

Of course, like every dry-fly angler I have cast the dry-
fly downstream occasionally when there seemed no other
way to get at a fish, but as a regular practice it seemed to
me a strange reversal of normality. This dry-fly fishing,
he went on to explain, was mostly for large Grayling, but
an occasional Trout would be obtained. He added that
any Trout under sixteen inches or about one and three-
quarter pounds must be returned. I was then informed
that the main fishing for the big Trout was done below
the weirs, and the lures were *Salmon* flies, fished wet.
The Trout, it seemed, were of three varieties: the biggest
were Alpine Lake Trout (*Salmo lacustris*), called *Lachs*
by the natives; there were also large Brown Trout; and
lastly a hybrid Trout derived from the other two. Dr.

Duncan provided me with four varieties of flies tied by himself. Two of them were on number one hooks[1] for daylight fishing, and were hackled flies of grey and brown tones; the others were winged flies on number four hooks, and represented two varieties of sedge. He said no other flies were necessary, and I must say I needed no others, nor have I ever seen flies with such excellent hackles and such resilience on the water.

I was then introduced to Pilz, one of the best ghillies, and arranged with him to fish that evening with the dry-fly. Dr. Duncan told me it was useless to expect anything before dusk, and suggested I should go and have a look at the *Behälter* if I had nothing else to do. I must explain that practically throughout Austria, wherever the right to fish can be obtained, there is a sacrosanct regulation, and a most peculiar one, that any fish taken must be kept alive and brought to the *Behälter* cr fish-tank of the owner. This is one of the reasons why a ghillie or *Träger* must be in close attendance, carrying a *Lagl* or small wooden barrel filled with water and, perhaps, fish. If the angler wishes to eat his fish he must buy it from the owner at the current market rate per kilo.

When I had got my tackle in order I took a stroll down to the *Behälter* hut where there were two tanks. In one of them there were some large Grayling running to about two pounds. The other tank had a grille over it, and when this was removed I saw nearly a dozen of the largest Trout I have ever seen alive. One of them was a seven-pounder, there were several over five pounds, and the rest were of about three or four pounds weight. I discovered later why there are such large Trout in this river. It appears that the Traunsee, which is the source of the Traun River, contains abundant food in the form of small fish – Dace, Miller's-thumb, and others – as well as snails, small

---

[1] For all hook measurements I have used the English numbers.

crustaceans, and a vast hatch of sedge flies. It is, of course, almost impossible in such a large lake to make a substantial catch of Trout, but fortunately the fish from time to time drift down out of the lake and station for a change in the river, where they can be more easily located. The record Trout (which was netted in the lake some years ago) weighed fifty-eight pounds, and this, it must be admitted, is a fairly good size. In the river recently the record fish caught on a rod weighed seventeen pounds two ounces; another of thirteen pounds seven ounces was obtained this year. These were all lake Trout. The record Brown Trout weighed nine pounds, and the best Grayling three pounds fifteen and a half ounces. I was told that during a season's fishing of, say, two or three months, an angler should expect about sixty fish averaging in the neighbourhood of five pounds.

Duly impressed by the contents of the *Behälter* (and who would not be ?), I put in the rest of the afternoon inspecting the river. It shows how different this fishing is from the general run that I completely overlooked, without even considering them, the best parts of the top beats. I was indeed puzzled by this river, renowned as the finest for big fish in all Austria. Of typical pools where one would expect to find fish I could discover none. On the left bank of these beats there is a footpath guarded by a rail, and the river-bank has been revetted with stone, the water having a depth of from three to six or more feet at the edge. Close to the embankment I did find some large Trout, as I had expected, but nothing to compare with those in the *Behälter*. Grayling I saw throughout the water, lying well submerged. The different beats I looked at varied in depth, but generally had an even flow. The top beat was deep and slow, then came a second weir at the top of the second beat, and below this the river widened and shallowed. Finally a third weir separated beat two from beat three, and this third beat had fast and shallow water narrowing into deeper runs in places. In the second beat I found one large Trout of about four pounds, with two slightly smaller in attendance, which for no apparent reason occasionally tried to encroach on the lie of the bigger fish. I could not determine why the four-pounder had chosen this particular place, as it did not seem to have any advantages over thousands of surrounding cubic feet of water.

At seven Pilz came for me and we walked down to beat two, which had been assigned me for the evening. We got into a light but roomy skiff, and my ghillie paddled out into fast running water with a depth of about three feet. In the air I could see cinnamon sedges dancing and occasionally lighting on the water. I put on one of the number one hook flies, while my ghillie lowered an anchor from the upstream end of the boat. Around us on all sides I saw intermittently the quick rises of Grayling. The speed and reflection of the water prevented me from observing the fish themselves, but I presumed they must be small. I began to put out a line to these rises, and at once found difficulties. Dr. Duncan had warned me that the fish gorged so much winged food that unless the fly came exactly over their noses they would not bother to take it. I confirmed this at once. Now the light skiff in the fast current was a by no means stable casting platform, but as a still greater handicap the swift water and an imminent drag made useless the casting of a straight line, unless the fly could be placed within inches above the rise. In a short time I had thus come to learn that I must cast a crooked line exactly over the fish from an unsteady position in order to have a chance of hooking one. As everyone knows, the rise of a Grayling is very rapid and requires an instantaneous strike; but how is it possible to accomplish such micrometric timing with the disadvantages presented? In my attempts to achieve this difficult feat I missed a dozen fish and was becoming quite discouraged, but Pilz told me that

MAJOR-GENERAL SIR WILFRID MALLESON,
HIS RECORD TROUT (17 lb. 2 oz.), AND PILZ

it would be easier at eight o'clock; and as it turned out he was right. He then suggested that I should change my fly to the larger pattern.

The sedges, which had up to now been coming down in tens, turned to hundreds, then thousands, and then millions. I will not go beyond these figures, but will only say that they became a brown snowstorm. They flew down one's neck, in one's eyes, ears, nose. I have never seen anything like it. The Grayling went mad; they abandoned all caution and, remaining close to the surface, kept taking the flies at intervals of a second. This mass of flies produced the inevitable result that there was too much food and too many rises. I did not know where to cast with this amazing *embarras de richesses*, and consequently cast haphazard " into the brown." It could scarcely be called fishing. Suddenly a Grayling made a mistake and took my fly. I did not have to strike; there was a ferocious and astonishingly heavy tug, and the fish was gone. I cast again, and in a few minutes the same thing happened. I continued my procedure; but there was now an interval and luck seemed to have departed; then again there was the same fierce pull – and again no fish. I could not imagine what was wrong; with such strong strikes all three fish should have been in the *Lagl* a long time ago. It occurred to me at last to examine my fly, and then, with my fingers – for it was quite dark – I felt at once what was wrong. The whole end of the hook was gone. Pilz told me that though Grayling have no teeth they have a hard, bony structure in their mouths which often breaks the hook. This explained the three lost fish. I put on another fly, but it was too late; this fantastic rise, which it appears is an ordinary circumstance here, was all over. An occasional dimple in the faint glimmer of the water showed that one Grayling at least was still not surfeited, but the hope of getting my fly to a particular fish in the darkness was too remote. Pilz poled me back to a small landing-stage. Below the stage was a slight back-current, and with my torch I took a look at the water. It was covered with sedges to such an extent that one could not dip in one's finger without having several flies adhere to it.

Having now made an attempt at dry-fly fishing down-stream, I was keen to have a go at Trout with Salmon flies. Pilz suggested that if I wanted to fish in the early morning without interference from other anglers he would come for me at 3.15. It did not give me much time for sleep but I agreed. By chance I had brought with me a large assortment of Salmon flies, and a short but strong Ogden Smiths rod would serve my purpose, even if rather on the light side. It was still dark when Pilz arrived, and, though we did not know it at the time, I was well advised to try fishing again that night as there happened to be no more good Trout fishing for several days afterwards. The hotel was only a short distance from the first beat, and we walked down through the sleeping town to the top weir, which, like the other two lower down, was a very complicated affair. The river itself was only about sixty yards across, but the weir, with its various channels, overflows, and outlets must have covered a distance of some two hundred yards. Pilz then told me that it was in the fast water below the weir that I was to fish. I understood now why I had failed to locate many big fish during my promenade of the day before as they were apparently mostly gathered in this swift and troubled water.

I had never previously fished a weir, and I was astounded to see the curious places where Pilz wanted me to trot a fly. We crawled about all over the construction while I cast out into the fastest water. It seemed quite wrong to me. I should have thought that the big Trout would seek the lazy bits where they would have little exertion to keep their positions, as do most big Trout, but in this fishing everything appeared upside down. Not only did Pilz fancy the swiftest water discoverable but he wanted me to work the fly up into the white foam of the fall, where I should not have believed it could be seen even if a fish were below it. Yet Pilz was the most experienced ghillie on the water, and the places to which he directed my fly must all of them have yielded Trout during the course of his guiding. Every well-known method of working a fly for Salmon was now employed, not to speak of several other dodges which the formation of the weir permitted

After I had accomplished numberless gymnastics around the weir we took to a skiff and fished the places we had not been able to reach before. Nothing happened. Pilz was bewildered by the lack of strikes, but finally, after trying everything, we went ashore and walked down to the next weir. There we repeated the same manœuvres. This weir was built on a slightly different principle for holding up the water, and since it was also in a narrower channel the water appeared to be dashing about in many contrary directions. At last, as I was making my thousandth retrieve of the morning, I saw a fish swirl near my fly. I cast again hastily, and just when the fly was returning to the same spot a vigorous tug announced a fish. It played beautifully, jumped and did everything a fish should do without escaping. I realised, however, that my cast was strong enough, and had no hesitation in getting the fish in quickly before it could tangle me in some sunken piles. I had previously made calculations of kilos into pounds, so when Pilz announced that it probably weighed seventy dekas I made a reply in German, which translated freely into English would come out as: " Only one and a half pounds? Throw it back, Pilz!" As a matter of fact I think he underestimated the Trout, which was as thick as a brick and in perfect condition. But I felt rather pleased with my remark, and considered afterwards that I had made a supremely magnanimous gesture. I hope, however, that having once released a one-and-a-half-pounder because it was too small, I shall not be called upon to do so again in the future.

I continued to fish with renewed hope. One of the little tricks they use here is to allow the line to be carried out a long way by the fast current, and then it is retrieved in slow jerks. I was in the midst of this stratagem when I got another strong strike. I could feel it was a larger fish, and, as it had already a lot of my line and some very fast water to play in, it gave me a terrific battle. My light rod stood up nobly, though why it did not get a set I cannot imagine. After about ten minutes I brought the Trout into a back-current and managed to lead it to the net. It weighed two pounds ten ounces, and Pilz was in no doubt about putting it in the *Lagl*. He then stood up, extended his hand, and with a broad grin of delight said: " Petri Heil! " It is the Austrian equivalent to " tight lines," and refers, I believe, to St. Peter, but the phrase is also used as a congratulatory expression. I replied correctly: " Petri dank," and shook hands with him. We were both well satisfied. There was nothing more to be done that morning and I returned to my hotel to try and catch up on my sleep.

That evening I was out again after Grayling. I had told Pilz that I did not fancy the fast water of the night before, and this time we went to the slow, deep water in number one beat. I liked it much better. The boat did not swing about so much, and it was easier to keep contact with the fly. Again I went through the process of missing a lot of Grayling which I thought small, till, perhaps more by fortune than skill, I hooked one. To my surprise it weighed one and a quarter pounds and was in excellent condition. We had reached the beat later than the night before, and we kept wondering when the great rise of sedge would start. For one moment a little cloud of them did come over, but that was all. The big hatch did not materialise, and we found ourselves under the necessity of pursuing an occasional rise with the boat. I stood up in the skiff while Pilz followed my directions. It was genuine dry-fly upstream fishing. Again the Grayling grew less nervous as night came on, taking my fly with a certain confidence. But it was no easy matter to find these gentle rises in the dark, and long before I was ready to stop we had to give up through lack of light. I finished the evening with one small Trout of about a pound, which was released, and six Grayling weighing seven and a half pounds, the best being one pound seven ounces. Pilz informed me later that I was high rod for the day with this catch.

My last experience with the Grayling took place the next evening. I returned to the same beat, but this time the light came at such an angle that I could see the fish under water. In a short time I discovered that the reason I had missed so many before dark the other evenings was that I could not strike quickly enough. Now that I could see them I watched the Grayling coming for the fly, and, just before they were about to take, I struck and netted five of them without a miss. It was fine sport. Once more there was scarcely a rise of sedge when it became dark – even less than the night before – and all I did during the rest of the evening was to lose two fish after apparently well hooking them. My five fish, including one very small one, weighed five pounds five ounces. The largest went to one pound eleven ounces.

It is noteworthy that throughout the world, wherever angling is much practised, there are so few small fish which can be considered in the category of outstanding game fish. In America there is the Black Bass and its family, and in Europe and America the Trout and its family. Finally there is the Grayling, whose great sporting qualities are not recognised as they deserve to be. There are many famous anglers, however, who consider Grayling to be the equal of Trout, both from an angling and eating point of view. The position which Grayling should rightfully occupy in the fish world has, indeed, been unfairly prejudiced by the fact that Trout and Grayling are usually found in the same water and that most people prefer Trout. If, however, the Trout enthusiast will for a moment forget his Trout, then a correct appreciation of Grayling establishes it at once as a splendid game fish which, for its size, ranks second to none.

I only fished once more at Gmunden, starting again at a quarter past three in the morning. I tried very hard, as it was my last chance for a big Trout; but though we went over both the upper weirs with great care I did not get a strike. My best fun on this occasion was an attempt on two four-pounders which lay just underneath the town bridge. Looking down from above I could see them clearly. They were poised in a perfect cataract of water which came so evenly through the weir as to form a clear, glassy glide. I showed them first a Salmon fly. They paid no attention. Then I decided to experiment with some strange lures they could not have seen before. I put on a weird kind of cork grasshopper, and they both moved, but thought better of it. Then I tied on a fly with long pale-blue streamers. This interested them considerably, but they would neither of them sample it. When I showed them an imitation helgramite, they decided they had seen enough unknown creatures for one morning and went off in disgust.

Thus I had to be content with my fish of two pounds ten ounces, but during those four days the biggest Trout caught was mine. One of the other anglers whom I met complained bitterly that he did not know what had happened to the water; he had never seen it so dull. Only the week before, as the *Behälter* testified, there had been some splendid catches made. It was, therefore, very fortunate that I fished twice my first night, and as a result had the opportunity of landing a very respectable Trout at Gmunden.

15

SHARK ! SHARK !

OF all the fish which swim the seas there are none which cause mankind the same horror and alarm as do Sharks, and there is good reason for the fear they create, in view of the vast numbers of people they have devoured. Sharks are uncompromising creatures, and I have never heard of anyone wanting to make a pet of a Shark.

In these days, however, when whitewashing seems so much the fashion that Burke and Hare have also their apologists, Sharks too, it is claimed, have their virtues, and it is loudly asserted that as scavengers of the seas they fulfil their duties with unexampled diligence and fidelity. It is further confidently stated, by those who remain on land, that Sharks never attack a black man, and only toy with white people if they insist on swimming where they have been warned that it is dangerous; but I doubt if the apologists themselves would be prepared to offer their own bodies for experimental purposes in Shark waters. I have been told that Sharks, when wishing to " play " with some adventurous soul who has decided it is smart to go out beyond the protecting beach barrier, generally take a bite out of the back part of the thigh. By this technique they sever the big leg vein, so that even if the fool is rescued he must die from bleeding in a short time.

If mankind generally has a just and reasonable desire to avoid Sharks, fish have a terror of them which would appear quite unreasonable if one did not reflect that the end for almost all sea fish is the belly of a Shark. Numbers of fish have their own special Shark which pursues them continuously like their shadows and remorselessly pounces on the stragglers. Other fish which do not shoal in sufficient aggregations to rate a special Shark for themselves still qualify as regular dishes on the bill of fare of the hunting or game Sharks. How many times have I had some fine fish lying on its side by my boat apparently completely exhausted and resigned to my gaff, when the approach of a Shark has suddenly brought it back to life so that it has thereupon offered a display far exceeding anything shown when freshly hooked. Whatever the fish may have thought of my hook, it has certainly not been terribly frightened. But the sight of its mortal enemy, the Shark, makes the fish realise at once the imminence of a swift and painful death, and that is a very different matter, which must be avoided if possible. Besides these hunting Sharks, which capture their prey by speed of swimming, there is that sinister company of carrion Sharks, which live on offal and into the maw of which arrive finally all diseased or injured fish, no matter how great their size. But these slow-swimming creatures can be of slight interest to the angler.

My first experience with Sharks was in Cuba in 1916. I had gone there to meet my friend Reggie, who had been excused further participation in the war owing to wounds, but was continuing to aid England by trying to sell his products to the Cuban Government, and thus carry on the British slogan of " Business as usual." The difficulties of his mission were prodigious, as it was necessary to mollify all personages who could possibly get a finger in the pie. I had come over to join him in Havana during an interval when nothing could be done commercially before he had interviewed an important official who was absent from the city.

One of us had the inspiration to break the monotony of

watching the rhumba danced at the Molino Rojo by trying
a spot of Shark fishing. Through Reggie's friend Padró,
we were introduced to El Guajiro (a fisherman), who stated
that he could catch us all the Sharks we needed. A few
nights later we met him by appointment at a small fishing
dock. The night was dark, without a single star, when we
embarked in his twenty-foot sailing-boat. The land breeze
carried us swiftly out to the harbour mouth, where an
anchor was heaved. El Guajiro then unwrapped from a
newspaper the cadaver of a fish already long dead, as we
could easily sense. It weighed about five pounds, I judged,
and was attached with strong twine to an immense hook
which was again attached to a half-inch rope, and the end
of this was then knotted firmly to the ship's mast. We sat
and waited. El Guajiro informed us that the Shark would
be as long as the boat, and showed us a small truncheon with
which he proposed to despatch the brute if, as, and when
he came. Reggie and I argued that we did not see how he
could get the shark on board with us as well, and that in
any event, if it was that size, it would prove bad company.
The rope was about fifty yards long, and about forty yards
of it were coiled on a seat, the rest continuing overboard.
Not far away the lights of the town shone bright and clear,
casting long reflections on the water. From a distance the
tinkle of a mandolin was occasionally wafted to us.

We had sat for an hour and were beginning to lose
interest, when El Guajiro showed us with his lantern that
the rope was beginning to run out slowly. The pace
increased, and Reggie, though he had been warned against
doing so, could not resist taking hold of the rope. It was
that slight touch which gave the Shark a hint that all was
not well, and it immediately speeded up so that Reggie got
his hand nicely burnt. In another instant the last of the
rope disappeared overboard, there was a fierce jerk on the
mast, and then silence. El Guajiro took hold of the rope

cautiously and began pulling it in.   There was no obvious
strain on the line, but he explained that Sharks sometimes
follow the bait right up to the boat.   El Guajiro was trembl-
ling with excitement, but at last the hook came in quite
bare.   How the Shark had removed the bait and the twine,
leaving the hook untouched, quite baffled us.   Our fisherman baited up again, and we settled down to wait.   As we
sat there in the stillness which then ensued, we became
aware of an intermittent swishing sound.   At first it gave
the impression, perhaps, of small waves rolling on to a
sandy shore.   But the noise became louder and closer, so
that we thought there must be a big sailing-boat advancing
at speed.   Then within fifty yards there was a terrific splash,
and we realised that some huge fish had jumped out of the
water about ten feet and fallen back.   We could see a great
white shape poised for a moment in the air, and then return
to the water with an even more resounding splash.   A
moment or two later we saw it again.   The splashes continued, appearing to come nearer.   El Guajiro said it was
Savalo (Tarpon), but no Savalo I had ever seen was so
huge, and I think now it must have been a giant Manta,
a fish much given to leaping out of the water.   After about
ten of these disturbances, which seemed to be always nearer
our boat, Reggie said he wondered whether it was the Shark
which was after us.   He said he did not like this preliminary war dance.   I said I thought Shark fishing was pretty
dull, and soon we were sailing back to the dock.

   It was some years later that I again had to do with
Sharks.   This time it was simply as observer when fishing
for Tarpon at Boca Grande.   Generally there did not seem
to be much trouble with Sharks there, but some days the
place seemed alive with them.   I can remember particularly
one occasion when, failing for Tarpon, our party kept
pulling in Grouper.   These were strung a little out of water
at the bow of the launch.   Suddenly we heard that cry

which can be the most terrifying in the world, " Shark! Shark! " and on looking over the other side of the launch we saw a great fin approaching us. Fortunately on this occasion there was no human danger, as it was a carrion Shark presumably; at any rate it swam slowly and unconcernedly up to our boat to take our Groupers. Our guide splashed an oar at the Shark and thus kept it away. It seemed, as I recollect it, to have been about twelve feet long. It continued swimming about among the other launches till a fisherman had several shots at it with a revolver, and caused it to depart. We had many subsequent experiences there with Sharks, as must everyone who has tried that fishing. Sometimes the Tarpon we were landing was bitten in half just before we got it in; sometimes the Tarpon, quite ready for the gaff, would become aware of its traditional fate, the Shark, and would come to life and swim away to temporary safety if allowed enough line.

It is a curious thing that the only Shark fishing at Boca Grande was done with a rope, whereas some of these Sharks might afford fine sport if taken on suitable big game fish tackle. All round the coast of South Africa a great deal of fishing with rod and line is done for Sharks with extraordinary results; witness W. R. Selkirk's 2,176 lb. Great White Shark taken from the shore on rod and line.

My next experience with Sharks was of a different character. I had gone to New Zealand to fish for Swordfish and also for Mako Shark. Mako[1] is the Maori name for the Mackerel Shark (*Isurus glaucus*). It is, I imagine, the gamest of all Sharks. In New Zealand there are several varieties which are considered game, but for really sporting purposes only the Mako qualifies, though the others can be extremely tiring to land. The Mako is different from most Sharks, as the two lobes of its tail-fin are of almost equal length. This makes for fast swimming, and in New

[1] Pronounced Mahko.

Zealand it is claimed that the Mako is the fastest swimming of all fish.

I did not have to wait long for my first Mako. It was the first day that I went out to the big game fish grounds. The weather was superb and the sea a bright Mediterranean blue, so clear that one could not determine how deep it was possible to see down. It is certain, however, that one could not see bottom, for that was six hundred fathoms away. That day I had done some trolling for Marlin without result, and finally at lunch-time my guide, Francis Arlidge, stopped the engine and put out two lines for me, so that we could make a drift. One of these lines was to be fished deep, the other shallow. The deep bait consisted of a live Kahawai, a fish of about six pounds, which was hooked through the lips. Kahawai are generally seen on the surface, but when frightened, as this one was by the hook, they go down to some depth. Our bait was thus swimming at about a hundred feet below the launch. The shallow bait was a dead Kahawai which was allowed to sink about thirty feet and was held at that depth by a small rubber balloon float.

The good Swordfish guide displays his skill in many ways, and in the selection of the proper place to drift a great deal of judgment is necessary. The ocean currents carry the launch along at two or three knots, and the usual drift takes about an hour. Thus a fairly wide stretch of ocean is covered, while the angler can rest from the fatiguing vigilance of trolling. The guides have a saying that to get a bite it is only necessary to start lunch; and Francis had just informed me of the saying when I saw my line on the shallow bait begin to run out. I bolted a hard-boiled egg and took up the rod, while with the thumb pad I maintained the slightest pressure on the reel drum to prevent an over-run. The speed of the line as it went out increased, but Francis told me to wait until about sixty yards had gone;

then he signalled to me to slap on the brake and strike.
Those who have not had the experience of a strike from
one of the great game fish can hardly imagine the sensation.
The tackle, for one thing, is immensely powerful, and is so
devised that, providing the line is not frayed and the reel
does not jam, a smash is scarcely possible. The rod is
attached by a harness to the angler's body, and so, when the
slack in the line is gone, the resultant momentum of the
fish on the rod tip can only be described as colossal. Nor
does this shock resemble other fishing strikes, for it is not
taken up by the arms but, owing to the harness, by the
whole body. It gives one, indeed, the sensation of having
been lassoed from a moving train.

I had braced my feet against the side of the boat, and
when the strike came I struck back. The line tore off the
reel against the powerful drag, and I was into my first
Mako. The Shark continued his run until a hundred and
fifty yards of line were out, and then I could see from the
angle of the line that the fish was coming up to the surface.
Another instant and he jumped clear, fifteen feet in the air,
and then turning entered the water again head first — a
most beautiful " breach " which was immediately repeated.
Twelve times he broke the oily surface of the sea in a
marvellous display. Then commenced a long submarine
struggle. Sometimes I would gain a little line, then out he
would go again as fresh as ever. Francis manœuvred the
launch so that if the fish did not swim straight away I could
recover line by cutting corners. In an hour and a half the
Shark began to tire, and soon after this the doubled line
appeared and then the aeroplane wire trace. I had already
had the opportunity to see a good deal of this fish from
different angles during his jumping, but I must say that,
as his huge form came slowly into view from the depths
and I realised that this fearsome monster was on the end of
my line, I obtained a thrill which I shall never forget.

My spare man then took hold of the trace (this is permitted in big game fishing) and hand-lined the Shark up so that Francis could harpoon it with a soft-iron whaler's harpoon. Once this was accomplished the Shark was snubbed in, and Francis administered the *coup de grâce* with a chisel-shaped lance. One expert blow at the base of the head, and the lance went right through the Shark like butter, severing the cartilaginous gristle which passes for backbone in a Shark. A gush of dark blood formed a great scarlet blotch in the translucent sea, and my first Mako was hauled on board.

Some people criticise this practice of harpooning Sharks before landing them but, as Francis explained, a Mako is too dangerous a passenger to have alive in the boat. Then, too, like all Sharks, the Mako has such a tremendous store of vitality that it would be an endless job to play him till dead. There may be a fish which gives a finer display than the Mako, but I have not heard of it. In this regard one thinks at once of Tarpon (that powerful and exquisite fish), but when one has seen a good Mako in action one forgets the comparison. It is not that the Tarpon's display lacks thrills, but the Mako is so much bigger, so much stronger, and so much more graceful. It will be noticed that I have said *good* Mako. This qualification applies to all fish, and very much so to Mako. For one thing these Sharks vary immensely in size. One may catch them from eleven pounds or less up to eight hundred pounds or more. The very small ones, of course, cannot perform well against the heavy tackle employed, while the very large ones are probably lethargic. For this reason a Mako of from two hundred to four hundred pounds gives an angler the ideal experience. My first Mako weighed two hundred and fifteen pounds, and did most of the things one could hope for in the way of fighting. I caught several other Mako before my New Zealand expedition was ended, and I was

THE 256 lb. MAKO WHICH ATTACKED OUR LAUNCH

able to experience the two other features of this fishing which makes it so unusual.

In common with other great fish of the seas, Mako, perhaps with more reason than others, is a fearless fish. It has, indeed, few enemies, and none which it cannot easily out-distance or defeat in battle. Thus, when Mako are hooked, they may quite well not seek safety in flight, but rather in fight. On one occasion, when fishing near Wangaroa, I hooked a hen Shark which, without making any attempt to swim away from the launch, remained instead jumping and diving in close proximity. It was rather alarming, as she could easily have landed in the boat from one of her high jumps. Under these conditions, too, it was difficult to exhaust her. Thus it happened that in a short time she was within landing distance, and Tui harpooned her preparatory to killing her. One would think that a harpoon would be enough to slow down a Shark, but the fact is that, unless the harpoon traverses a vital part, it seems to have little effect. As this fish was quite fresh, the harpoon only infuriated her the more, and she turned on the launch and attacked it with her teeth. We could hear the stout boards of the understructure rending, and the sensation was most unpleasant. Francis was prompt in the emergency, however, and with a well-directed thrust from the lance killed her before she had bitten through the planking. We found afterwards that she had broken eight teeth in her attack.

This peculiarity among Mako, though remarkable, is not unique: in New Zealand, however, they are credited with a tactic which, if they actually adopt it, would tend to prove them the most intelligent of all fish. It is said that they swim up the line and bite it off ! Many fish, of course, appear to try to fall on the line while jumping (Tarpon, Salmon, Black Bass), but I have heard of no other fish which frees itself by biting the line. I myself had two experiences which seemed to verify the contention that they actually do carry out this decisive stratagem. On one occasion it was possible that some other large fish had fouled the line and broken it, or that it had simply parted through some weakness. The other instance was, however, different. I had hooked a fine Mako which had given a good jumping display. The water was clear and calm, so that if other fish were in the vicinity they would probably have been observed. My Mako was at about eighty yards from the launch, when suddenly I felt the line go slack. I reeled in frantically, and with the big multiplying reel I could retrieve very fast. Then there was a fierce jerk, and my line came in apparently cut above the trace. Now the trace used is twenty-two feet long, and above this is a double line of some twenty yards. It was this doubled portion which was neatly sheared off, leaving two strands of equal length. It looked to me very much as if the Mako had swum up and bitten off the doubled line at that point. If fish think, I dare say they consider we take many mean advantages of them; but if a Mako bites off an angler's line, it can scarcely be called cricket.

I fished for various other Sharks in New Zealand, and landed some of them; but, as I have said, the Mako is without equal among them all. The variety esteemed in second place is the Thresher Shark. This fish averages generally much larger than the Mako. It has the peculiarity of possessing one immensely long lobe to its tail,[1] the lobe being about the length of the fish itself. With this lobe the Thresher stuns or disables small fish, so that it can eat them at its leisure. Naturally under these conditions it is not a swift-swimming fish, and the fight it gives is consequently not exciting, though, owing to the size of the fish, it is generally long drawn out. I hooked one of these

[1] All Sharks have heterocercal tail fins, the upper lobe being larger than the lower, and containing the prolongation of the vertebral column. This formation is most noticeable in the Thresher and least obvious in the Mako Shark.

H. WHITE-WICKHAM AND HIS WORLD RECORD THRESHER
(The record has since been broken by a 915 lb. fish)

Threshers at Wangaroa in rather a rough sea, and played it for forty-five minutes before it got away. The fight was typical of the fish. As is usual, the Thresher struck my bait with its tail and entangled itself either with the trace or the hook. It must have been a fish of some five or six hundred pounds, but its fight was not impressive, consisting of a series of small diving runs without any jumping. As the Shark was thrashing about with its tail I kept getting the typical jars and shakings on the rod which such a fish produces. Towards the end I could feel that the trace was unwinding from the tail. There would be a curious shock, and then the line would suddenly come in a foot. I had a triangle and a single hook on the trace, but neither of them took hold properly and finally, after a sudden jerk more violent than the rest, my line reeled in quite free. I found the trace all in coils like a watch-spring.

Another Shark commonly found there is the Hammerhead, which swims a good deal on the surface, and to this extent is interesting. It is curious to watch a Hammerhead when it senses the effluvium of the bait. It seems to nose after it like a well-trained retriever dog. Another rarer Shark is the Blue Shark, which swims, too, mostly on the surface, but fights in a dull way, without jumping. As these Sharks may be very big, they sometimes take a lot of time to dispose of when one could well be fishing for some more sporting fish, and are thus avoided, if possible, by the angler. This also applies to the Reremai Shark, which, however, has not even the virtue of giving a surface display. Finally there is the Sand Shark, which has no good qualities at all from a fishing standpoint. The only Sand Shark I caught took just five minutes to account for, whereas a Mako of the same size would have required two or three hours. Such can be the margin of difference between a game and non-game fish.

There are many other varieties of Shark in these waters,

but those mentioned are the kinds most commonly encountered. One may enquire what is done with a Shark when it has been captured. Any Shark offers a fine trophy for the angler, if its jaws are removed and divested of flesh, the teeth making a magnificent and gruesome ornament for the billiard-room.

Sharks are among the most ancient of all fish, for fossils of the Elasmobranchs have been found dating from the Devonian period and these differ only in minor respects from living examples. It is curious that a creature was evolved so long ago with such practical development that it still remains numerous in most seas.[1] But Sharks, thanks to their armament, have had few enemies. It was not till the advent of shagreen for commercial and decorative purposes that Sharks came to be pursued consistently by man in various oceans. The Chinese, however, discovered centuries ago that, if Sharks like men to eat, the Shark, too, makes a fine dish for man. I noticed that my guide, Francis, used to cut off the fins of my Sharks, and I asked him why. He told me that Shark fins always command a steady price in the fish markets of China.

In Pekin, some time later, I sampled the dish and found that the Chinese were sound as usual in their gastronomic judgment. In fact, Shark's fin well prepared by a Chinese chef resembles in appearance, tastes very like, and is perhaps even more delicious than, that famous French dish, *Raie au beurre noire.*

[1] See Appendix Note, p. 298.

16

EVERYBODY TAKES A DRINK

MY first angling experience out of the Perch class took place some years ago at the Isle of Pines, south of Cuba. I had gone there with my friend Reggie to put in a few days' fishing while a deal he was trying to conclude should have time to mature in a land where nothing should be done in too much of a hurry. We had crossed from Havana to Batavano by train and had to endure a longish wait for the grapefruit boat which was to take us to the island.

To fill in an hour or so we wandered down to some neglected little piers, constructed, no doubt, when sailing-boats required such facilities, and watched a small boy apparently trying to catch Tarpon (immense ones) with a string hand-line. About the pier the Tarpon sported without paying much attention to the small boy's bait. It was my first sight of really big game fish. How wonderful they looked! There are few fish so narrow through for their length as Tarpon, and yet possessing such tremendous muscular strength. From above, looking down on them, their grace was exquisite, while the beautiful sage green of their backs and the huge scales which cover them so perfectly formed a fantastic pattern against the golden sand of that shallow bay. As they turned and gambolled, rolling out of the crystal water in playful loops, we occasionally obtained glimpses of that silver armour which sheaths all but their upper portions with a brilliance surpassed in no other creature. We could form no opinion as to what kind of fish they could be; in fact, except for a few pioneers, nobody really knew what a Tarpon was in those days – a strange name for a fish, anyway!

At last our steamer arrived, and we reached Nueva Gerona, the capital of the island, in due course. As neither of us spoke Spanish we wandered about carrying our suitcases till we found an American bar. The bar-tender spoke a little English, and after some enquiries he told us that there was only one man on the island who did any fishing, a Señor Thomas Upton, and he gave us his address.

The next morning we chartered a car and went inland some way to his house. We found Upton was an Englishman – and a very jolly one too. He was soon telling us that he would be ready to take us out the next day. We enquired the price, and he explained that if we would pay for the petrol he would provide the rest. This seemed fair enough.

At ten the following day we met Upton at the dock. His launch was a sturdy and seaworthy craft, and we were quickly aboard. As we edged out into the stream he passed to each of us a hand-line, to which were attached piano-wire traces with large silver spoons, and told us we could begin trolling at once. He cautioned us to be prepared for a strike, as it might come hard, and then, throwing in the clutch, we started downriver for the sea. As we approached the river mouth the mangroves increased in density, till we found ourselves shut in on two sides by the coiling, "Laocoön" roots of these sinister trees.

"Look out! " shouted Upton, and at that moment Reggie was fiercely startled by a big fish which hit his spoon. For a moment it seemed that Reggie would be overboard, but then, getting his foot against the back of the boat for leverage, he began pulling in his line. There was a great splashing behind, and we saw a Barracuda twisting and leaping, as Reggie brought it in hand over hand. He managed to haul it into the boat with some trouble, for it was a ten-pounder, and once aboard it proved an ugly customer,

UPTON AND SOME SPANISH MACKEREL, YELLOW TAILS, AND BARRACUDAS

with huge teeth snapping in every direction. We succeeded in killing it at last with a small club.

I had retrieved my line when Reggie's fish struck, so as to avoid getting in his way, and I was about to let it out again when Upton called out, " Just a minute." He grinned broadly and then went on: " There's only one regulation on this boat and that is when anybody gets a fish everybody takes a drink."

He then pulled out a large demijohn, which he passed round. It turned out to contain Bacardí rum. We considered that we had made an excellent start for a fishing day, but, alas, we could not long continue the sport. There had been warning of a hurricane which Upton considered unlikely to occur, but soon black clouds began to appear and he decided it would be more prudent not to go out to the main fishing-grounds. We caught a few other fish (including two Yellow Tails) trolling along near shore, and then as the air became sultry and oppressive we decided to take a swim. A small bay was at hand, and there we anchored in shallow water. It was not long before we had stripped and jumped in. We were no sooner in the water than a tropical rain poured down on us. We were astonished to find the rain so very cold, to such a point that we remained submerged in the sea in order to keep warm — an unusual reversal of the accepted order of things.

We had expected to continue fishing after our swim, but as the wind was increasing momentarily we were forced to give up our excursion and in some haste returned to the lodgings we had obtained in the town. For the information of those planning a trip to Nueva Gerona, I should explain that the living-arrangements there are different from most places. We had secured, after some bargaining with a landlady, a double room which faced the street. All the houses on the main street are alike. They are only one storey high and the front bedroom to which we were assigned was similar to many others. It was a large room with a high ceiling, but it had the peculiar feature of lacking one wall. In place of the wall which gave on to the street it had, as sole concession to privacy, an immense mosquito net which closed it in completely, as far as a mosquito net may be said to close anything. This arrangement was splendid in the matter of ventilation, but might prove an annoyance to those squeamish where modesty is concerned.

As it happened, the hurricane missed the island in the end, and the next day we went out fishing again. The weather turned out to be glorious after the uncertainty of the previous day, and the fish seemed to appreciate it. Before we had got out of the river we had three fish, one of them a seventeen-and-a-half-pound Barracuda. Each fish, according to the regulations of the launch, was duly saluted with Bacardí. We made for the Keys, which con- sist of a series of mangrove islands with deep channels between. Below through the translucent water we could see great fish patrolling lazily, without seeming even to notice the launch. Every time we went through a channel we caught at least one fish. Once we hooked a Tarpon which shook off, and then a moment later we brought in a twenty-pound Yellow Tail and a Spanish Mackerel at the same time. The sport was becoming fast and furious and, Upton being a stickler for the regulation, we began to be feeling the effects. Suffice it to say that in an hour we had seventeen fish, and Reggie and I were ready to stop. It was not that we did not enjoy the fishing, but the regula- tion was too severe. We accordingly suggested returning to the silver bay where we had swum the day before, and to this Upton agreed.

We must have gone in bathing with our clothes on, as we have never otherwise been able to account for the fact that, when we came to ourselves next morning, we found them lying in great disorder on the floor, wringing wet.

17

ESTANCIA LA PRIMAVERA

THERE are many famous railway journeys one can
take on this earth which, even in these days when
everybody has become air-minded, well compensate the
land traveller for the extra time. In the train one may
obtain among other advantages, for instance, greater
creature comforts or a more intimate view of the people
or better scenic glimpses or an appreciation of difficult
engineering problems successfully surmounted.

Three such journeys which occur readily to mind are
the Canadian Pacific, the trans-Siberian, and the trans-
Andean. It was to this last that I had been looking forward
with keen anticipation for some months while visiting
Argentina, and yet in the end I crossed the Andes by
another route. It was only a short time before my departure for Chile that I met W., an enthusiastic angler, who
was responsible for my change of plans. He informed me
that in the Neuquen Territory of Argentina there was good
Trout and Salmon fishing. He then asked in an engaging
manner why I did not come and try it, and added that he
was going down in that direction in a few days. I was torn
between missing the railroad trip or missing some fishing,
but eventually decided that the fishing could not be resisted,
and I was also influenced in my decision by the prospect
that in going via Neuquen I would have the opportunity of
seeing something of the pampas and of Patagonia.

One afternoon a few days later we started our journey,

travelling south by west from Buenos Aires. With us was
N., the manager of a great sheep ranch, "La Estancia
Pilcaniyeu," where they raise half a million sheep – " Quite
a flock," as he put it. To reach the fishing we had to travel
in a south-westerly direction to " Kilometre 585 " : the
terminus of the railway which is, except for a short spur
in Chile, the most southerly line on any continent in the
world. Soon after leaving Buenos Aires we entered the
pampas. The land was very flat, and the next morning it
had become flatter still, and very desolate. Of pampas
grass, which I had been eagerly expecting, I saw not a sign;
instead, the inhabitants were attempting to raise crops by
the dry farming method; but to my eye the crops appeared
already ruined. The dust was appalling; it came seeping in
through the screened windows of the train and covered
everything with a thick beige layer. To distract ourselves
from discomfort we put in our time playing the South
American game of *bidou* (the best of all dice games), first
for the drinks, then for more drinks, and then for the meals.
It is the only dice game I know in which judgment and
psychology have a chance to tip the scale against luck.
During the morning we stopped at Bahia Blanca, which is
quite an important wine centre, and then continued to
Patagones, where we made a motor connection with
another train at Viedma. I found that I had a companion
in my compartment for the following night. He was the
editor of the local paper at Viedma. I noticed as I was
turning in that he was wearing rimless spectacles, and I was
much astonished on waking the next morning to find him
asleep with his glasses still on his nose.

We were now passing through the valley of the Rio
Negro, and the country appeared more fertile, but soon it
changed to a desolation which must be seen to be believed.
We continued to play *bidou* in a desultory fashion, and
between times listened to yarns which N. spun us of life in

Patagonia. For twenty years he had lived in this wild country, and his tales, some of them no doubt true, were fascinating. One I remember is worth retelling, as it shows how little this country is known, even to the Argentines. Near N.'s old home at Maginchao is a small and deep lake which was unremarkable until one day an old pedlar arrived in the neighbourhood. He was a scoundrelly old blackguard, and very fond of the vitriolic red wine of the country. In a drunken state one evening he wandered down to the lake, from which he returned to the nearest village staggering, trembling, and out of breath. When partly recovered he announced between gasps that, while sitting beside the lake, an enormous and fantastic creature had emerged out of the water and had tried to seize and devour him. He claimed that he had escaped miraculously, thanks to the Virgin Mary and the intercession of numerous saints. The natives were delighted with his adventure, and he found that whenever he told the story it was good for a round of drinks. Further, with each repetition the tale became more authentic and more decorated with specious details. He would, perhaps, have remained there for the rest of his life, with all his needs provided for by his story, if one day another villager had not also seen the monster. This obvious falsehood of the villager enraged the pedlar, and cut down his free drinks considerably. But, what was worse, soon one native after another saw the creature, so that in a short time his entire livelihood was taken from him. He moved to another town, but his story was there received with laughter, and without refreshment. Then inspiration came to him. He got hold of a cheap photographer who took a snapshot of the pedlar with a borrowed gun, apparently shooting some obscure object in a lake. The photographer then supplied him with a thousand postcards, depicting the episode, on a fifty per cent commission basis. The pedlar now found his fortune was made. He wandered freely about the country selling the postcards and telling his story. Life became easy for him. At last the tale reached Buenos Aires, and through official sources was referred for comment to the director of the museum. After consideration the director opined that it was possible that a Plesiosaurus still existed in Patagonia. Things now began to move fast, and soon 10,000 pesos were voted by Government for a scientific investigation, and a platoon of soldiers was detailed to accompany an expedition to bring back the Plesiosaurus dead or alive. The end of this adventure provided, alas, an anticlimax. Guards had been posted at all vantage-points and a continual watch was kept while drag nets and grappling-hooks were manœuvred about the lake, without fishing up the Plesiosaurus. This had been going on for three weeks. The soldiers, who had been at first impressed by the accounts of the local inhabitants, were beginning to weary with the monotony of their duties. One of them, however, had decided to take no chances, and when it came to his turn to keep watch one dark night, he climbed a tree and stretched out on a limb overhanging the water. He must have dozed off; he fell into the lake with piercing screams and much splashing. The soldiers, thus rudely awakened, came tumbling out of their tents and commenced a furious bombardment in all directions with their rifles. It was only at dawn that some sort of order was restored, and then it was discovered that no serious damage had been done. The Plesiosaurus was still apparently hiding in the depths of the lake, and the only casualty was a soldier who had been slightly wounded in the pants. The expedition remained a few days longer, but when the funds grew low it returned to Buenos Aires. W. and I were much amused by N.'s recital, and asked when all this had happened, to which he replied, " About six years ago." We pressed him to discover whether the whole story was his own invention, but the only reply was the sober comment (to which I am willing to subscribe) that he could well believe there still exist prehistoric monsters in this vast and mysterious continent.

We passed another night on the train, and in the morning found the landscape had changed to a rolling formation of rocks and lava. Here and there small bushes grew in thick clusters on the barren ground, while occasionally we came to more level slopes. On one of these I saw my first guanaco. This animal is the " llama which gallops," and for which there has not yet been discovered a human utility. Inasmuch as each guanaco eats the forage of three sheep a day, it is being rapidly killed off by the ranchers. The skin of the young guanaco can, indeed, be employed for mats and rugs, but the hair of the older ones is too rough even for that purpose.

At four o'clock we arrived at Kilometre 585. N. had already asked me to spend the night at his house, and I accepted with pleasure. He warned W. and me to put on our overcoats, and when we descended from the train we appreciated his advice. We had reached latitude 41 degrees south, and the " roaring forties." As we stood on the temporary platform, we wondered if our own weight could hold us down against the terrific blast of wind which howled round us. We took cars and were driven to the Estancia, which was on the east side of a slope; N.'s house had, in addition, large wind-breaks constructed round it to keep out part of the gales. On our way I saw more sheep together than ever in my life before. The flocks gave the appearance of vast perambulating blankets as they moved along slowly grazing. I have already described how the rolling lava formation of this country leaves the slight eminences completely bare of vegetation, but in the hollows there is rich grass which supports easily the huge flocks of Australian merino sheep.

That evening we dressed for dinner, which was served

with all the embellishments and with as much care as if we were in London. After the savoury we had coffee and Courvoisier, while the conversation turned to fishing. I had come all this distance with nothing definitely planned. I knew that Trout could be obtained near Lake Nahuel Huapi, and I was intending to interview the chief of the fish hatchery at Bariloche to see how I must go about getting some fishing. N. suggested that a better idea would be to go straight to see Guy Dawson at the Estancia la Primavera, and find out if I could not secure my fishing at the Estancia. Dawson was a sheep rancher, and was also just getting ready to form a club and take in fishing guests. I decided to try this plan, and W. said he would accompany me.

When we left the house the next morning we were again assaulted by the same overpowering west wind. I turned to N. and asked: " Doesn't this fearful gale ever let up ? "

To this he replied: " My dear fellow, it isn't windy to-day. We call this a calm."

The trip to Dawson's was uneventful, except for the alarming character of the road. We crossed the Rio Limay by ferry, and then followed the river which flows from Lake Traful to Estancia la Primavera, which is some distance from the south end of the lake. It was this last bit of road (constructed by Dawson himself) which proved so exciting. W. said that it was *more* than an engineering feat, and it was really a miracle that it could be used at all. At several corners where the road was cambered the wrong way over a precipice, our chauffeur descended and went forward to look over the situation before advancing. He would return to the car muttering, " *Muy feo,*"[1] but he was a good driver, and got us to the ranch for tea.

Dawson was away, but Mrs. Dawson received us very kindly and agreed to take us in for a few days. We were

[1] Very ugly.

GUY DAWSON WITH A 25lb. "SEBAGO"

introduced to her adopted daughter, "Blackie," and after tea we started off with her for the river. It proved a good two-mile walk before we got to it. This is the river from Lake Traful which joins the Rio Limay further down. Neither of us knew quite what was the procedure, but we had Salmon spinning rods and various spoons, with which we worked two pools until quite exhausted. It was not easy casting, as the cursed west wind still pursued us, though in a slightly diminished degree. At last Dawson appeared in his car. He was a fine big chap, a New Zealander, as are so many of the ranchers in this region, and he was astonished and disappointed that we had secured no fish. After expressing his regrets he drove us back to the Estancia and consoled us with a " tot," as he called it. He told us he had been living some time at this ranch, and had known about the Trout in the river for a number of years. Occasionally he used to go out and catch some for dinner. One day, however, when he was fishing, he got into something which he realised was no Trout. He had a fearful time with it, but finally landed a fifteen-pound Salmon. It was a peculiar-looking fish, and he had subsequently discovered that it was a land-locked Sebago Salmon. Since that time he had killed many. Usually he fished with a spoon, though a Devon or other artificial was also satisfactory. Nobody seemed to know how the Salmon had got there, but it was surmised that Salmon eggs had by mistake been mixed with Trout eggs sent from North America many years previously.

There were two other guests at the ranch that evening; one was a sheep buyer come to inspect the stock, the other a Chilean consul, who entertained us greatly by dancing, with Blackie, the Chilean national dance, called the *cuaca*. Dawson had to go away on business the next day, so his wife volunteered to take us fishing. As we were to go to that part of the river where it debouched out of Lake Traful we wanted horses. Among the semi-wild creatures brought up for our selection I picked out the one which appeared the most docile, and the others permitted me, as a non-equestrian, to set the pace. We were quite a cavalcade, with several Gauchos carrying provisions, and a pack of no less than seven dogs in attendance. Mrs. Dawson explained about the dogs. They were all half-bred, except the parents. The father was an Alsatian and the mother an English foxhound bitch which had lately littered seven more puppies. Dawson was trying to produce a breed of lion dogs from this cross, and I must say I have never seen a finer combination than some of the offspring. They had the colour, brains, and courage of the father, and the ears and modified nose of the mother. The animal hunted was the puma or " lion " of that country, of which Dawson had already bagged several.

Nellie, the six-year-old daughter of the Dawsons, was quite an annoyance to me, as she kept enquiring why we did not gallop. She was riding a half-wild horse without a saddle, and at last Mrs. Dawson told her to gallop if she wanted to. She was off like a flash, lying full length on the horse's back; how she kept her balance I cannot imagine. If she ever wished to she could get a job in any circus.

We crossed a small river which came up to my horse's girths and, after what seemed an age, reached the outlet of the river from Lake Traful. It is a very pretty stream, some twenty yards wide, with deep transparent pools. On the left bank are some high rocks which made fishing impossible, but from the right bank we could get a line out when the wind permitted. W. and I tried very hard without luck till lunch-time, when Nellie came to fetch us. Mrs. Dawson had prepared a marvellous repast. It was called an *asado*, and consisted of half a lamb split lengthwise and skewered on a long sword, which was planted upright in a smouldering wood fire. I never expect to taste anything better. According to local custom, each guest was provided with a hunting-knife with which he hacked off a piece of meat, which he then devoured while holding it in his fingers. It was primitive and wonderful.

The great valley in which lies the Estancia is most beautiful. The surrounding mountains, composed of grey rock, reminded me of the Dolomites. They are very jagged and rise against the skyline in mighty bastions and pinnacles of weird and fantastic contour. Far above us, as we lunched, two huge birds wheeled in great spirals. We were told they were condors, of which there are many in these regions. We continued fishing afterwards, but still with no success. I tried various spoons without result. That night when we returned to the Estancia and told of our failure, Dawson was quite disgusted. He said he would take us out the next day himself, and it would be quite different. No doubt we had struck an unlucky fishing period, but I dare say our methods were partly to blame. Dawson showed us photographs of some of his catches. One, I remember, contained five Salmon averaging thirteen and a half pounds, and nine Trout averaging four and a half pounds, all taken in two hours. Four of the Salmon had been killed in one pool.

The following morning we started out in a truck, and though the water in the river came up almost to the top of the wheels, the motor pulled us through all right. Our programme was the same as the day before, but at lunchtime we still had nothing to show for our labours. Dawson had made several changes in our tackle, but even these did not seem to help. He told us we had put a spell on the fish, and that he had never seen such a blank day. Just to show us what bad fishermen we were, he then put up his own rod and caught three fish — a small Salmon and two nice Trout — in a short time. We were ashamed of ourselves, but try as we would we could accomplish nothing.

Dawson by now had decided that only heroic measures would suffice for us, and the next day we left camp after lunch on horseback, with the truck loaded for spending the night out. The river, which we had crossed with so much difficulty the day before, had continued to rise, so we left the truck at the camp site and crossed on the horses. Dawson chaperoned us over the river, which had become very deep and rapid.

We had naturally discussed the night before what we could do to entice the fish, and Dawson had enunciated the theory that our spoons were too bright. The spoon he found most successful was a small brass one which, owing to long use, had become very dull. Acting on this tip I painted the convex side of my Pfleugers dark grey. When we reached the river, Dawson accompanied me to the top pool and I put on his brass spoon. Almost at once I got a strong strike from a Salmon, but it threw the hook with its first jump. I had raised my rod with the jump, as is usually done with Tarpon; in Salmon fishing the reverse seems to be correct; at any rate the fish got away. We decided to change the spoon, and I put on one I had painted. With my second cast again a fish took, and this time, though I made the same mistake, it stayed on. The fish gave me a splendid fight in the swift water, involving considerable manœuvring about the bank and passing the rod round trees and bushes; but it gave up in the end and was gaffed by W., who had come running up. Dawson, having caught a fish for me, went to help W., and I continued by myself downstream. After a while I came to a fine pool, but one very difficult to fish. It meant wading in water just below the top of the waders, always an uncomfortable proceeding, and it also involved left-handed casting with very little room to get the spoon back. Again, using the same spoon, I got a strike with my second cast. This fish was even better than the last. It jumped beautifully eight times

all over the pool, and then decided to go downstream. I
was in a very bad position, as it was impossible to follow
the fish, and I simply had to hang on and hope. Just as I
thought my chances of holding it were gone, the fish
suddenly grew tired, and I was able to humour it upstream
and finally beach it.

It was now getting late, and after trying a little longer
without result we decided to return to camp. We weighed
the two fish and found that they both went twelve pounds
two ounces, our scales being unable to discriminate between
them. W. had failed to get a single strike all day, but he
had kept to a bright spoon, so it looked as if the theory of
a dark spoon in the clear water was responsible for my good
fortune. This time on the way back Dawson refused to
trust me to cross the river alone, and I mounted pillion
behind him. As we were going into the water he remarked
that it was all right so long as the horse did not stumble,
but that if it got its nose under it was all over. He then
asked me if I could swim, to which I replied, " Yes, but I
don't want to." Luckily there was no necessity for me to
display my aquatic prowess.

We reached camp and found everything had been prepared for our reception. A great wood fire burned bright,
and the savoury odour of roast lamb whetted our appetites,
already well sharpened by the exertions of the day. My own
spirits were, indeed, subdued by the thought that train
and ship schedules did not permit a longer sojourn in this
entrancing land, for Lake Traful is only the beginning of
one of the most beautiful countries of lakes and mountains
in the world.

The sun was setting behind the mountains, and as it
disappeared it cast great streamers of gold and orange tints
into the darkening azure overhead. Gradually the light
faded, and the moon crept up to share our solitude and with
its soft radiance to outline the towers and minarets of the

cordilleras in silver relief against a blue-black sky. As we sat admiring the beauties of that Patagonian night, one of the Gauchos emerged from the surrounding shadows and with a gently murmured " *Por favor*," joined our circle. Beneath his arm he carried a guitar, and then with great simplicity he commenced playing for us the sad and romantic melodies of that wild country. A long time we listened peacefully to his music, until slowly the camp fire began to dim, and then we, weary at last, sought our pine-bough beds and tranquil slumber.

18

A VERY CURIOUS EXPERIENCE

SOME years ago I had the pleasure of meeting in Buenos Aires a gallant colonel (retired) of the British Army. His job involved constant travelling over the South American continent. He was a keen angler, and thus it happened that when I told him I was going to Chile he was able to give me an introduction to another enthusiast named Smith who resided in Valparaiso. The colonel informed me that there was wonderful Rainbow fishing in Southern Chile, and also some fishing for small Trout in the streams near " Valpo." As my chances for Trout had hitherto been limited I decided that this less ambitious angling would suit me well.

My journey from Buenos Aires was not by the usual trans-Andean railway. Instead, I went south into Patagonia and then across the continent through the " Argentine Switzerland " of Lake Nahuel Huapi and its chain of sister lakes. The Andes in this latitude are not so high, but the actual pass which skirts Mount Tronador must be traversed on mule-back. I entered Chile at Casa Pangue and continued by boat and car through the country which surrounds the extinct volcano of Osorno, reaching at length Puerto Varas and the railway. This is almost the southern terminus of the Chilean system, and the journey north proved most interesting. Particularly noticeable were the ulmo trees, from the bloom of which bees manufacture the finest of all honeys. Along the track wild digitalis grew in masses. It was curious to see that in the south these flowers were mostly a lovely mulberry tone, with here and there a cream-coloured one. Further along the two colours were about equally mixed, while in the northern extremity of their range they were mostly cream with only an occasional one of the mulberry shade. The other commonest flower was the wild fuchsia which differed in no way from that of the European garden.

The country changed frequently as we went north. At first there was a rolling landscape which looked like England with the cultivation of the United States. Then the country reminded one of Italy, with vineyards, tiled houses, and poplar trees, so that after a while one could hardly distinguish it from the foothills of Northern Italy. Then again it changed to a North American landscape, with the digitalis all gone and in its place a yellow flower like golden rod. Once more a change, and this time one might think of the wheat-fields of France filled with cornflowers and a scarlet flower of the colour of poppies.

In the train the women's strident Spanish voices (surely the world's most unmusical) pierced the ear; but I found respite in the smoking-car where a fellow traveller was playing a guitar and singing beautifully – for his own pleasure, it seemed. The songs, either sentimental or passionate, were loudly applauded by the other passengers.

At Valpo I looked up Smith. He turned out to be a dark little man with one eye slightly cocked. His private office was only separated from the reception-room by a wooden rail. As I was not sure that it was he, I informed his stenographer in broken Spanish that I wished to see Señor Smith. She returned to the gentleman and handed him my card. Smith at once became galvanised into action, and dictated three letters, two of which were to renew subscriptions to foreign magazines, while the other was equally unimportant. I was impressed, as no doubt was intended by this business camouflage. I was then admitted through a swing gate to the sanctum.

I said, " My name's McCormick. I want to talk to you about fishing."

" About what ? "

" Fishing," I repeated.

Smith threw his feet up on his desk, leant back, and shouted, " Why didn't you say so before ? "

I explained that the colonel had sent me, that I wanted to try for Trout near Valpo, and that I had just come up from Puerto Varas.

" Well," said Smith, " you might as well go back again. There's no fishing here. The only good fishing in Chile is just near Puerto Varas at Villarica."

I told him I would go to-morrow and asked for details. Smith was still fearfully busy in theory. He remembered that he was expecting important European cables concerning big transactions at any moment. He found time, however, to accompany me to several shops where tackle could be obtained, and, in fact, did not leave me all day. At intervals he kept repeating how busy he was, and how much he wanted to get some fishing. Finally at tea-time he announced he was coming with me. He said he thought business could spare him for a short period.

Two days later we got off the train at Temuco and took an appalling road in a fearful car for Villarica. I have never seen such fences as they have there. They are composed of huge logs, some of them a yard thick, laid in five-foot sections along the ground. In every direction these fences extended, though the value of what they purported to divide off we could not perceive, as a poorer-looking land could scarcely be imagined. We continued on to Pucon, making a circle round Lake Villarica, and put up that evening at Otto Gudenschwager's hotel.

The next morning, though it was pouring rain and very

windy, we prepared to fish. There were only two guides available: Elicio, the star guide of the hotel, and an under-nourished boy of fifteen named Alesandro. Though Smith had already often fished these waters he said he would take Elicio. We were intending to fish that part of the Cautín River which flows into Lake Villarica from the east. At the west end of the lake it continues on as an outlet, eventually reaching the Pacific Ocean under the name of the Rio Toltén. Twenty or thirty years previously the river had been stocked with Rainbows and Brown Trout which had thriven splendidly. After the manner of Rainbows, those which had reached the sea returned later as Steelheads, attaining sometimes noble proportions; fish of ten or twelve kilos being reported occasionally. Besides these foreigners there was also a native *Trutta Criolla*, a kind of Perchy fish of little sporting worth.

Putting on waterproofs, we started shortly, and after walking through a small pine forest arrived at the river inlet to the lake. It was not easy fishing, for the rain came driving down between the gusts of a piercing wind. My wretched Alesandro, who I believe had never guided before, did not possess even a *poncho* and was soon dripping and shivering. I commenced fishing with a spoon and a light Salmon spinning rod, for all this water was either of spinning or wet-fly type. Nothing came, however, and we returned fishless to the hotel for lunch.

In the afternoon we crossed a corner of the lake in rowing-boats, thus saving some time, and began again at the same spot. Elicio had soon taken Smith upstream to try in some likely places. I must explain that at this time I had no knowledge of wet-fly river-fishing; my only previous experience had been a few days with a dry-fly on the Esopus; Alesandro appeared to know even less. It was thus in a very tentative manner that I advanced upstream, fishing down where I imagined a Trout should lie.

I must have sought for fish in quite impossible waters. At last I came to what I considered a very favourable pool. I was proceeding to fish it when Smith arrived with the information that he had caught a four-and-three-eighth-pound fish. His delight savoured almost of gloating. He then went to the head of my pool and commenced to fish it down. At this stage Elicio came over and told me I was using the wrong kind of spoon, and selected another one for me. I went up to the middle of the pool, leaving the upper half for Smith, and made a cast. To my surprise the new spoon, a Pfleuger No. 5, immediately hooked a fine fish. I was using a nine-and-a-half-foot Trout rod of six and one-eighth ounces, and the fight which ensued was glorious. The fish first ran downstream and then turned and ran up again, interspersing its manœuvres with numerous jumps. In the midst of the fight my reel fell off, but in the end Alesandro managed to net the fish, after several attempts – three and three-quarter pounds. Returning to my position I shortly landed two more of two and a half, and two pounds. This was all I found in the bottom part of the pool, but when I moved upstream to look for other water Smith rushed down to go over it once more. Of course with my present experience I would never have continued to fish a river in this way with a companion. Two methods which are both delightful are either to divide the water by the spin of a coin into two stretches, remain on the stretch drawn for a fixed part of the day, and then change stretches; or (perhaps the more pleasant) to fish the same water taking either alternate casts or alternate fish. Some time later I returned to the pool and got two more out of it, one of one and three-quarter pounds and a small three-quarter-pounder.

It was getting dark, and as we walked back to the hotel Smith remarked: " Well, that isn't so bad, nine fish the first day." I never did see two of these, though I observed him making a great fuss over one very small fish. As a matter of fact he had scarcely been out of sight all that afternoon. One of my fish was a Brown Trout, and we had it for dinner. Very delicious it was, with a wonderful red flesh.

That evening in the bar Smith was kind enough to instruct other anglers in the art of fishing, referring at intervals to his large fish.

The next morning we took boat again for the river, and, though Alesandro almost managed to upset me in the rough water of the lake, we arrived wet, but safely. The weather turned out even worse than the day before. During the morning I had two strikes, and Smith caught a two-pounder. I then went home and Smith came back later with a two-and-a-half-pound *Trutta*.

The following day the weather was still dreadful, and we decided to wait for the afternoon. I had developed a bad cold, so after catching a two-and-a-half-pounder I returned to the hotel. Later Smith appeared, and in answer to my enquiry described exultingly a two-pounder he had captured. At dinner they served my fish. Smith looked at it in surprise as it was laid before us. He cocked his weather eye a little more than usual, and then asked, " What fish is that? "

" My fish."

" Your fish ! Which fish ? "

" The two-and-a-half-pounder I caught to-day."

" You never told me you had caught a fish," he said.

" You never asked me," I replied.

That evening I discussed with another angler the question of flies. I had already tried several varieties, but had had small success. From my fly box he selected a weird blue, red, and yellow affair, which was called a " Hair Basser." It was a fearsome contraption intended for Black Bass. The next morning I decided to experiment with it.

This day, as it was to be our last, we took our lunch with us. We were going to try much higher up the river. I should explain that this river was very rapid in some parts, but contained nice pools here and there. It was in these pools that we generally found the fish. The method of procedure was for the guides to put us ashore and then row upstream where possible. If, however, the current became too fast, they would go ashore and pull the boats up by hand in the shallow water along the banks. Elicio with his superior strength and skill had soon out-distanced Alesandro. Smith, too, was shortly out of sight, while I remained behind essaying some places which looked likely, without success. At last I came to the pool where I had had my good fortune the first day. It was not a very long pool, perhaps sixty yards in all. At the top of it I saw Smith putting up another rod. I called out to him to find out if he had fished the water.

" Oh, no," he said.

" Do you want to fish it ? " I asked.

" No," he replied, " I will leave it for you."

He then jumped into his boat hurriedly and crossed to the other bank.

With my very first cast the Hair Basser got me tied up with a lovely fish. It put up a magnificent fight, and although Alesandro again missed it in the netting I finally landed it. It turned out to be a Steelhead of six and a quarter pounds, the best fish we had during the whole trip. I fished down the rest of the pool and hooked another of about two pounds which came unstuck after I had had it on for five minutes. As we were leaving the pool, I asked Alesandro, who had been waiting for me there already a long time, whether the señor had fished the pool before I arrived.

" Si, señor."

" What with ? The fly or the spoon ? " I asked.

" With both, señor."

I could see that our fishing must remain, at any rate from Smith's point of view, a contest without mercy. I therefore determined to try my hardest to give him some competition. But this was not to be. One of those periods now arrived during which the fish would not stay on the hook. In different pools I had four strikes in succession, and each time after a moment or two the Trout departed. At last I caught up with Smith, who had by then captured two fish. I was on the opposite bank to him when another fish took my fly. Smith and Elicio watched with interest as I played it for some minutes, and then again the fish kicked off under water. Our boat was soon left behind once more by the others, nor did we see them again before I judged it time to return. During this period I had had many strikes, strong ones, some of them with considerable subsequent battles; but almost every time the fish got away. I should perhaps have landed twenty fish; but two, of three and a half pounds, and two and a half pounds, were all I netted.

Our journey back proved exciting. While going upstream I had observed the rapids which I passed on dry land, but it had not occurred to me that we should have to go back over them by water. I got aboard and Alesandro turned the boat upstream and let it drift stern first with the current. In a moment we were carried away. I must say that in this voyage my boy guide showed himself a fine waterman. He sat facing downstream, and with his oars, when necessary, steered the boat to avoid anything menacing. We went tearing through currents and between rocks in a manner quite impossible, but we floated over all without a touch. At last we got into deeper water, and at my lucky pool I told Alesandro to stop for a final try. Once again, as if to emphasise my demoralisation, I lost a fine fish under water. What was the cause of this? Perhaps I was trying too hard, or striking too soon or too late; perhaps I was holding the fish too strongly or not strongly enough.

Perhaps the hook was too small or was strained by my big fish. It did seem slightly pulled out, but it was the only fly of that pattern I possessed, and other patterns appeared less successful. Nothing I did succeeded, and my total catch for the day amounted to only three fish. At last Smith returned to the hotel. He had seven fish with him and said he had released three others. This time I was forced to believe him.

I told him of my extraordinary sequence of lost fish, and he explained that it was because I had not held my rod up straight enough. He said that on the occasion when I caught up with them and lost my fish before their eyes, Elicio had remarked to him that I would lose all my fish for that reason. Elicio contended that in that strong water, with those extremely lively Trout, the rod must be held very straight or the fish would surely get off. I do not know whether this was the reason; at any rate I should have liked to have been informed of the theory. As for Smith, he claimed that he had not lost a single fish. That day I shall always remember, and also lesson number one – when a Trout is hooked to *keep the rod tip up*.

Smith got a little drunk that night, so the repeated recital of his exploits must be forgiven.

Four days later I sailed from Valparaiso. I had seen Smith frequently every day, and I must say that he had tried hard to make my stay agreeable, but incidents continued to occur which showed his peculiar character. The reader will no doubt have been wondering why I had accepted Smith's companionship to begin with, and why I did not relinquish it long before. The fact is that if the incidents were not taken seriously, then they were really amusing, and, indeed, I have ever since looked back on my association with Smith as a pleasurable and very curious experience.

19

A SLICE OF SCOTCH SALMON

IT is sad the way friendships sometimes lapse never to be renewed, or, if ever, then with so much missing during the interval that they can never quite regain their former charm. There are two reasons why we must lament the verity of this trite dictum. One is ourself and the second is the other person.

My companionship with M. was not interrupted by neglect or by any of the usual causes which destroy such friendships, but simply by war and dividing oceans. We corresponded for a while but then other distractions intervened. She was married; and I – after an extended trial – had had my shackles removed before we met again. It was at Ciro's Club in London that an acquaintance happened to re-introduce us.

We talked of old times, of course, and then got caught up on the years between. When one gets down to it, if one has led a normal sort of life, there is little to tell – a few facts, yes; the war and so on; but unknown lands and unknown people are not of much interest even to old friends. In a very short time we had arrived at what we did yesterday.

As it so happened the day before I had leased a beat on the Dee, in Scotland, with the idea of some Salmon fishing. I was complaining that though the water could carry several rods I had discovered nobody to accompany me, when M. remarked that she thought her husband, V., would be very glad to do so. Now Dame Rumour, on whose lack of accuracy it is no longer necessary to comment, had informed me that V. was a very difficult man to get along with; but I was in need of a companion and, having had successful dealings with many funny ones in the past, I was ready to take a chance.

We arranged that I should meet him for tea to discuss the project. Needless to say I found V. to be a most charming man. As the saying goes, I could not fault him, nor indeed was there any reason to try; for his fine qualities shone out at once. He was keen to go with me and in a short time we were ransacking the tackle shops for necessary equipment. Neither of us had ever fished Salmon before, nor had we the vaguest idea of how to employ the spinning and double-handed fly rods recommended. We had about a week of grace before starting north and, having found a professional instructor, put in several days trying to learn the technique of casting. Our tackle was similar: ten foot eight, medium, spinning-rods with Silex reels and sixteen-foot greenheart " vibration " rods for the fly.

The spinning was not so difficult, but I proved extremely stupid with the fly rod. V., on the contrary, showed a natural aptitude and got along quickly. The professional too, though a famous teacher, did not seem to be able to convey his art to me. About the third day he was in such despair that I found myself having to console him with the assurance that I would get it in the end. To add to the difficulties, my water consisted only of the right bank of the river, and from this it followed that most of our casting would be left-handed. By chance it happens that I am far from ambidextrous. It took me years to acquire the proper use of a fork. My innocence of Salmon fishing can be further judged by the fact that I had not even noticed which bank was offered me in the lease and had to look up the question when the professional enquired. Naturally, there was not sufficient time for me to learn the cast on both sides, but before we departed I managed occasionally to get out some sort of line, left-handed. The method of instruction which I found most profitable was to stand behind and to the right of the instructor, and to follow the exact movements of his rod with my own. Sometimes he would get my hookless fly in the back of his neck; but though he objected strongly to this, I could not help feeling that he should consider it one of the hazards of his profession. It was curious that I proved so awkward, for, though not a great expert, I could already wield a nine-foot Trout rod with fair skill. But I, at any rate, found the double-handed rod a very different proposition. It was obviously impossible to learn all the necessary casts but I did have dinned into me in the end the ordinary " overhead," and had acquired a slight notion of the " switch " and the " Spey."

Giving ourselves two days for the trip, we motored in V.'s Rolls to Scotland and reached Banchory on the 28th of February, the day before my lease commenced. There we put up at the Brig o' Feugh Hotel which had been recommended to us, with good reason.

The Dee is not a big river, being only eighty-seven miles long; it is, however, celebrated for its fishing and for the famous places along its banks, among others the royal castle of Balmoral. My fishing started immediately below where the Water of Feugh, a tributary, joins the Dee. I had a mile and a quarter of bank.

For those contemplating Salmon fishing in Scotland there is one important consideration: that is, whether the Salmon will be where you expect to fish at the same time as yourself. Salmon (those which are not netted at the river mouth) enter the Scotch rivers at different times of the year. They proceed upstream in a leisurely or possibly rapid manner. They are influenced in their decision as to when and how fast to go by many conditions, especially the weather. If

MAJOR KERR ON THE DEE

the year is an early one, the Salmon will come up early. The
flow of the river and other circumstances determine how
rapidly they will swim and in what pools they will rest
during their journey.   The records of when and how many
fish were taken in previous years serve as a rough guide to
show what one may expect in a particular water at a certain
time; but though the records are surely accurate one cannot
count on the fish with confidence.

I was aware that my beat was too high up for March
fishing unless the weather became very favourable, and,
for that reason, I paid only a moderate sum for the privilege.

We had arranged for a couple of ghillies and they appeared early the following morning. We tossed to see
who would get Blacklaws, a typical Scot, with a long
drooping red moustache, and he fell to my lot, while V. took
Shaw, a younger man with a shock of black hair.   They
were both very doleful.   Blacklaws said there was a fearful
lot of " grrrue " on the water.   We went down to look at
it, and discovered that " grue " meant floating ice cakes.
These were not large but they would certainly cut our casts
and freeze our lines; in fact it was impossible to fish.   We
spent the day going over the water, being told the names of
the different pools, and getting our tackle ready.   The
ghillies pointed out several Salmon to us, which looked
encouraging.

The next day we started fishing.   There had been a
slight thaw and the grue was gone, but the water was still
discoloured.   I had drawn the lower half of the beat.   As
this meant wading, I had put on my heavy waders in preparation and had to walk a long distance thus accoutred.   I
did not made the same mistake again.

Blacklaws proved merciless and sent me out immediately
with the fly rod into the Floating Bank Pool and thirty
inches of water.   Though he was tactful enough to make
no remark I am sure my first cast disillusioned him at once.

I tried, to begin with, right-handed and then on the other side, which went better. I put everything I had into it, but after two hours I seemed to have nothing left and there had not been the sign of a fish. I was about ready to give up when I saw a huge fish rise. I cast again quickly and by chance exactly over it. Whether the fish struck or not I cannot tell, but at any rate I struck, and I had my first fish on. It appeared enormous and I was in ecstasy till it dawned on me, partly from Blacklaws's evident indifference, that I had hooked a kelt or " spent " fish. The fight which ensued was, however, well worth the experience, for, when the fish was finally tailed, it turned out that it had been foul-hooked. The encounter lasted fifteen minutes and included several interesting manœuvres. Blacklaws released the kelt with appropriate Gaelic regrets reflecting on the nature of the fish, its uncleanliness, and the tragedy that it was not fresh-run. If the fish had been in condition it would have weighed twenty pounds.

In the afternoon I changed beats with V. and started in the Kirk Port Pool. This was much more difficult as the water was deeper. My arms were so tired by now that I could scarcely cast at all. I kept at it, however, with the fly, and also tried spinning a golden Sprat. After what seemed hours I finally got another strike. That this was a fresh fish I quickly realised, and it gave me a splendid fight, though it only deigned to indulge in a couple of jumps. This contempt for my inexperience was, however, misplaced, as I landed it in the end, after a considerable tussle — my first Salmon, but only six and three-quarter pounds. V. in the meantime had enjoyed better fortune and had killed a ten-pounder and tailed two kelts.

As I have said, we had arrived much too early to expect many fresh fish so far up-river, and as the days wore on we kept putting back numerous kelts. From further downstream reports of catches came dribbling up to us. They had had so many fish of such weight, the biggest was so much; we could only hope that if any were left they would run up to visit our pools. Alas, it was a vain hope. The weather continued cold and blustery and we began to feel that we had got all the fresh-run fish out of the beat.

One day we had a great treat. An old friend, Alister, came over from Aberdeen and gave us an exhibition of what casting could be. I believe he is one of the world's best, and we were quite willing to abandon fishing and watch his performance – in particular his switches and Speys with a fifteen-foot vibration rod. I will explain, for those unacquainted with these rods, that they are made of selected, greenheart wood in three pieces. Instead of fitting together with metal joints like the usual rod, the pieces are trimmed off flat at the joints and then spliced together with raw-hide thongs. The theory is that they thus possess one continuous curve and have no stiffness at the joints. The taper of these rods is immensely important, as this governs the action. Alister used to test dozens of them in a year and claimed that he rarely found a perfect rod.

Two days before we left I did manage to kill another small fish of seven pounds, but this was positively the last, though kelts continued to visit our lures to the very end.

The evening of the day before my lease expired I finally got on to fly casting. My mistake all this time was simply that in the forward drive of the rod I had been trying to propel the line with the rod tip. By chance I discovered that if I made the drive employing the lower end of the rod to get the power, the whole difficulty was solved. It was curious that not even Alister had spotted my fault. The last day I was able to verify that this was the solution of the problem.

V. and I were well satisfied with our first attempt at Salmon. We had killed few fish but we had had a lot of fishing. We had fished with spinning and fly rods from bank and boat, we had waded in shallow and heavy water; and though we had done all this in cold and difficult weather, we regretted that our stay had been so short. Of the Scots and Scotland I could find naught but praise; a more charming people and more picturesque and delightful country I never expect to see.

On the 21st of May I was back again. This time I was V.'s guest for a week on the Lower Durris beat. We found we were nine miles below the previous fishing and the water was of a very different character. Previously, the river was fairly narrow and contained eight small pools in a mile and a quarter; this new beat was wider and possessed only four pools, but each one of considerable extent. The whole beat had a length of about two miles.

Again we had the right bank to fish, but as the river was bigger and more open it was possible to do more casting with the right hand. I had, as ghillie, Davie Nicol, who was sixty-eight years old then and had been keeper of the beat for forty years. V. had Robertson, who was considered one of the best ghillies of the Dee.

Conditions had now completely changed. The kelts were all departed and the spring run of fish had already gone through. Whereas, before, the catches reported were below us, we now began to hear tales of sport on the water above. There was no spinning done on Lower Durris at this time of year; besides this, our tackle was all fined down. No longer the heavy sixteen-foot rod and two-inch fly, but a light fourteen-footer and the flies only half an inch long. The flies were mostly dressed with grey wings and light blue hackles, the bodies being varied: silver, claret, or other colours.

We did a considerable amount of boat fishing and wading in water which was still cold, but of bank casting there was not very much. I started off in the Boat Pool and to my surprise caught no less than ten small Trout in the morning, while V. had a seven-and-a-half-pound Salmon and a pound-and-a-half Sea Trout.

It was the third day before we had another Salmon and this one fell to my rod. I was fishing the lower Floating Bank Pool and the morning had passed without the rise of a fish. At one o'clock I changed from a silver and blue fly to a yellow and grey. Almost immediately I had a strike and it was a Salmon. It was, however, a very lethargic one. I went ashore to play it from the bank, though, until I saw its large tail fin, I thought it was a big Trout. It was amusing to see Nicol, nimble as a goat, trying to find a good place to gaff the fish. I was disappointed with this Salmon, as it only weighed eight and a half pounds and was very black.

After this first success I returned to the same pool and in a short time had another strike. This was a very different encounter, the fish being both strong and vigorous. It was so strong, in fact, that in a moment it had broken my cast. Nicol was almost beside himself at this misfortune, which he said was due to my not holding my rod up straight enough. It may have been so, but the fish got off with insufficient pressure to have broken a sound cast. I think that the cast must have been frayed by the first fish. In any case, we should have examined it before resuming fishing. Whether this fish left the beat thereafter or not, I do not know, but at any rate we failed to kill any others during the next two days, though we tried hard enough.

The last day, I must confess, we spent after Trout. Thus ended my first season on the Dee: three fish in three weeks. Not a brilliant record, but one which points the moral that to kill Salmon one must be at the right spot at the right time. Since then I have taken other Salmon and concur with universal opinion that it is a noble fish and appears to be more intelligent than most; but as far as strength and ferocity are concerned I could name other fresh-water fish which surpass it, and, of course, it is not in the class with many sea fish, which have no river current to aid them.

What then is this quality of intelligence which has been specially accorded to Salmon by many anglers and has been equally denied it by others ? There are some, indeed, who claim that it is an extremely stupid fish, and that the killing of a Salmon is merely a matter of chance and may be compared to the luck required to back number seventeen *en plein* at roulette and win the coup. If the Salmon is so clever, then surely it must require great corresponding skill from the angler; but this does not appear always necessary.

I was told recently the story of a famous Salmon fisherman who one year took his wife, who had no angling experience, to Scotland with him. He had a well-known beat of the Dee which necessitated a certain amount of boat work. During a fortnight's fishing his wife killed six Salmon and never missed one; while he lost several and had, to his fury, to content himself with a single small fish. One of his wife's fish, and the largest of those obtained on the beat that year, hooked itself on her fly when she had carelessly left it trailing a few feet behind the boat. Not one of her fish had required the slightest skill in casting (for she had none), whereas her husband, who was a first-class expert, could do no good with all his wiles. How account for such results except on the theory of pure luck? I am inclined to think that this reversal of the law of probabilities could scarcely occur in dry-fly Trout fishing. In Salmon fishing it is, of course, likely that the expert caster, being able to cover more water, will go over more fish with his fly; but he still has to contend with the " chancy " temper of the Salmon, as shown in the above anecdote.

If, then, mere good fortune can defeat the expert, it does not seem likely that great skill is required to hook a Salmon. It is rather in the subsequent battle that the fish's intelligence comes into evidence. There is no doubt that the

Salmon does, during this stage, display considerable resource if the water is strong enough to give help, and I imagine that its struggles and manœuvres after being hooked have earned Salmon its renown as " the greatest of game fish."

Apart from the question of how much intelligence the fish possesses and how much the skill of the angler enters into it, Salmon fishing has a charm all its own. Generally, it takes place in wonderful surroundings, and then there is, too, the interest and healthy exercise of the casting. To my mind, also, a diverting addition to the sport is provided by the association one has with the ghillies. These honest men, at any rate my two, could not have been finer types nor more entertaining. Their dignity, their keenness, their pawky humour, the heights of joy and depths of despair to which they were driven by the trivial incidents of the angling day, compensated me generously for the lack of a more imposing catch.

I will recount but a single episode. It was one of those long days on Lower Durris when I was fishing down the Boat Pool. My ghillie had long before refused to consider a single one of the selection of flies I had brought with me from London and continued instead to try over and over again the three or four patterns which he considered alone worthy of *his* Salmon of *his* beat. I had been casting for about four solid hours without anything to encourage me, and Nicol for the third time that day was going to let me have " a half-hour with the silver and grey." Now I had with me a tackle box containing all manner of gear for all manner of fish. Happening to open it, I noticed a small golden spoon designed, no doubt, for the enticement of Black Bass. I said:

" Nicol, I'm going to put this on."

My ghillie looked at me at first with surprise and then, seeing that I meant it, with disgust. Finally he handed me the end of the cast, at the same time betraying the resignation of some kind of super-saint. As I prepared to make my first cast his pent-up emotions could stand it no longer, and he interjected:

" Ye'll no get anything wi' that."

Needless to say, the miracle occurred. My spoon hardly touched the water before it was seized violently by a large Salmon. Now this little gewgaw was never intended for the taking of a Salmon, and the fish went off at once with hook and spoon.

No artist could have rendered the expression on Nicol's face, nor his tremulous anxiety as I pretended to search my tackle box for another golden spoon. Of course I would never have played this outrageous trick on him again. If I had hooked a second Salmon with such a lure it would have broken my ghillie's heart.[1]

---

[1] There must be some lesson to be drawn from this anecdote. It has, apparently, not yet been decided why a Salmon rises to a lure in fresh water ; but, if it is not to feed, then it must be due to caprice and, if Salmon are thus temperamental, it would seem advantageous for those seeking to kill Salmon to show them as many varied causes for capriciousness as possible. In this connection I have been informed that last season twelve Salmon were taken in one day by an angler who used American Black Bass plugs instead of the usual Eel tail or golden Sprat. The one most effective was made of transparent celluloid (a quite new invention) which gave from underneath a very different appearance from that of the usual wooden plug. I am told that this lure is also deadly for Pike.

20

RIVER TEST, TEST RIVER

WHEN C. Ernest Pain wrote his book *Fifty Years on the Test*, he expressed his diffidence in writing of the river inasmuch as so many greater fishermen and writers had already done so. How much more is my own diffidence, with a mere five seasons' experience. It is, therefore, with due humility, yet with the usual temerity of the novice, that I would offer a few comments.

In what respects is the River Test superior, and why have I called it " test river "? I will say at once that it is not because the Trout there grow bigger, that they fight harder or are better eating, or that there are more of them, or that one can catch more of them. It is simply that they are harder to catch.

The Test is a small river some sixty miles long flowing through Hampshire and discharging into Southampton Water. Most of its course it runs through chalk downs. It is not a surface-fed river, but rises from springs along most of its length. These springs percolate through the chalk, so that three months after a rain the water finally issues crystal clear into the Test to make its journey to the sea. Owing to the transparency of this filtered water the fish can see the angler easily, and this is the main factor which makes the fishing so difficult. The Test has, however, been fished so steadily and by so many anglers for so many years that the Trout have also become highly educated. It is an old jest that a Test Trout can distinguish between flies tied by Hardy, Ogden Smiths, or Farlow, while they can be seen to turn down their noses disdainfully at home-made flies as being unworthy of attention.

The Test is a dry-fly river, the only wet-fly used being the sunk nymph, which is fished upstream and is even more difficult than the dry-fly. The water flows with a smooth even current between curving banks. Along most of its course, rolling downs border the valley at no great distance. The river is mainly shallow, its banks fringed with reeds. It gives one an intense impression of peace and contentedness. While one is fishing there will probably be no spectators except an occasional water-keeper or fellow angler. The scenery is most beautiful, and the river valley is the home of a vast quantity of bird life. Thus, apart from the fishing, there is a great joy in a day on the Test. There are other fine chalk streams in England, such as the Itchen and Kennet; but " the Test is best."

Practically every foot of the Test, its feeders and side-streams is either owned by or leased to anglers. Each such piece is called a " water " and is generally divided into parts called " beats." I have fished three different waters and have walked along, or observed, practically all the rest of the river. In its upper reaches the river is shallow; lower down it attains to perhaps twelve feet in depth. Nowhere is it very rapid. Almost everywhere it has a quantity of river weed growing in it. This weed forms the home of the innumerable Ephemeridæ, flies, snails, shrimps, and other creatures on which the Trout feed. For this reason the river supports a great number of fish.

The price of fishing varies in different parts of the Test. Some of it is quite unobtainable unless one buys the castle which goes with it. Other parts are owned by syndicates or clubs. One may obtain a rod (the right to fish) in more modest parts of the river for £50 and upwards for the season from May to September, but a good fishing will cost about

NEW STREAM ON NUMBER ONE BEAT, PORTSMOUTH WATER

£150. This will probably mean a rod in a syndicate owning some four to seven miles of river, including the carriers. The water will contain several beats and the rod will fish the beats according to a pre-arranged roster.

The first fishing I took on the Test was just above Mottis-font Abbey. I had a rod on it. It was called the Halford water, after the famous F. M. Halford, doyen of dry-fly fishermen, who had the water during the latter part of his life.

I was then a complete tiro with the fly rod. That is, I could cast a fly well enough to catch Black Bass, I had fished the Esopus indifferently, and I had landed some wonderful Rainbows and Steelheads with the wet-fly in Chile, where they were big and strong but callow. I must say that with this background and my experience with many other game fish behind me, I did not approach my first day on the Test with too much confidence.

I remember it well. I had all the equipment — an excellent rod, and the finest line, casts, and flies which could be obtained. I had also a creel, for even modesty could not temper optimism. I would remark that to this day, as on that occasion, I always shoulder my creel with trepidation. It does seem somehow to be tempting the fates to laugh.

That day the wind was moderately gentle from the south-west. As the river runs south and I was fishing upstream, this would have been favourable if it had not been for that west quartering. There were plenty of fish in the river — I could see them. In this fishing one never casts without first seeing the fish or a rise. One rarely fishes the rise without taking the precaution of seeing the fish, for any-thing under three-quarters of a pound has to be returned.[1] I had asked the water-keeper before going out what was the best fly for the day, and he had advised a medium olive.

[1] Where a size limit is imposed for takable fish, this limit is frequently on a weight rather than length basis. If the angler is in doubt as to the legality of a fish, he can easily weigh it in the net by subtracting the known weight of the wetted net from the total shown on his spring scale.

As I did not know one natural fly from another I saw no reason to change. There were flies about, there were rises, and I fished all day like a demon. I failed to christen my new creel. I never got a rise. No, that's wrong. I did hook a swallow and played it for six yards in the air; then the hook came out. I suppose the peculiar gyrations of my fly attracted the bird. Curious, that this should have happened my first day on the Test and never since.

The Test is tended as no great social beauty ever was. All through the year the keepers are trimming banks and cutting weed. Away from the bank one can walk with perfect ease, but at the very edge there is purposely left a fringe of reeds, weeds, and whatever else may be growing. It serves the double purpose of sheltering the fish and hiding the angler. Now, the fish mostly lie under one bank or the other. If the wind is from the left and one is on the right bank near which the Trout lies, one never seems to be able to get the fly close enough to the bank to go over the fish. If one purposely casts too far to the left, relying on the wind to carry the fly to the fish, it just doesn't happen that way, and the fly and cast are all tangled up in the reeds. If the position is changed to the other bank for a fish on that side, then the fly is blown into the reeds just the same. Finally, if one tries to cast across the river to a fish on the other side or one in the middle, the fish sees the angler first and at once has a " date " in Iceland.

There are very few parts of the Test where one is permitted or is able to wade, so that the bank-growth problem is a permanent one.

Then there is the question of " drag." If the line is pulled by the current faster than the fly (and it is astonishing how often this can happen), the fly is dragged across the surface. This causes a slight disturbance of the water, and one may as well start looking for another fish.

Then there is the question of how the line, cast, and fly

fall on the water. If the line splashes, or the gut flashes, or the fly fails to light as a real fly would, it is again time to look for another fish.

The final question is whether the fly on the cast is the right one. Assuming that all these difficulties and problems have been overcome, and that one has actually presented the right fly to the Trout in a proper manner, it by no means follows that the Trout is hungry just then. If he is, he may take it as a Trout should. But, if he is a Test Trout, the odds are he will let it pass right over his nose and will then turn majestically round and follow it downstream, inspecting it the while with minute care. This is the biggest thrill of all. The angler can apparently read every thought in the Trout's head. He seems to be thinking, " Well, that one looks all right. Hmm, I'm not sure; shall I risk it ? I am hungry. Yes, I think it is a real ' iron blue.' " And then he takes it very gingerly with his lips. Now is the time *not* to strike. Wait till he turns back, and then, if he has not already spat it out, he will be hooked. But as likely as not a Test Trout will not take it in the end, and instead will turn back with a look of disgust in every fin and resume his former position.

The angler is further handicapped in his endeavour to capture fish by the tackle which is forced on him. He is undecided whether it is better to employ a gut so fine that the fish will not see it, or so stout that he has a chance of holding a big one. This is a problem which solves itself if the water is not gin clear. In that case 2x or even 3x will hold the big fish, but in brilliant water one really needs 5x. For myself, I started with 4x, but soon decided to risk 5x. I later tried 6x, but found it really too feeble, though it certainly seemed to give an advantage in bringing the fish to the fly. The hook, too, is another problem. Of course, if one is using a large fly, one can use a large hook, say size 1 or 0, but a good part of the time I found the best fly was the smallest, and that meant a ooo hook, which is so small that it has practically no " take hold," and an active fish soon gets rid of it.

My second day on the Test was a really bad one for weather, with a blustery wind and rain which was practically continuous. That day I could have caught as many fish from a balloon.

The third day I did catch a fish. I think I was more surprised than the Trout. I was fishing the Oakley stream, and he was lying close under the left bank, on which side I was fishing. He was lying quite still and not rising. He was close to me, but the wind was again from the west and that meant either a left-handed cast or—— Then I remembered something I had read. I retired backwards to the right and cast the line along the bank so that only the gut fell into the water. It was a good cast, and I distinctly heard the Trout take the fly. There was a short, sharp struggle, and then I had my first fish in the net. Just over the limit in weight.

That season I did not catch many fish, though I tried hard enough. I think they must have cost me £3 each.

The second season I took a lease on a house past which flowed the river, and had the right of fishing a rod. Living on the water, I could go out and fish at whatever time seemed likely. I fished pretty continuously. I was able now to observe much more closely the baskets of my fellow anglers in the syndicate, and was impressed by the fact that with less time to fish they caught more and bigger Trout.

One evening two members of the syndicate who were old friends came in for a drink after fishing and discussed a fish, a *particular* fish which stationed always in a corner of the Roundabout (a small carrier). I had fished this corner intermittently almost for a season without realising his presence. I must explain, for those unacquainted with Trout ways, that the biggest and strongest Trout takes the most desirable retreat in the river, the next biggest the next best place, and so on. Each fish keeps his selected position until chased away from it by some more powerful fish. Thus, season after season the same big Trout stations within inches of his lie of the previous year. He isn't caught, for three reasons. First, he is rarely discovered by anglers; secondly, the position is probably unassailable with a fly; thirdly, the Trout is too clever. I never did find that fish. I had to go away for a day or so, and when I got back one of my friends had netted a two-and-a-half-pounder.

This set me thinking, and from then on I paid much more attention to seeking specially good fish than to catching ordinary ones. At last I had found the real interest of Trout fishing.

Towards the end of that season one of the syndicate members told me about a fish near the cattle bridge. He said that he had hooked the fish, a five-pounder at the very least, six times. Naturally I investigated that place the next day, though unsuccessfully. I began to think the fish was a myth when much searching proved of no use. But the evening before the last day of the season I asked for further details and was told that he rose with the faintest dimple just to the left of the third post which supported the bridge near the right bank. The next evening, my last, I was there, of course, and there was the fish. He made such a gentle and unobtrusive rise, such a tiny bubble in the smooth where the water slid below the bridge, that I had never noticed it. I took infinite pains preparing my fly and determining from what position I must cast. So as to avoid overcasting, I made a series of casts, each time lengthening the line a yard. At last I was ready for the decisive one. By a miracle it was perfect. There was really only a leeway of three inches in any direction. The Trout took it, and I was on.

I showed my inexperience by not having planned beforehand for the battle. I knew, of course, that the fish would go round the far post and downstream, as he did, in a rush. Instinctively I galloped over the cattle bridge, tearing off line from my reel until it was clear of obstructions, with the rod held practically upside down and the tip in the water. The Trout had not gone very far and I began to take in slack. Suddenly I felt the fish and thought I could hold him. Of course this was folly; the moment he had something to pull against he pulled, and my 5x point broke at once. What I should have done was to have stripped off twenty yards of line, then passed the rod under the bridge and fought the fish in the open water below. One learns things slowly, but it was the best day I had that season.

The next year I took a house much higher up the river on the Portsmouth water. I had half a mile of my own fishing and seven miles in a syndicate. This water was much smaller; that is, the river was not so wide. Though wading upstream was not permitted, one might always step into the river to get at an awkward fish. There was, however, an extra handicap in the trees and foliage which overhung the river in many places and forced one to consider first the back cast before casting at all.

I fished this water with great pleasure, and to me it appeared ideal. During the latter part of my stay I rarely fished for the pot; my guests took care of that for me. Generally I was off on a fruitless stalk for one of the five really big fish which I had located in the water. Only if I was satisfied I could do nothing that day with the one selected did I turn to more humble game. My results with the big fish were practically nil. I hooked three of them at various times, two of them twice, and rose a fourth once, but always something happened. As far as I know they are all of them still there in their chosen refuges. My last season I did, however, get the biggest fish caught in the water during the year. I discovered that in spite of this obsession for big ones the cost per Trout was much reduced.

THE CATTLE BRIDGE WHERE THE BIG TROUT LAY

I have spoken so far of Trout in the Test, but it also harbours other fish. There are Pike, for instance, in some of the waters, and these are, of course, snatched or shot by the keepers as soon as they are discovered. There are Salmon also, and good fishing for them as far up as Romsey; but above there I have seen a lordly Salmon ruthlessly netted out and killed like any other vermin. After all, the Test is a *TROUT* river. Then, too, there are Grayling, which at the proper season are netted, very often with considerable ceremonies, including sweepstakes on the extent of the catch and subsequent dinners to the farmers of the neighbourhood. The small Grayling are a fearful pest, but the large ones afford excellent sport when the Trout season is over and a fair day and fishing can be synchronised.

I recall one Grayling in particular which still swims in a memory that many a Trout has forsaken. He was lying a little below the bridge forming the boundary between my own fishing and the club water above. The day was cold, and I had entered the river to try for a Trout which was rising regularly but, on closer inspection, did not appear large enough to suit me. I was cold and rather disgusted at having been put to so much trouble, when I suddenly observed, very close in front of me, the orange fin of a large Grayling. I stepped backwards very gingerly in the deep water and put out a medium olive. There was not the vaguest interest shown. The fish was down about two feet, but I could see him very clearly. I changed the fly, according to the well-worn formula for Grayling, and had knotted on something with a red tag to it, when the keeper, Wilkins, came up. I put out this fly several times, but again there was no response. Grayling can be very infuriating. Under such conditions they often seem to be more alert than Trout, which one might very well not even attempt at that depth. But the Grayling looks all the time as if seeking food; his body moves about perceptibly, and one cannot help thinking that he is really feeding. When the new fly had passed over this fish enough to discourage me, Wilkins suggested a nymph, and I looked through my fly box and found a green one which W. J. Lunn had tied for me. I find fishing the sunk nymph very difficult. One must first estimate the depth, then one must somehow watch the fly under water and manage to notice if the fish has taken it. When my nymph had drifted by the Grayling several times, I decided that I would go on at it until I either put the fish down or hooked him. Twenty times I cast to that Grayling, and twenty times he made no move. Wilkins had given it up and had proposed trying a rise he could see further along, when I perceived the slightest side movement of the fish. I raised the point of my rod and in due course netted a one-and-a-quarter-pounder. Why is it that I particularly remember this fish ? There was nothing very striking about the episode. Yet some fish remain in one's memory. Again I ask, why ?

I found throughout my five seasons on the Test that each year my fishing steadily improved. This was shown not only by the smaller cost per fish but also in my relative basket as compared with those of my guests and fellow anglers. Though, fortunately, there was never an element of competition about our sport, I constantly noticed that the captures of my guests and myself invariably corresponded to our relative fishing capabilities. It was interesting thus to be able to measure the skill of my guests. Even if the water was quite unknown to them, those with class shone out at once. This kind of fishing is the only sort I know in which beginner's luck enters scarcely at all. To the beginner will remain only the good stories of the fish he did *not* catch. The fish that are taken are those merited, and it is for this reason that I have called the River Test " test river."

21

A FISHING ON THE ITCHEN

MY friend F. is a splendid fellow, possessing several assets which I covet much.

If it were not for two of them I would forgive him his good fortune in the others; but these are really so enviable that I am only ready to grudge them to him because his chief pleasure consists in sharing their amenities with his friends.

To begin with the less important of the two: he has laid down a very fine and well-selected brandy cellar. Now it so happens that I once spent six months within walking distance of the village of Cognac, and my official status was then reputed so puissant that the mere sight of my uniform uncorked for me the choicest bottles of the whole country-side. I can remember one occasion when the wealthiest man of the district was under the impression that it depended entirely on my decision whether he would have to face a firing-squad at daybreak. With tears in his eyes he offered me first one and then a second glass from a bottle which he claimed his grandfather had distilled in 1810.

After the second glass I remitted the offence with a caution that I would have to return and review the case from time to time.

I have given these details to show that training has enabled me to judge the merits of my friend's cellar and I would add that his brandies have never failed to delight my palate.

F. has, however, another possession which is even more enthralling: he is the owner of one and a quarter miles of the Itchen. It is a treasure of great worth.

Rivers can sometimes be described by a single adjective which fits them so well that further delineation appears unnecessary. Thus one can speak of the " mighty " Mississippi, the " roaring " Colorado, or the " peaceful " Test; but I think there is scarcely a river which can be more aptly depicted by one epithet than can the Itchen.

The Itchen among all rivers may most justly be styled " cosy," and F.'s piece seemed even to bring out still more the snug purport of the term. I have been in love with other parts of the Itchen before, but when I saw his water I lost my heart at once. Like much of the river between Itchen Abbas and Winchester, it reminded me, from an angling standpoint, of a miniature edition of the Leckford water. It lacked, however, the broad stream and open reaches of the middle Test, though, for its size, it was deep in places and contained many large Trout which were entirely wild-bred.

I cannot forget the fishing the first day of that week-end. I had hurried down to the river alone, in fear that I might be too late for the evening rise, while F. stayed behind to welcome some other guests. He had given me directions as to where I should turn off the Winchester road, and said that I should continue down a small lane till I reached a bridge. I could fish up from there, he told me, and he advised a silver sedge when it grew dark.

I found the place without difficulty and, normally, would have been switching my fly with small delay, but on this occasion I could not bring myself to the task. Instead, I found myself entranced by the charm of that lovely stream. It flowed with a dark but transparent graciousness through the little valley whose green meadows contained and embraced it with a delicate and affectionate caress. On the

A VIEW OF THE ITCHEN

right bank a fringe of trees seemed to help the illusion that
the river was longing to be cuddled, while beyond, the pink
and lilac tones of the setting sun reflected soft rainbow hues
through the shimmering foliage of the poplars.

I might have remained a long time thus, wasting the
precious minutes of the evening rise, had I not been recalled
to action by the faint plop of a feeding fish. Below me,
under the left bank, a large ring dimpled out in widening
circles and betrayed the disturber of my meditation. I put
on a small dark sedge and began a stalk. It was not easy.
There was first some wire to be negotiated and then a
bramble which trailed out just short of where I wanted to
cast. It was, besides, a left-handed affair. After some other
difficulties I was at last ready for the cast and the fly sailed
out and settled exactly six inches in front of the victim. He
came up like a lamb and took it with dignity. Down the
stream he went, and I, with the rod at arm's length, held
on and hoped. But this Trout showed no desire to distress
a stranger, and with slight coaxing he came back again and
was soon resting panting in the net.

I lit a cigarette and walked up a piece. How pleasant
had been that little encounter, and how comforting the one
and a quarter pounds now added to the weight of my
creel! Before me, along the slower water which hugged the
bank, I could see many rings, but I had already become
particular. Now I could face my host without abashment
and I would either capture something fine or fail with
honour. I inspected each rise with care, and though there
were many Trout which merited attention, yet I was not to
be quickly satisfied. At last I found what I was seeking.
Below the point where a small carrier came in to add its
quota to the main stream, a slow dimple betrayed something which looked important, and, on closer inspection,
there could be no doubt that this fish possessed the guile
of experience.

Against the sky, in the failing light, I held up the eye of a silver sedge. In a moment the knot was tied, a spot of oil to make the hackles float high, then a short series of false casts and the fly went on its mission. In the shadow it was hard to see where it had lighted. Was it in the water or was it caught up in the overhanging reeds? Suspense — and then the Trout rose again, but it was not to my fly. Again I repeated the cast. I strained my eyes but could see nothing. The fish came up once more, and if my cast was right it must be to my artificial. I raised the rod, there was a solid tug, and the fish plunged away. He was firmly on, and all that remained was to play him and keep on at it till he was tired out. I exercised great patience, and after many minutes and much angry battling he came reluctantly to the net.

I had then enough to satisfy me — a brace of pretty fish, the last just under two pounds — and back I walked to the house, strolling contentedly along the cosy stream.

That was an ideal evening, but Itchen Trout are not always so accommodating. The next two days I was warned there would be no evening fishing, as dinner-parties were arranged and the ladies of the household must be entertained. An angler and fellow guest exchanged glances with me across the breakfast-table when we heard the news. We both smiled, of course, and in our duplicity murmured gay and enthusiastic phrases of delight which we hoped did not sound too hollow.

The ladies smiled also, and, in fact, the prospect of two evenings in stiff shirts quite enchanted the fishermen. That morning there was golf to be played and we anglers toiled out to the course. I suppose that we, too, must be altruistic sometimes, though it would appear with such sacrifices we shall attain beatitude much too soon.

It was thus not till after lunch that we could return to the fishing, and, alas, the weather was no longer so favourable.

An east wind had sprung up. I have often heard it said that an east wind is the worst a fisherman can endure, but that did not disturb me. I have, indeed, gone to the trouble of analysing the effect of an east wind on Trout over a five-year period on the Test and have found that, as far as that river is concerned, excellent catches can be obtained under such conditions. In fact, if one takes into consideration that the wind blows more rarely from the north and east than from other quarters, it will be found, when one takes count of the fishing days, that those days when the wind comes from a " bad " quarter often seem to bring the angler more and bigger fish.

On this day, however, the wind was too strong, and the Trout were only rising in a spotty manner which allowed no time for the angler to try out a fish before it had already lost its appetite. My companion and I had tossed for beats, and the one on the main river fell to my lot, while he walked over to a side-stream. At four-thirty we were to change beats, so as to equalise our chances.

He was one of those heaven-blessed persons who had fished for Trout all his life and, though perhaps not so celebrated as he deserved to be, still ranked at the very top as an angler. When we were about to separate at the lower end of the water, he caught a passing fly expertly and pronounced it a blue-winged olive. I was thankful for the tip and tied one on. He went off with a cheery " Tight lines," and I set myself to the business in hand.

I found at once that the fishing would be difficult. The wind was from the right and slightly downstream, and, though it came in gusts, there was still no satisfactory diminution of intensity between times. The sky was bright, with large white clouds drifting across the sun at intervals. I chose the right bank, as it is easier for casting purposes when the wind is from the right, though the fish are more likely to be found under the lee of the left bank. There was very little happening on the water. After a longish wait I saw a rise some way up and advanced to it carefully, but the Trout would not come again though I gave him every opportunity to show himself. Finally I could not resist having a look for him, and there he was just where I thought he must be, but he saw me, too, and was away in a rush.

The next rise I marked well; it was conveniently just below a broken reed in a small alcove and I must have cast twenty times to that fish without response. I dare say one of the casts was too clumsy, but I had to give up in the end, and when I sought for him he was not there at all. Across the meadow I observed the gleam of my companion's rod planted upright in the grass while he sat smoking with his attention on the water. Some anglers do a great deal of this contemplative work and I presume they thus save themselves much exertion without prejudicing the ultimate burden of their baskets. Being, however, one of that school which takes its fishing hard, I never stop trying until my arm is numb and my legs can no longer support me. Thus I prefer to do my contemplation when there is no fishing-tackle to hand, at which times I can sit watching a stream interminably.

Continuing further, I came shortly to a place where some trees and undergrowth on the opposite bank sheltered a slow-flowing run on my side, so that for minutes on end not a ripple disturbed it. In this mirror surface, to my delight, I observed numerous dimples which, in an encouraging manner, kept repeating themselves. There did not seem to be any special fly in demand, so I tried the first rise with a B.W.O. The fish came in a moment to the fly, but when I raised my point nothing was adhering to the hook. I cast again, with the same result. It is unnecessary to detail what followed; suffice it to say that every rise was tested in turn and, though different Trout responded to several casts, not one of them could be induced to pay more than lip service to the various patterns with which I tried to lure them.

If my host had not informed me that his water harboured no Grayling, I should have thought that these small, quick rises were due to that elusive fish; but I observed one at least of my adversaries and verified that it was a noble Trout of interesting proportions. This peculiarity which Trout frequently exhibit of " coming short " when the B.W.O. is on the water has been noticed by several authorities and, though I am an infidel when it comes to such tenets, I must still offer this experience to reinforce arguments to which I do not subscribe in principle.

I continued for some time longer attempting to glean success, despite obscure inhibitions, until I saw my fellow angler approaching for his turn on the main beat; and so, crossing the meadow, I examined the prospects of the side-stream. It was a very pretty piece and in parts much deeper than I had expected. There was one pool which I fancied greatly, and after close observation I found it contained an immense Trout which patrolled imperially a limpid recess in the left bank beneath the overhang of a willow. I imagine this veteran must have rejected a thousand artificials in his time, but such considerations did not deter me, as I would far rather lose in such an encounter than capture less educated opponents. The problem he set was most interesting, since, as in the case of most exceptional fish, it was the defences of his retreat which accounted for his continued safety. From below there was no chance of presenting a fly; while from above, the willow branches blocked off every avenue except immediately in front of the fish, where the angler must perforce be exposed. Creeping up on hands and knees, for an hour I continued unavailing efforts to entice him, but only once did he pay me the compliment of inspecting my fly. My heart was in my mouth as he came up to a special Coch-y-Bonddu which, I have found, will sometimes rouse a *blasé* fish from its indifference. His curiosity did not, however, go beyond taking this close-up of my offering. I accomplished nothing more that afternoon until it was time to return for dinner. On the way home I caught up with my fellow angler and, to my surprise, discovered that his success had been on a par with my own. He reported the same shyness among the fish and the same exasperating short rises.

The following morning we fished again and found conditions similar to those of the day before. The wind, if anything, was stronger and the fish were still suspicious of the fly. As I was searching the left bank of the main river I did nevertheless obtain one small and undeserved victory. It was while I was retrieving a long cast to a Trout which lay in midstream. The line did not pick up from the water as neatly as it should and the fly, carried by the wind, skittered across the surface with an exaggerated drag. This clumsy performance proved more seductive to a three-quarter-pounder than all the wiles I had previously employed, and the fish hooked himself forthwith. He was released at once, being under the limit, and will no doubt avoid repeating his mistake. I have on several occasions caught fish in this unorthodox manner, but they have always been small and I can only put down such captures to the folly of youth. My companion had not even the consolation of a fluke fish to relieve a blank morning, and at lunch F. was so distressed at our plight that he offered to guarantee us some large fish if we would try again that afternoon.

It seemed to us that, in view of our recent failures, he was straining optimism too far, but after lunch we discovered how he proposed to fulfil his promise. As I have told, he is one of those charming people who delight in giving pleasure to others, and it had occurred to him that, when he asked a friend down to fish, the guest would be all the more grateful if he actually caught something. F. had therefore arranged to secure this ideal climax by stocking a stretch of his side-stream with a large supply of Rainbows. The fish were fed on cockles and horseflesh until the fishing season opened, and thereafter were left to pick up their own living. Naturally in a short time they became ravenously hungry, and ready to devour almost any fly, no matter how presented.

My fellow guest and I had been sufficiently humbled by the wild fish of the river to be anxious to take our revenge on the residents of this duffer's paradise, and that afternoon visited it in turn, netting a brace each without too much trouble. It was not perhaps as glorious a termination to our week-end as we could have hoped for, but we had to do something to re-establish our angling self-respect.

22

THE GREAT PACIFIC

TO reach New Zealand from Europe or America requires a lot of voyaging, no matter from what port one sets out; but if one wishes to experience some of the world's greatest fishing one must make up one's mind to take the trip. My own point of departure happened to be from Valparaiso, that great harbour which, I think, for beauty surpasses all others, especially when night brings out the lights of the city and creates a vast illuminated amphitheatre crowned by the imposing foothills of the Andes. Beyond the hills, if one is fortunate with the weather, one may see the snow-covered summit of Aconcagua, highest mountain of South America. I had had many opportunities to view it, but clouds always intervened, and it was not till I embarked in the S.S. *Orbita* that I was at last favoured with this exquisite spectacle.

The ship rolled slowly to the great ground swell of the Pacific, which took us abeam with a not unpleasant motion as we steamed north for Panama. I remember that the first evening for dinner we had *langoustes* brought over by fishermen from Robinson Crusoe's island in the Fernandez Group. This sea journey which I was taking was only to last fourteen days, but there are few such voyages which are more interesting. The ship was designed for passengers, but had occasion to load or discharge cargo at ten different ports before reaching Balboa, and for those who have not made the trip I will digress a little and describe it.

Our first stop was at Antofagasta, where we soon found how difficult it is to land at these coastal towns of South America. Owing to the fact that there are but few natural harbours along the seaboard, it has been necessary to take advantage of whatever small bays or indentations are available. Antofagasta has thus no protection from the great combers of the Pacific, and the small bay catches the full sweep of the waves if there is any sea running. A few years ago a breakwater was built, but it was broken in half by three rollers a short time later. The method by which visitors go ashore at each of these ports is similar, but with variations. There is generally a good ground swell, but, if it is not too big, passengers can descend by the ship's ladder and take a power boat which has been sent off from the shore. It is quite a trick to calculate the moment to step into the launch, but this should be attempted at the moment when it is on the top of a wave. At the shore there is generally an iron pier running out to sea, and it is again difficult to disembark on the pier. Our experiences that morning were sufficiently exciting, but later the sea got up, as it usually does in the afternoon, and when we wished to return to the ship we had more excitement than we wanted. I was lucky, but one of my companions got very wet when he tried to board the ship, and another only just missed falling into the ocean. A lady passenger became quite hysterical at the mere thought of the alarming gymnastics which were required of her.

I went ashore with one of the residents, who kindly showed me the various buildings of interest, the racecourse, and other sights. Later we had lunch at his club, where the conversation went something like this:

" Have you seen Smith lately ? " " No."

" Is he in Valpo ? " " I'm not sure. He may be at Salaverry."

" Where's Brown ? " " I think he's in Callao."

" Oh, I thought he was at Mejillones.   How is Jones ? "
" He's all right; he's at Mollendo."

" Is Robinson still at Iquique ? " etc., etc.

And so the conversation continued through several brandies and a couple of cigars.   At Antofagasta one sees the first of the desert country of Chile, where it rains only three times a year, and where anything would grow if there were sufficient moisture.   The hills which lie immediately behind and close to the town are a yellow-brown in colour and bare of any vegetation.   They look quite smooth, and the effect is heightened by huge signs traced on the cliffs advertising drinks and other commodities.   The immense lettering appears to be done by digging trenches and filling them with sea-shells or white stones.

That night we sailed through a yellow-green sea, and this colour, sometimes turning to blue-green, continued along the whole coast, making a peculiar contrast to the deep ultramarine of the South Atlantic.   Our next anchorage was at Mejillones, where there is a fine harbour; thence we continued to Iquique, and, a few hours after leaving that port, began to see white patches on the still barren cliffs. These patches turned out to be, as I suspected, the beginnings of the guano deposits.   I was fascinated by this first sight of one of the world's wonders.   The effect was that which one often sees when a slight snowfall has thawed away except in a few places.   I was astonished, however, not to see any of the birds responsible for this white gold. That afternoon we reached Arica at four o'clock.   As we approached the anchorage we passed through a sea almost the colour of claret.   This red tone, which detached itself in long lanes against the pale yellow ocean, was made by uncounted millions of plankton – tiny sea creatures, sometimes called " Whale food," which are also the food of the fish on which the sea-birds prey.   Outside the roadstead is an island, with a lighthouse on it, which was quite white with guano. On the shore-line of the island we could see a large herd of seals lying in the sun, and occasionally swimming in the surf. One or two of them were out near the ship when we dropped the hook.

Arica, which had its day of prosperity when the commission was there to settle the famous boundary dispute, is now once more lapsing into a forgotten town. There was nothing more of interest except huge jelly-fish which floated around the ship, looking like mutilated corpses in the transparent water.

The following day, when we reached Mollendo, the first Peruvian port, we discovered that the *laissez-faire* system of other South American states was to be replaced by red tape. I was told that all the passengers would have to be medically examined and their certificates of vaccination inspected. In a short time the ship was in charge of the Peruvian army. Soldiers with rifles patrolled every deck and the passengers were warned that if they lighted their cigarettes with pocket lighters these would be confiscated. In fact, during our voyage through Peruvian waters on a British ship, only Peruvian matches were permitted the passengers. I went on deck and observed the town. Everybody reviles it as one of the wretchedest places in the world, and I must say it is not beautiful, consisting as it does of a sad little collection of wooden houses drawn up in a straggly row on the top of a stony cliff. There was no doubt now about the guano; for miles along the sea-front the rocks were covered white with it. It was thicker in the rocky parts, but it also spread over the smooth land near the coast and extended up the mountain-sides in the sheltered folds of ground, where the birds apparently seek protection in bad weather.

Between the ship and the shore lay a considerable fleet of barges used for loading cargo, and the edge of each barge was lined with ordered rows of sea-birds. I counted the barges and found there were sixty. I counted the birds on an average barge and found there were a hundred and fifty. Taking into account the birds flying and those resting on buoys and other floating platforms, I estimated the birds in the bay would number about ten thousand. I am not an ornithologist, nor could I find anybody on board who could help me with the names of these birds, but from what I could observe there were a few grey pelicans, small penguins and diving-birds; and there were three varieties of gulls: the large black-backed, a small grey-brown gull, and a black-and-white gull, whose wing-tips had a black-and-white chequered pattern. There were also numbers of cormorants. The birds, however, which sat on the barges were none of these; they were of a black or dark grey colour with a white edging to their wings, which were long and pointed; they resembled a large swallow both in conformation and flight. That was all I could make out through my binoculars, as the birds were very timid and did not fly near the ship. I think, however, that they were the same birds I saw at Mejillones, and that they have feathers, like whiskers, which spring from the corners of a reddish beak.[1]

We left Mollendo at two, and for the rest of the day the coast was covered with guano. It was astonishing that we saw so few birds considering the evident traces of their numbers. The next morning we had another surprise. There was no more guano on the cliffs but, as if to make it all the more mysterious, we began to see the birds themselves. Early we saw a great many pelicans and various gulls, then cormorants appeared in large numbers, with a few boobies, the first I had seen. The cormorants became more and more plentiful, flying in long lines of a hundred or so. Then we witnessed an extraordinary sight. In the

---

[1] I have since been able to identify some of these birds. The grey pelicans were *Pelecanus thagus*. The greater black-backed gull is properly known as the Kelp gull (*Larus dominicanus*), the small grey-brown gull is *Larus modestus*. The swallow-like bird is known as the Inca tern, *Larosterna inca*.

distance there appeared on the sea a great moving blotch, like a vast, black blanket. It consisted of perhaps two hundred thousand cormorants. These birds swim very low in the water, with only the head and neck showing, yet they were packed together so closely that one could see no space between them. In patches some of them would start to fly, and the water would boil with the splashing of their legs and wings. As the ship approached, the leading bird of this vast concourse decided to fly across our bows, and at this the rest concluded to do the same. As they started they formed into a great black column some twenty birds in line. Since there were so many of them, those towards the end of the procession had to fly about a mile to catch up with the ship. It seemed to be a point of honour with the birds not to break their column, and so by the law of velocities a time arrived when they could no longer pass in front of the ship. I was watching this strange proceeding, and as the last birds which could manage it flicked across our bows, I was wondering at what instant the ship would begin knocking down those which could not pass. The birds, however, provided another surprise. Just when some of them should have hit the ship, they dived. Under the ship they swam, and then, nicely calculating for what distance it was necessary to submerge, came up again and rejoined the line of flight, thus continuing their uninterrupted parade. This was only one of many similar flocks of birds we saw during the day. They seemed to be almost all cormorants of two varieties; one with a reddish beak, and the other with a white breast. Generally I noted that leading each of these great assemblies were a few boobies.[1] There were also many flocks of pelicans, but they kept mostly to themselves.

After some time we came to the San Gallan and Chincha Islands, where again we could see the guano deposits, which

[1] The reddish-beaked cormorant is known as the " red-footed " cormorant (*Phalacrocorax gaimardi*), the white-breasted one is called the " Guanay " cormorant (*Phalacrocorax bougainvillei*); the boobies were probably *Sula variegata*.

appeared very deep. The deposits used to be more than a hundred feet thick on these islands, and this gives some idea of the centuries necessary for the making of them, and the numbers of birds involved in the process. That afternoon we reached the roadstead of Tambo de Mora, where I saw two large Hammerhead Sharks, the first I had seen in the Pacific. The next morning found us anchored at Callao. When we were leaving this port the following day I noticed that some Peruvian officers had come aboard to say good-bye to their comrades who were going further north. When they parted I observed that large tears were rolling down their cheeks, and that they wiped them off unconcernedly with dirty pocket handkerchiefs. We continued to see guano islands, which stood out more and more clearly as the sea at last began to turn to a deeper blue. After anchoring for a short time at Supé, we reached Salaverry the next day. It was there that disembarking was most difficult, and we had to be taken off the launches in buckets which were let down from cranes on an iron pier. There, too, we visited the pre-Inca ruins of Chan-Chan, where the buildings, though only made of mud, were still wonderfully preserved by that dry climate; and where the skulls of the old inhabitants lay exposed in hundreds to the view of the casual tourist.

We only made two more stops, at Eten and Paita, before leaving the Peruvian coast and laying a straight course for Balboa. I put in several days there and at Colon fishing for Tarpon; but that interlude is described elsewhere so I now pass on to my next Pacific voyage.

At Panama I went on board the M.V. *Rangitane* for the trip to New Zealand. She was a new and well-appointed ship, but there were not as many passengers as one would have expected. Among them I found S., who was taking the trip chiefly for its own sake, but also with the idea of doing some fishing in New Zealand. It was not long before everybody knew everybody, and all found themselves in the position of having to make the best of their fellow passengers for a crossing of twenty days, or do without company. It was amusing to see how even the most grouchy soon had to face this situation and became noticeably more agreeable, and finally as meek as lambs and as garrulous as parrots. By the time we had reached Wellington we had all developed into one big, happy family, whose members appeared to have always lived amicably together.

For myself, I put in a lot of time training for the big game fishing. I used to run a mile or two round the ship every morning, and spent hours on a rowing machine trying to strengthen my body and arm muscles. This is a precaution no one should neglect who desires to fish for really big game, as otherwise the sport can prove more exhausting than pleasurable.

Two days after leaving the canal, steaming south, we crossed the "line" at thirty minutes after midnight in longitude 88° 55' west. That morning I was amazed when I looked out of my porthole to see land on our starboard beam. It was Hood Island, of the Galapagos group, that small series of fly-specks in a vast ocean made famous by Darwin and Baroness de Wagner Wehrborn — isles of romance, of tragedies, buried treasures and giant tortoises. Through my glasses I observed that the land was barren and rocky, with high cliffs falling straight to the sea, except in one small space where a beautiful waterfall glistened down at a steep angle.

It was a week later that we again sighted land: this time Pitcairn Island, another world-renowned atom, famed, beyond all proportion to its size, for the strange and cruel drama of the *Bounty* mutiny and for its half-breed inhabitants sprung from an unusual miscegenation. When we had anchored, most of the islanders came aboard our ship, rowing through a swelling sea in long whaleboats. They were of every shade of colour, some dark as their maternal ancestors and others with clear skins and straw-blond hair. All that I heard the names of were Youngs, as was the " Magistrate " or Governor of the island. Most of them had various island products to sell — necklaces of local shells, curious tropical fruits, and carved walking-sticks — but, most astonishing of all, some of them handed us tracts with the idea of converting us to Seventh Day Adventism. Why they wished to proselytise us I could not determine. At last our siren blew, and they quickly joined their boats. I watched them as they rowed away singing some melancholy old-time chanty, boldly daunting the huge breakers which preserved the only land they knew.

As we each day made southing, I asked the first officer when we would encounter albatross. We had already long passed latitude 20° south, to the north of which the albatross[1] never fly, and I could scarcely restrain my impatience to view the most wonderful of all sea-birds. At last the idea of a small bet induced him to offer me even money that we would see them the next day. He had calculated that we would meet the *Ruahine* coming north that morning, and that she would be likely to bring albatross with her. His confidence was justified. I may say that the bet was well worth the spectacle these birds afford. There is no creature, in my opinion, of more majesty and grace. It is said that albatross sometimes attain a wing spread of fourteen feet, but I did not see such giants as those. That day they kept a long distance astern, until, as the first officer explained, they were convinced that this was a genuine high-class ship with plenty of garbage. Then they came up closer until there were eight of them circling the ship, and occasionally lighting in the wake to pick up what they considered choice titbits. I saw none whose wing span exceeded, as I judged, about ten feet, but that was enough to impress me. The

[1] *Diomedea exulans.*

wings of the albatross are most unusual. When the bird settles on the water it is fascinating to see how the wings fold up, giving the impression of a concertina. One of my knowing fellow passengers told me that it was because the albatross have an extra joint in their wings, and after watching them I could well have believed it. It is not so, however. The curious effect is caused by the disproportionate lengthening of the middle section of the wings beyond that of other birds, so that when the end section is finally brought in to the body it appears as if it were not properly belonging to the bird, or as if it should already have been tucked away long before.

As I was watching the albatross the second day, I witnessed a very amusing incident. The log line of the steamer trailed behind out of water for some distance, and one of the albatross, in swooping down, caught its wing-tip in the line; the resultant tumble to the water was so undignified that it must always remain for me an outstanding example of a descent from the sublime to the ridiculous.

After three more days we reached Wellington and our little company of friends divided up on their several courses. I went north to Russell for the big game fishing, while S. remained at Wellington with the intention of touring the island. It was some weeks later that I saw him again. He and his wife had spent a few days at Lake Taupo, where they had done some Rainbow Trout fishing. The method seems very unsatisfactory. He told me that Lake Taupo is roughly circular, with a diameter of some thirty miles. His fishing had been from a launch. The general procedure is that one or two anglers hire a motor-launch and sit in the stern with stout nine- or ten-ounce rods. The launch then starts off at a good pace, while large flies are harled behind. In a short time by this dull method many magnificent Trout are obtained. When an angler gets a strike the launch is stopped and the fish is played; but, owing to the heavy tackle and the dead water, it cannot give much of an account of itself and so these fine Trout are quickly hauled in by sheer force as if they were so many Mackerel. This curious way of securing Trout, which average over four pounds, may, indeed, be justified in the case of an occasional visitor; but I understand that it is the regular practice there. However, for visitors to New Zealand who want to capture large fish on Trout tackle, let me suggest a trip to Russell, where I had an astonishing experience with another kind of fish. One day there was a glassy calm which did not seem propitious for big game fish. Though we had searched the sea for miles not a fin had been seen. Even Francis, my guide, was discouraged; and yet, after the manner of all good guides, he refused to give up. In the launch with me was a nine-and-a-half-foot, six-and-an-eighth-ounce Trout rod, and to his obvious chagrin I said I would like to try to catch a Kahawai with it. The schools of Kahawai swim on the surface in great numbers, feeding on plankton, which they suck in without exerting themselves. These schools remain always in certain places where their food is in evidence, and it is these Kahawai which are caught as bait for the big game fish. The Kahawai resembles a large Mullet, but is more streamlined in shape. It is a silvery-brown fish with large scales and a forked tail.[1] The usual method of catching them is to troll a wooden " dummy " or plug through the school. The fish are all so busy feeding that the approach of the launch only frightens them momentarily. I imagined that it would not be necessary to choose any particular fly for my cast, but decided on a large brown one which I had bought in Panama. There was no hesitation when I dropped the fly in the water; the nearest Kahawai took it instantly. I had no difficulty in the hooking; all I had to do was to raise the rod tip, and I was on.

The Kahawai, which are in shoals, weigh between four

[1] The Kahawai is of the Perch family.

THE 5½ lb. KAHAWAI TAKEN ON A FLY ROD

and seven pounds individually, an average fish being about five pounds. So I was fighting a fish of approximately the same size as those caught by S. and his wife at Taupo, and I must say I had never had as strong a fish on that rod. Not only did it fight desperately but it displayed all the tricks a fish could show in deep water. It jumped; it ran; it dived, jagged and plugged; it tried to fall on the line; and all with more vigour than, for instance, the six-and-a-quarter-pound Steelhead which I caught in Chile on the same tackle. And this Kahawai had no fast water to help it. Usually I have found that a Trout will give a series of jumps and then, perhaps later, another series; but this fish gave five series, each of them quite protracted. I timed the fight and found that it lasted twenty-seven minutes. My guide simply could not understand the affair, and became more and more impatient as he did not realise that my tackle forbade simply hauling in the Kahawai as he was so used to doing with a hand-line. In fact I did finally strong-arm the fish, taking advantage of my Salmon cast. When I got it on the scales I found it weighed just five and a half pounds. I did not have the heart to continue this fishing, as I am sure it would have driven my guide frantic. I am convinced, however, that in six hours' fishing one could land twelve fish after twelve magnificent fights; in fact one could land a fish every half-hour as long as one had the strength. Naturally with stronger tackle still more fish could be secured. Here, then, is a suggestion for launch anglers: that they leave the Taupo Trout, and that they turn their attention to Kahawai, which exist in inexhaustible numbers and will provide a better fight than the Rainbows without the trouble of having to troll for them.

I regret very much that I did not have the opportunity to try Trout fishing in New Zealand, as I understand that in its rivers there are immense fish, and that the technique and difficulties of obtaining them make the angling as fascinating as one could well desire. But even in Taupo itself there is a method of shore fishing where at any rate a premium is placed on the angler who can put out a long line. This little philippic is only directed against launch trolling, which is, indeed, necessary for some kinds of fish, but should surely not be employed against the noble Trout of Taupo.

There are other great game fish which suffer from technical or man-made inhibitions, so that they are prevented from displaying their true worth or giving their all in their last struggle for life. The Black Bass of the United States cannot well defend itself with a five-inch plug and several triple hooks in its mouth; the Tigerfish of Africa cannot be properly hooked on a light rod commensurate with the fish's weight, owing to the bony structure of its mouth and the formation of its teeth. If it were not for the friability of gut casts, the Salmon would be hopelessly handicapped on a sixteen-foot rod; but here the cast restores the balance of power, though a light rod provides better sport if it is practical. Another family of fish, the Spearfish, have the unfortunate habit of fighting so hard on the hook that it is generally impossible to release them alive because they are nearly always dead when brought to the launch.

In time the disadvantages under which some fish labour will be eliminated to a great extent, either by new developments in tackle and technique, or by man's own appreciation that he is spoiling his pleasure by making the sport too easy or too brutal. In recent years the education of the angling public has gone forward very rapidly, and it is noteworthy and laudable that the average man is apt to learn in a single lesson what is implied by the elegant term " fish-hog." It is simple enough to avoid taking too many fish, but to preserve an equilibrium between fish and tackle is much more difficult. It is foolish to use tackle too light for the fish. That is a snare into which it is very easy to fall in one's desire to be sporting. On the other hand, when one is trying for a record fish one is likely to employ tackle too heavy for the fish one may normally expect. Under these circumstances one can only compromise with weapons adequate for the best that can be hoped for, trusting that these will be the only fish to be tempted to the lure.

23

A WHY, WHAT, WHERE, WHEN, AND HOW OF BIG GAME FISH ANGLING IN NEW ZEALAND

TO repeat a plagiarism which every writer on fishing has surely expressed in some form or other: angling for sport is simply a question of obtaining a proper relative balance between the tackle employed and the quarry in view. The small boy's bent pin and the modern whaler's harpoon, with its explosive charge, are both adapted to the same purpose – the end-all of this pursuit – namely, " to get your fish." Between these two extremes there are innumerable stages, dependent, for merit or pleasure, on the fish which is being pursued and the method of catching it; and these two factors in turn are determined by the mental attitude of the angler.

The man who is only seeking sport, and whose livelihood does not depend on it, prefers, where possible, to devote himself to a game species of fish. He then matches his weapon to his proposed victim, and in this manner assures both pleasure for himself and a fair chance for the fish. The limits to which such adjustment can be extended are wide enough, enabling even those who cannot manage distant travels to find in their own neighbourhoods angling experiences of worth and interest. With a one-and-five-eighths-ounce rod and 5x gut, I once had five thrilling minutes of Tuna fishing. Magnificent runs, plugging drives, boring, jagging, sounding – all the tricks known to that dogged fighter – were gallantly displayed. At last I landed him – a four-ounce Sunfish. Quickly grasped with a wet hand, and released from the hook, he was returned to the water none the worse for the battle. If Sunfish have memories, that one will know better another time than to try to swallow that kind of bug. Advancing up the scale, no one need be ashamed of catching a two-pound Small Mouth Bass on light gut, with a three-and-a-half-ounce, nine-foot rod. In Salmon fishing the gut cast, and not the rod, becomes the determining factor; while all Tuna and Tarpon Clubs prescribe weights of rods and line strengths for those seeking buttons of merit or other official recognition.

In all these forms of angling, therefore, besides the skill requisite to hook the fish, the determining factor is the tackle employed. In other words, will the tackle hold or break?

The human factor has never been in doubt. Man is, however, hardly to be satisfied, and is always seeking new worlds to conquer. When, therefore, the big game fish of New Zealand were discovered, from an angling point of view, it was at once realised that here was a bigger and better fish, a fish so big and so strong that not only could it strain the most powerful tackle, but could test the angler himself to the last ounce of endurance. This, then, is a sport which appeals in a different way. There is a fascination, not found in any other form of angling, in the mere fact that the fisherman can put all the " beef " in him into the fight, and may still find, at the other end of the line, an opponent stronger than himself. Anyone who has experienced the first run of a great Swordfish knows already the " why " of big game fishing, but for those who have not, perhaps I have made it more clear.

As to the " what," big game fish can be divided into two categories. In the first I place the jumping fish: the Black Marlin Swordfish, the Broadbill Swordfish, the Striped

Marlin Swordfish,[1] and the Mako Shark. In the second category are the under-water fighters: the giant Tuna, the Thresher Shark, and the Hammerhead Shark. All these fish, except giant Tuna, may be found in New Zealand waters. It will probably be admitted that their qualities, from the sporting point of view, rank in the order in which they have been named. Personally, I should prefer to capture one of the jumping fish, though other anglers may not share my opinion.

Among the Swordfish, the world records of Captain Mitchell's 976-pound Black Marlin, of H. White-Wickham's 673-pound Broadbill, and Zane Grey's 450-pound Striped Marlin, all caught within the last few years, give an idea of the size of these fish. C. H. Dunford killed his record 873-pound Mako during the 1926 season.[2] All these fish were taken on the east coast of New Zealand.

Zane Grey's Striped Marlin seems to have been an exceptional fish for those waters, and its weight will probably hold the record for some time. The other three records may be upset at any time, and by considerable margins. Of course, record fish are what an angler hopes for; but for practical purposes the sportsman may be more interested in what he is justified to expect as regards size and numbers if he undertakes the long trip to New Zealand.

The average weights of fish for the Bay of Islands, in the seasons from 1925 to 1929, were as follows:

Fish	Total Number	Average Weight, lbs.
Black Marlin	27	493
Broadbill	4	416
Striped Marlin	531	260
Mako	381	$213\frac{1}{2}$
Thresher	5	466
Hammerhead	37	313

[1] Properly speaking only the Broadbill is a Swordfish; the Marlins and Sailfish are really Spearfish.
[2] See Appendix Note, p. 299

A LUCKY DAY.   205 lb. MAKO AND 292 lb. STRIPED MARLIN

In the report of a more recent season (1934–5) these averages seem to have been maintained. It is noteworthy that Tigershark have been added to the game fish captured, one of 801 pounds being listed.

As will be seen from the above, the fishing consists mostly of Striped Marlin and Mako, with the added thrill of an occasional big fish from the other varieties. It must be remembered, however, that the above list scarcely does justice to the larger species, as a far greater precentage of these are hooked, but not landed, than of the smaller fish. Thus, out of twenty-two fish which I had on in five weeks' fishing – apart from strikes when the fish were not hooked properly – three were apparently in the 500-pound class, and were lost.

Taking the 1928–9 season as an average, 195 big game fish were killed by ninety-nine anglers fishing from Bay of Islands as a base. Unfortunately, there is no method of determining fishing days per angler, nor how many fished without success.

This does not appear a very imposing average – less than two fish per angler – but a great many anglers seem to attempt the sport more in the spirit of " I'll try anything once," and, having obtained their first fish, depart. If, however, an angler seeks more than the experience of capturing one solitary fish, and arranges to be at the right place at the right time, he should average three fish a week. With luck he may do better, but one a day during a protracted period will be about the limit.

These big game fish are encountered in many parts of the world, yet, up to the present time, the east New Zealand coast undoubtedly offers the most promising waters in which to pursue this sport. Not only are six of the seven recognised big game fish obtainable in New Zealand, but there, too, these fish run to greater size. There is no other well-known fishing-ground which yields such a variety of the largest fish.

New Zealand also offers many other advantages. It is easily reached by fairly frequent steamship connections; the country is healthy and civilised; the angling is thoroughly organised; excellent fishing-boats are obtainable, manned by expert boatmen with a thorough knowledge of the sport; and, finally – a very important consideration – there is never any difficulty in securing the necessary bait.

When these advantages are considered it will perhaps be conceded that no waters equal those of New Zealand. For instance, to make the most obvious comparison, Catalina is more easily reached, and the living accommodations are, perhaps, better; but from a fishing standpoint the only feature in which Catalina surpasses New Zealand is in the more frequent capture of Broadbills. Against this it may be pointed out that these Broadbills average much smaller than in New Zealand, as do the Catalina Striped Marlin. As for Black Marlin and Mako Shark, Catalina possesses neither of these grand fish; while the Tuna fishing, for which it is perhaps best known, does not include the giant Tuna but a smaller migration which is not in the category of big game fish. The same observations might be made about Miami and Bimini, where large Tuna may be obtained but Mako and Broadbills are rare.

Granting that New Zealand is the best place for big game fishing, there is still a choice of three main bases organised there for the sport.

Whangaroa, the most northerly, is best in the early season or in a year when the usual seasonal run of fish does not occur. During the season which I spent in New Zealand there were more fish at Whangaroa than elsewhere, and they averaged larger, the fishing being particularly remarkable for the unusual number of Black Marlin and Thresher Shark hooked. The accommodation is not palatial, consisting of one small inn – the Marlin – of which the best feature is the bar. Whangaroa has a well-protected and beautiful harbour, but the entrance is so narrow that in some weather launches cannot get out. The fishing-grounds are very wide. There are two main reefs where fishing is carried on, but they are without shelter, so that a strong wind will make fishing impossible, except in the lee of Stevenson's Island, where, indeed, little can be expected at any time.

Striking south-east from Whangaroa in two and a half hours' trolling, the Cavalli Islands offer the next fishing-ground. Lying half-way between Whangaroa and Bay of Islands, they form a neutral ground fished from both bases. There are no living-quarters; in fact no houses at all, though there are land-locked bays in which a launch can be moored if one desires to camp out.

Another two and a half hours' steaming takes one to Bay of Islands. It was from a base there that Zane Grey and Captain Mitchell made their remarkable records in the 1925–6 season. The Bay of Islands consists of a large bay containing exactly twelve dozen islands and islets. Within the bay lies Russell, the first capital of New Zealand, now only a small village. In the Bay of Islands there are four camps or inns for fishermen, the two best being Otehei Bay on Urupukapuka Island, and Deep Water Cove. The Otehei Bay camp was specially built for anglers on the site of Zane Grey's original camp. It is charmingly placed, completely land-locked against the sea. The camp consists of a series of huts and a central bungalow for meals, baths, and other comforts. There is no licence, and drinks must be obtained from Russell. In Deep Water Cove there are only a few rooms in a small inn, but it lies nearest to the main fishing-ground.

From Bay of Islands, beside the Cavallis, there are five other fishing-grounds, at Ninepin Rock, The Twins, Bird

Rock, the Tide Rip, and Piercy Island. Bay of Islands offers a great advantage over all other bases inasmuch as a part of the grounds is fishable in any weather barring a north or north-east gale.

There are, besides those above-mentioned, many small bases from which fishing can be had in New Zealand, but the only other one of note is at Mercury Bay, near Auckland. There the hotel is so far from the fishing-grounds that the usual practice of anglers is to camp out on Mercury Island. The fishing-grounds are off Red Mercury, and are very much exposed to the weather. In a south-east wind, which is the prevailing wind, it is frequently impossible for the launches to go out at all.

The big game fishing season lasts from the beginning of November till the end of May. In New Zealand, November corresponds to our June, and February is generally the warmest month. The weather, however, is never oppressively hot. In arranging a fishing trip to New Zealand, the expedition should be planned so as to make February 15th the middle day of the time allowed for fishing. The year I was there the season was so late that the fish had not yet run down by the end of February. In a normal year, however, there is good fishing in January and March as well.

Owing to the distance, and the necessity of booking accommodation and launches before arrival, it is not feasible to delay making plans in order to find out how the season will be. It is a great mistake to plan for less than four weeks of big game fishing. In any case, three weeks should be the absolute minimum. Unless sufficient time is allowed to provide a reasonable insurance against bad luck and bad weather, it is quite possible that one may have to go away without having got any fish.

The launches for fishing are mostly owned by the boatmen who operate them, and, as these launches are engaged frequently from year to year by different anglers, July is not too early to arrange for a launch for the following February.

The boatman who runs the launch also acts as guide. If it is desired to do the fishing with a maximum of comfort, an extra or " spare " man will be found helpful. He will act as a sort of fishing valet, taking care of the manifold odd jobs which require constant attention, leaving the boatman free to do the navigating and finding of fish.

The tackle can generally be hired from the boatmen, but very often it will be of the English variety, with the reel below the rod. This is quite adequate, as many record fish have been caught with this arrangement. The average angler, however, if he desires to bring his own tackle with him, will probably do better to purchase reels which fit on top of the rod in the American manner. It will be found that this system is simpler and easier to manage once one has become accustomed to it. An automatic release fitted to some of these reels is a useful adjunct.

Two rods are always fished at the same time, so that rods and their appurtenances must be purchased in duplicate if one is keen on one's own tackle; otherwise one will discover that all the fish take the bait on the hired rod, as is the perversity of such things.

The climate is very equable in New Zealand – in fact, no special clothes are needed. It is, however, important to bring a sou'-wester, a waterproof jacket of the pullover or double-breasted type, and trousers of oiled silk or rubber, with boots not above the knee. All these must be definitely waterproof. The footwear problem is difficult; on a wet deck almost any sole material skids except felt and rope. I found the best arrangement was to wear rope-soled slippers over waterproof wading socks.

Nowhere does the sun blister so fiercely as it does in this angling. In a day one's whole face will peel, leaving a raw surface ready for frying on the morrow, and one must therefore be careful to possess an adequate preparation to guard against such an unpleasant eventuality.

Black glasses will be found a great relief from the water's glare. One must be sure that they have no colour tint at all, as it is important to be able to distinguish colours, and only a pure black has that quality.

So much for a brief survey of a sport which has as yet been only vaguely exploited. In these waters fish have been observed surpassing any of those captured. To the lure of anyone may come a world record. A tantalising prospect.

24

WHAT HAPPENS IN NEW ZEALAND BIG GAME FISH ANGLING

IF you travel up from Wellington, arriving at Opua by the five-thirty-five train, and your boatman has been notified, he will just have time to take your luggage aboard his launch and get you to English's Hotel before the bar closes. It is here, should you be staying at Otehei Bay Camp, as I was, that you will lay in a preliminary stock of such wines, spirits and liqueurs as will enable you to mitigate the legal aridity of Urupukapuka Island.[1] An hour's further steaming brings you to the camp, where you will have dinner and an opportunity of exercising your first choice between roast lamb, roast mutton and roast beef — the eternal triangle of New Zealand cooking. The rest of the evening will be spent in deep consultation with your guide. If you have brought tackle with you, it is unpacked, and he will inspect it with intense interest. You may also be sure that far into the night he will be getting it in order; indeed, much preparation is necessary, as reels must be attached to rods, and then filled, and hooks must be soldered to traces. In fact no detail can be overlooked which will prejudice the taking of a world's record fish on the morrow. This is not an idle jest. I know of two anglers who captured fish of over six hundred pounds their first day out, but of that later.

Your night will no doubt be restless; for who can sleep

---

1 A Maori name which means " Lovely, lovely island."

calmly with the immediate prospect of an attempt at really big game fish ? In the morning, if you have not been already roused by what you take for the buzzing of innumerable bees, the camp gong will get you up at six-thirty. You will hurry out shortly for an amateur meteorological observation. There is the scent of wild honey in the air. This, the national smell of New Zealand, does not come from bee-hives, but from the ti trees; and the buzzing does not come from bees, but from blowflies. You have thus been fooled twice before you are fully awake. If you have a sense of orientation you will now examine the breeze which ruffles the placid surface of the little bay and, having noted that the wind is in the east, say, you will be fooled the third time. When you have had breakfast, and reached your launch, your boatman will inform you that the wind is in the south-west, or some utterly contrary direction. Having by this time received three distinct setbacks in your judgment of things antipodean, you may perhaps have reached the humility of spirit properly necessary for successful co-opera-tion with your boatman in the capture of big game fish.

All the gear having been stowed aboard, you will no sooner have taken a chair than the launch is off swiftly for the fishing-grounds.

The spare man now exhibits considerable activity. The bait-box is filled with water, traces are attached to the lines, bait-lines wetted and coiled, and finally the needle-points of the big hooks are filed for an even quicker penetration. In a short time the launch, having passed the small islands which form a barrier against the Pacific ground-swell, is headed for Bird Rock. It is here that bait is generally caught. Bird Rock, as its name indicates, is usually covered with sea-birds, and until it was washed clean in a big gale some years ago it presented all the characteristics of a guano island. In half an hour the launch has arrived and hand lines are put out for bait. The bait consists principally of

Kahawai, a fish resembling an overgrown Mullet, weighing between four and seven pounds. The smaller are preferable. Schools of Kahawai and Trevalli can be seen around the Rock, surface-feeding on small Shrimp. The schools sometimes cover an area of an acre or more and contain perhaps fifty thousand fish. As the launch approaches the school, the fish flare in a great rush and sound for a moment or two, reappearing shortly a few yards further on. It does not take long to catch the bait; chugging slowly over the school, two or three are hooked on each troll. These are Kahawai, as the Trevalli do not take the spoon or " dummy." If it is desired to catch Trevalli, they are taken by foul hooking or jagging; a cast being made haphazard into the school with a large triple hook which is suddenly jerked and pulled in quickly. It is surprising how easily Trevalli can be captured in this manner. In five minutes, with a supply of six or seven Kahawai, everything is ready to commence fishing.

There are probably by this time half a dozen other launches out; some are still getting bait, one or two may be trolling, while others have already started their " drifts." The opinions of boatmen are divided on the merits of trolling; some do little of this type of fishing, believing it of no value; others find it produces good results. It was Zane Grey who first brought to New Zealand the trolling system now used, and demonstrated it with such success that those who fished with him employ it frequently. Among others, my boatman, Francis Arlidge, had the benefit of this experience with Zane Grey, and is a master of the art. His custom, then, is to start the day's fishing with a little trolling, to see if he can " raise " some fish, and to enable him to sense the " lay " of the water. The main fishing-ground at Bay of Islands is off Piercy Island, which lies a mile or so from Bird Rock, and a troll to Piercy is thus often taken as a preliminary to some subsequent drifting.

The procedure is somewhat different from Sailfish trolling, but along the same lines. One of the Kahawai is killed,
and then hooked through the lips; the launch is then started,
and steams at about five knots, the baited hook being let
out the length of the trace. On either side of the launch
two poles are extended, each four feet long, from the ends
of which, on stout cord, are attached large hookless plugs or
" teasers." As the beam of the launch is nine feet, the
teasers, about seventeen feet apart, follow bobbing in the
wake some twenty-five to thirty feet astern. The most
common teaser is silver-bodied, with a red head; others are
green or blue, to simulate small fish. These teasers sometimes bring a Swordfish up from great depths to have a
look at them. The angler now has his rod attached to the
harness, and sets his reel with the drag off, the line being
held only by the leather thumb pad.

Though a Swordfish may sometimes rush the bait, he is
usually first seen by the boatman following one of the
teasers. The " Swordie " is at this time completely submerged, and appears only as a purple shadow which is quite
invisible to the uninitiated. Only once did I thus see
a fish before my boatman, and on that occasion the boatman
was not looking. This, indeed, is the main difficulty of
trolling. The boatman must have an eye like an eagle,
trained by constant practice, to be able to spot the fish at
the critical moment. If a willing fish is located, the angler
will generally be roused from a dreamy reverie by the thrilling cry of, " There he is! " It is hard to see the fish, even
knowing he is there. Everyone in the launch is galvanised
into action, the launch is slowed down a trifle, the two
teasers are gradually brought in to the launch, and the
angler, letting out his bait, tries to present it to the fish as
a substitute for the teasers. The difficulty of this is more
real than apparent. The bait, while the launch is travelling
at trolling speed, has been planing along the surface on its

side. With the rod tip held well up, and only the length of the trace out, it is a simple matter to keep the bait thus in position, but with the two new factors, that the launch has been slowed down and the line has been lengthened, the bait has a tendency to sink below the surface, and, once it has done this, it will begin to revolve, a fatal motion which will almost invariably put down the Swordfish. Assuming, however, that the angler has successfully presented the bait to his quarry, four different things may happen. The Swordfish may merely take one look at the bait and then leave it, or he may take a vague interest in the bait and follow it for some time and then go down. In both these contingencies the fish is probably lost. If, however, he evinces a real interest, following the bait with apparent eagerness, the launch is slowed still more, and if the fish shows a tendency to go down all pressure is completely removed from the reel, and the bait at once sinks. At this stage the Swordie may take it ever so gently; or in the fourth, and most thrilling case, he may grab the bait in a great swirl at the moment of substitution for the teaser.

If the bait has been taken, the angler now permits the line to run out freely for what appears an appalling distance; while he must at the same time exercise the greatest care not to get an over-run. When the fish has taken off some sixty yards of line, the drag is slapped on, and the moment the line comes taut the angler strikes with all his strength. There is no mincing of words about this strike, which should be repeated several times. The reel will have from six to eight pounds automatic brake on the drum. This gives from thirty to forty pounds at the rod tip, allowing the angler every opportunity to exhibit at this moment whatever gorilla qualities he possesses. If by any chance his hook has taken hold, and this is his first Swordfish, the next few minutes will be the most crowded of the angler's life.

It is difficult to describe the first run of a great Sword-fish. The display is magnificent and impressive. and must be experienced to be believed. I will not attempt the impossible but will merely offer a catalogue of some of the manœuvres to be expected in a typical encounter with Striped Marlin. Let each reader imagine breath-taking thrills to suit his fancy. The Swordfish, having actually taken the bait, will probably make a short run of sixty yards or so. There is then frequently a pause when it is imagined that he is swallowing the bait. He will then start to move off again, and it is at this moment that the strike is made. With the strike the speed of the run increases immensely, and almost immediately afterwards the fish makes his first jump or " breach " – generally in an unexpected quarter, causing a large loop in the line. The breach may bring him completely out of the water, his action somehow reminding one forcibly of a bucking bronco. The jump has a peculiarly flattened apex at the top of the parabola, the fish returning to the water in a manner colloquially described, I believe, as a " belly flopper." If he does not completely leave the water, a good part of him will show, and at this stage he will be seen to be shaking his head violently from side to side in an endeavour to throw the hook. There will now follow a series of breaches, and then the famous " run on the tail " in which he moves forward at perhaps fifteen knots with all his body out of water except the tail.[1] This is something which must be seen to be believed. Sometimes he will run thus for a hundred yards, interspersing the tail running with gigantic leaps. After one or two final breaches he will sound. Up to this time the launch, though following him at full speed, will have been quite outdistanced, but now there is an opportunity

---

[1] It is peculiar that this idiosyncrasy seems common to most of the fish with spears, and may be observed in the Sailfish and even the tiny Piper and Needlefish, though they are not related to Swordfish.

to catch up with him and place him, if possible, on the beam. If the launch takes a position with the fish on the starboard beam, say, an attempt is made to keep him always to starboard, so that, in case he has been foul hooked, there is less chance of the hook pulling out.

It is during this stage that the angler's stamina is tested. The fish must not be allowed to catch his wind and line must be recovered so that the angler must set to work with back-breaking pumping. This may go on for hours, depending on various factors. The angler will put in his time, between pumps, cursing and praying for the hook to stay in and the tackle to hold. I have found that cursing seems to answer best, as Swordfish apparently do not believe in the efficacy of prayer.

After perhaps half an hour of pumping, the Swordfish may be expected to come up and give another exhibition of breaching. During this second display it is unusual for him to do any tail running. The fish is tiring but by no means finished. He will now sound again, and the pumping will continue. Unless the angler is much experienced, by this time his throat is dry, his arms and back are aching, and he has developed several big water-blisters on his hands (memo: wear leather gloves). If there is a heavy sea running and the deck surfaces are wet, he will begin to be occupied with the probabilities as to whether he is going to get the fish or the fish get him. In the meantime, his boatmen, with exasperating calm, are preparing ropes and gaff. In an agony of terror at such obvious tempting of providence, he begs them to do nothing of the sort till the fish is dead alongside. It seems only necessary to touch the gaff for the Swordfish to break loose. At last — and here I have omitted a long pumping interlude — the angler feels the fish is weakening. With every downward bending of the rod the line comes in quicker. There is a shout when the top of the " double " appears. Fifty more feet, and the trace comes to the surface. The spare man now grasps the trace and draws the fish to the boat. He takes care to let the free trace fall back overboard while the angler releases considerably the drag on the reel. These are necessary precautions, for should the fish not be "ready" a sudden plunge might prove disastrous. The fish, however, is ready this time, and the boatman gaffs him skilfully. Soon the Swordie is roped across the poop astern. All that remains to be done is to hoist the Swordfish burgee.

It will, perhaps, be asked, how is the fish killed? The answer is that he dies fighting. It is almost invariably found that Swordfish are practically lifeless when brought to gaff; they are reduced to such a point, indeed, that usually they do not even exhibit those last quiverings of a dying fish when laid on the poop.

Over periods lasting occasionally for several weeks it will be found that Swordfish do not rise to the teasers. At such times drifting will be employed almost exclusively both for Swordfish and other game fish. The method is far simpler than trolling.

The boatman, having determined the direction in which the sea currents are flowing, shuts off the power at such a point as to let the boat drift across that part of the fishing-grounds which he thinks most likely. Both rods are now baited, one is fished "deep" at fifteen to twenty fathoms, the other "shallow" at four to five fathoms. The deep bait will probably be a live Kahawai hooked through the lips, the shallow or "balloon" bait may be a dead Kahawai, a balloon or cork keeping the bait high in the water, at the same time allowing it to drift away some thirty yards from the launch. The angler takes one rod, his boatman the other. The drag is thrown off the reel and the line is held in the hand. Complete relaxation ensues, except that the fishermen must be on the alert for a sudden strike,

with the consequent danger of an over-run. A drift will
last from three-quarters of an hour to an hour, when the
launch will be returned to another station and the drifting
resumed.

It was on the second day of my New Zealand fishing that
I was fortunate to have an encounter with a Striped Marlin
which presented some really unusual features. There was
only a moderate sea, but I thought it was quite sufficient,
having not yet experienced a gale in those waters. We were
drifting near Bird Rock, and in close proximity to another
launch, when there was a peculiar commotion between us
and the rock.

My boatman shouted, " Watch him! He's chasing
Piper! "[1]

I saw a huge fish leap through the trough of a wave and
dive. The fish seemed to be heading towards where the
shallow bait should be, and in another instant my line
began running out rapidly from the reel. Francis was in a
frenzy, which communicated itself to me, so that I was in
a daze of excitement without quite knowing why. The next
moment Francis flicked on the brake of my reel and told
me to strike. I did so, with all my strength. There was an
increasing strain as I saw the line looping in a great curve
towards the other launch and then, as the slack was taken
up, I felt, for the first time, the colossal power of a fine
Swordfish. He was heading straight for the other launch,
but the anglers in it were extraordinarily quick in grasping
the situation and were already winding in their lines so that
the fish passed under their boat without getting entangled.
The other launch moved off and we began to move too, so
as to turn in the direction the fish had taken. The line had
gone slack and we could not make out whether the fish was
free or where it was. Then Francis exclaimed, " There he
breaches! " and the Swordie appeared out of water on the

1 A small beaked fish on which Swordfish prey.

other side of our launch. He was shaking his head and then suddenly he started on a long straight run towards Piercy Rock.

First he came out and ran on his tail for fifty yards, then he began breaching in a series of splendid jumps, and then once more he ran on his tail. Our launch was now roaring after him, at twelve knots, and getting left behind. There were two hundred yards of line out and more being taken against the drag every second. It seemed as if he would never stop, but some more breaches helped us to catch up somewhat.

Then he decided to get right away from us and, still continuing his run at great speed, left us further and further astern. My line kept dwindling on the reel, and it looked as if he would take it all and escape. There must have been five hundred yards of it in the water when the Swordie slackened speed. By now he was approaching Piercy Rock and we were fearful that he would turn the corner of the promontory and cut the line. But the fish provided an astonishing finale. Suddenly speeding up again, he dashed himself head first into the rock. We saw a great flurry of foam and the line went slack once more. The shock must have finished him, for in a minute or two we were quite near where he had disappeared and on reeling in the line the fish came up, quite dead, with his spear broken off.

This, my first battle with a Swordfish, was also the most spectacular of all those I experienced. His run had covered some three miles of sea and terminated, as I have told, with an amazing suicide which deprived me of his spear — the trophy of victory.

Stories of " the big fish that got away " always bring a smile, but I will now relate an adventure with a Black Marlin, which escaped me, because I have only had the pleasure of hooking one of this variety. We had gone one day to the Cavalli Islands where we anchored in a small

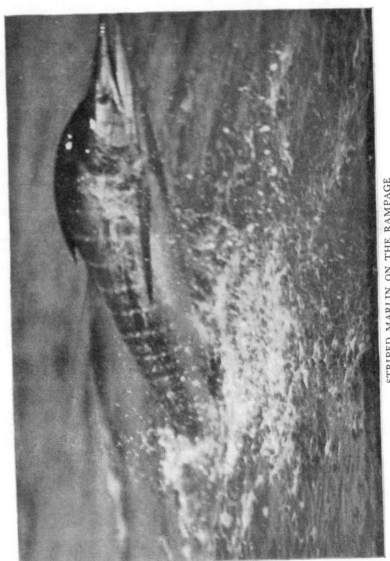

STRIPED MARLIN ON THE RAMPAGE

bay to pass the night on board the launch. That evening before retiring I landed three horrid Sea Snakes, two of them black and stubby, the other a sickening yellow; all of them, I was told, were very poisonous. The next morning we put out to the Cavallis.

The day before we had been pestered there by Reremai Shark.[1] I had killed two, the larger running to more than four hundred pounds, and lost two others. We were expecting, then, a continuation of this undesired sport, but were hoping that we might also get a chance at a Mako. It was only nine-thirty when I got my first strike. We were drifting, and the fish took the shallow bait. I could not make out what it could be. First there was a series of small tugs and then a short run. I thought it was a Reremai again, and was preparing to " give it the butt " when the fish made a nice long run and then showed on the surface for a moment. It was a Striped Marlin, and I at once struck with everything I had. The fish provided a fine fight with six jumps, but did not last long. It weighed two hundred and thirty-six pounds and only took twenty-one minutes to land. The weather began to be threatening after this; but, though it was quite windy and a little rain fell, conditions were not so bad as I had often endured in this fishing.

It was not till after lunch that anything more happened. At two o'clock my guide saw the line running out with the deep bait, and handed me the rod. After waiting the usual time for the fish to gorge the bait, I struck. Now, though all these fish are immensely strong, one can still detect some difference between a really big one and one of, say, two

---

1 I have been unable to identify these Sharks. W. J. Phillipps, of the Dominion Museum, Wellington, informs me that the Reremai is *Cetorhinus maximus* (the Great Basking Shark), but *C. maximus* feeds on minuscule fish or plankton, and, as I caught these Sharks with five-pound Kahawai, either Reremai cannot be *C. maximus* or else the Sharks I caught were not Reremai. In the latter case the boatmen of Russell must be using the Maori name " Reremai " for the wrong fish. I believe the Reremai is either a Porbeagle or a species of *Odontaspis*.

hundred and fifty pounds. The response to my strike was so solid that I knew at once I was into a very big fish. This fish did not play like any of the others, but stolidly and without apparently paying much heed to the hook, it turned north and headed for the open sea. Only once did it come up to the surface, but on that occasion it displayed the immense sickle tail of a Black Marlin. I hung on, and then to my horror I found that the reel (a hired one) took this crucial occasion to get out of order. Till then I had had no trouble with it, but now every hundred yards or so the brake would fail to hold and the line would slip out freely, causing imminent danger of an over-run. Francis, in despair, tried to tinker with it, but this was hopeless at such a time. I found that I could still recover line if I went at it gently, but any extra pressure brought a terrifying clutch failure.

Thus we continued to keep the fish on our starboard bow for three-quarters of an hour. Whether the heat developed by playing the fish was taking up the slack in the reel clutch, or what it was, I do not know; but at any rate it seemed to be working better and I was beginning to have hopes of doing something with the fish, when suddenly, with full strain on the line, there was a disgusting jerk, and the hook came out. At such moments there is very little one can say. I do not believe that my boatmen uttered a single word. I myself felt that not even swearing would afford me any relief, and I accordingly retrieved my line in silence. When I got it in, Francis caught hold of the trace and examined the hook. It was then seen that a minute fraction of the extreme point was broken off. Not much, but enough to make all the difference to the penetration. It was possible, Francis explained, that I had hooked the fish in the spear and that the hook point had been broken off in that manner. Again, the slipping reel may have afforded the fish the opportunity of a slack line to get rid of the hook.   At any rate, this was my first and only chance at Black Marlin.

I had, as I have described, hooked two fish in one day each on a different bait while drifting, nor does it ever seem possible to predict whether the deep or the shallow bait will be favoured, but having the lures at two levels undoubtedly gives a better coverage of the surrounding ocean.

Drifting, besides being much less tiring than trolling, has other advantages.   For one thing, the angler never knows what he may hook.   The game Sharks are caught almost exclusively by drifting.   Then again he may hook a common Shark, such as a Reremai or Sand Shark, or he may get a momentary thrill from a large Yellow Tail[1] (called " Kingfish " in New Zealand).   There is, therefore, the charm of the unexpected to drive off slumber.   Thus all day long he sits glued to his chair, perhaps without a single bite, till approaching darkness terminates a fruitless day. It would seem impossible that such a result could leave the angler otherwise than disheartened, and yet the experience has not been without pleasure.   In this kind of sport continuous action can hardly be anticipated, and there is really plenty of distraction to drive away monotony.   Joking with the boatmen, and interminable discussions on tackle, fishing methods and tactics fill in many long periods.   Then the other launches must be closely observed.   If they are fishing on a different drift, it is most important to notice the exact spot where they get a strike.   Some boatmen are very clever at thus locating in a wide sea the small area in which fish appear to be taking.   By shifting position quickly to these places a fish may sometimes be picked up.   The sportsman has, however, in addition to the altruistic diversion of watching other anglers play their fish, much else to distract him.   Apart from the glory of the sea itself, the seabirds, for instance, are an ever-present source of enjoyment.

[1] *Seriola grandis.*

Over these waters are constantly winging forms of bird life, unfamiliar to the landsman. Shearwaters of three varieties (including that superb acrobat of the air, the mutton bird),[1] pink-billed gulls and boobies are in abundance, while stormy petrels and an occasional albatross afford him from time to time a close view of rarer species. The mutton birds, I was told, have a peculiar method of rearing their young which is also observed in the case of some other sea-birds. The young are tremendously gorged by their parents during the early part of their lives, but are deserted when they still require about ten days to complete their flight plumage. They must, therefore, survive by absorbing the fat which they have stored, without further nourishment. It is when the young birds are at this stage that the New Zealanders collect them, and, having killed them, render the fat, which is of superb quality, for various domestic purposes. The mutton birds are quite fearless, and to amuse ourselves we caught them occasionally by throwing out a hookless line with a large piece of fish tied to the end of it. The birds would swallow the bait and, having once got it down, would refuse to part with it, so that we could pull them in to the boat without further trouble. When they were thus taken, they would scratch and peck their captor with a ferocity which seemed to show that they considered themselves capable of combating any man on level terms. But all these birds appear very confident in their own powers as well as quite trusting of men. On one occasion a magnificent albatross circled our launch, and when we threw out pieces of fish it came down to a perfect landing beside us. I estimated it had a wing spread of more than ten feet. With such a span it seems like a kind of conjuring trick when the wings fold in sections and finally disappear into the perfect streamline of the body. This albatross swam right up to the launch and greedily

[1] *Pterodroma tenuirostris.*

took chunks of fish out of our hands. It would have been an easy matter to have stroked the bird were it not for the risk of a possible peck from its formidable mandible.

Drifting, as I have said, is the best method of catching the game Sharks, and sooner or later the angler will thus have occasion to try conclusions with a Mako. As a rule a Mako takes the bait firmly and immediately makes a good run at no great depth. At this time it is hard to know whether it is a Mako or a Swordfish. Then there may be the same pause that a Marlin gives, but generally after a shorter run. The Shark, however, very often reveals its identity by terminating the run in a gorgeous jump. There is then no question about it, and the angler at once strikes with all he has. Mako vary a good deal in behaviour, and very much in size. They have been captured ranging in weight from eleven pounds to eight hundred and seventy-three pounds, and this fact accounts for the low average weight of these fish in a season. With the heavy tackle employed, a fish under one hundred and fifty pounds does not put up much of a fight, but if the angler is fortunate enough to get into a *good* one, there is no doubt that he has also hooked a Tartar. They are probably the most superb jumpers of all sporting fish. Their display is dazzling, and as their run is usually short, and the breaching at close range, the angler's admiration may sometimes be slightly modified by alarm. A Mako will occasionally jump twenty feet in the air, possibly turning to re-enter the water head first. As he may be a four- or five-hundred-pounder, it is usually considered advisable to get out from under. Though the angler's alarm may be, perhaps, groundless, dangerous incidents have occurred. On one occasion a Mako fell into the cockpit of a launch; fortunately no one was injured, but the heavy metal chairs were crushed like paper and everything within range was smashed to splinters before the Shark could be subdued. A Mako fight, in addition to breaching, will include a certain amount of jagging and running. The great speed of Mako and the quickness of their manœuvres makes a taut line imperative at all times, and difficult to maintain. But it must be mentioned that, owing to the large size of their mouths, they usually take the whole bait in one gulp, and the hook with it; consequently there is less danger of losing a Mako than a Swordfish. When a Mako is brought to the launch it is harpooned and then killed with a chisel-shaped lance. It is too fearsome a beast to be handled otherwise.

I had one infuriating experience with Mako. It is again the story of a big fish which got away, and I feel I should really apologise for telling it. The weather on this occasion was most unpleasant, and a high sea was running. We had gone to the lee of Piercy Rock which sheltered us somewhat, and were making a series of short drifts from comparatively smooth water out to sea and then back again. It is very peculiar to come thus suddenly out of waves, say, six or eight feet high, into a series more than twice as big. During the entire morning nothing had happened, and it was not till we were in the midst of lunch, and at the moment within eighty yards of Piercy Rock, that the line on my boatman's rod began to go out slowly. Francis handed it to me and, after waiting a suitable interval, I gave the strike. The resultant sensation I received was most strange. It felt exactly as if I had driven the hook into solid ground. There was no counter pull, but there was also not the slightest yielding. I gave another violent jerk on the rod, but again obtained a negative response.

I was entirely baffled, and, turning to my boatman, said: " Francis, I've struck bottom."

He laughed, and replied: " There's no bottom for half a mile."

He took the rod from my hands, gave several strong pulls, and then said: " You've got a world record fish."

He gave me back the rod, and by this time I was shaking with excitement. Just then the fish began to move. Slowly and majestically it started out to sea. In a moment we had entered the big waves and my task became more difficult. Every time we rose on one of them, the line ran off the reel against the brake, and when we descended into the trough I could feel once more the heavy dead weight of a gigantic fish. This went on for five minutes, and then, as we were rising on the crest of a wave, the tension ceased. There was nothing to do but reel in. Now on this occasion the bait happened to be a Trevalli, which is a flat fish some seven or eight inches across, and when I had recovered the line I found that half the Trevalli remained still fast to the hook. The tail end of the fish was gone, but along the upper half were furrowed the crimson wounds of immense teeth. A Mako's teeth are long, and resemble somewhat the teeth of poisonous snakes, but there are five rows of them, one behind the other. It is only the front rows which are employed by the fish, the back rows being stored in a cavity of the jaws ready to come forward for use if the outer teeth are broken off. As the Mako grows in size the teeth become longer and spaced further apart. We were thus able, from the imprint of the teeth, to estimate the size of the Shark. Francis told me that the marks on the Trevalli appeared further apart than the teeth of Lord Grimthorpe's six-hundred-and-thirty-pounder, at the capture of which Francis had been present, and indeed it seemed likely that I had thus lost a world record Mako.

There are two other methods of securing fish which combine in varying degree with trolling and drifting. Frequently, while drifting, a fin or fins may be seen on the surface, which may belong to any of the great game fish except the Thresher Shark, which never shows above water. Again, and most probably, they may belong to a giant Sunfish. These fish will not take a bait, and are not game fish anyway. If it is the fin of a sporting fish, it is at once pursued and, when the launch is near enough, the fish is either trolled or drifted for, according to its species.

A last method, and a very successful one, is called " fishing the schools." When it is seen that the schools of bait are very disturbed, frequently flaring and going down, it may be deduced that they are being pursued by big fish. Making a large circle round them, a live Kahawai, hooked through the lips, is then very slowly drawn through the school on a long line. It is astonishing how often a Shark or Swordfish will select from fifty thousand Kahawai the one that happens to be on the hook. This is a very amusing way to fish, as the angler is kept constantly alert for the thrill of a heavy strike.

It is impossible to give the details of angling for all the big game fish in New Zealand waters, but I must tell two stories about Black Marlin, " the world's greatest game fish."

A friend of mine related the following experience: He came up by boat from Auckland two seasons ago to have his first try at big game fish, arriving late at night. The next morning the weather was perfect; other boats were catching fish but nothing would come to his bait. By three o'clock in the afternoon, tired and disgusted, he was contemplating a return to camp when he had a strong strike. The fish did not show, but, as is the manner of most Swordfish, headed north for the open sea, at a fair depth. My friend, being a novice, was exerting himself unnecessarily, and after half an hour had made no impression on the fish. The boatman now suggested that he should work harder, to which the angler replied, with some asperity, that he could not. After an hour it was apparent that this was no ordinary Striped Marlin. At six o'clock it had been on for three hours, and my friend said he did not care if he caught it or not. At seven o'clock he was sure he did not want it.

By this time the boat was some twelve miles out to sea, and darkness was fast approaching. He told the boatman to cut the line, but the boatman talked him out of that. By eight o'clock it was quite dark, the angler's hands were one solid blister, his back felt broken, and his arms were numb. He began to look about furtively for a knife. The boatman produced a bottle of whisky, and the fight went on. After this my friend does not remember much. All he knows is that at eleven the whisky was finished and the fish was gaffed. He was helped into bed about two-thirty, and remained there for three days. The fish was a six-hundred-pound Black Marlin.

It has been objected by some that big game fishing does not require much skill on the angler's part, that the tackle is too heavy, and that it is the boatman who kills the fish with the launch. I am prepared to deny that; certain it is, however, that the launch plays a big part, as the following incident illustrates:

A well-known international character was fishing at the Ninepin some seasons back when he had a strike from a Black Marlin. The fish went off at great speed, breaching heavily from time to time. The boatman tried desperately to get his engine running, but without success. The angler, being a man of means, had the very finest tackle, and a reel with six hundred yards of line on the drum. A lot of line was out, and he told the boatman to hurry. There was nothing to be done, however; the motor simply would not start. In an incredibly short time the line on the reel shrank to nothing, and finally parted at the knot with a loud pop.

"Thank God it's gone!" said the sportsman. "That wasn't a fish, it was a tidal wave."

25

I'M A BIT OF A LIAR MYSELF

I PRESUME that any man who has done a fair amount of sea travelling must have had at some time a view of the sea serpent. I cannot keep out of this category, so I will relate my experience.

I was fishing for Swordfish in New Zealand. We had been through a period of rough weather, which I shall always consider must establish my claim to possessing patience, that quality expected of fishermen. For fourteen days running I had fished continuously in mountainous seas which sometimes towered twenty-five feet between crest and trough. It is, perhaps, difficult for those who have not encountered such weather in a small boat to appreciate the extraordinary contortions one undergoes. If it were not well known that only adverse currents or shallows can turn a big wave over, one would also, no doubt, be thoroughly alarmed. Actually, once I had become accustomed to the motion, I enjoyed the great swell of these waves. It was very pleasant and beautiful to watch them when the sky was clear and when the wind was not strong enough to lash off the tops of them in our faces. There was only one part of our cruising under these conditions to which I never became quite inured, and that was when we had to collect bait. Francis Arlidge, my guide, used generally to stand barefooted on the seat in the cockpit, controlling the steering-wheel of the launch in a casual manner with the big toe of his left foot. That was all very well in an open sea but, when catching bait, the launch was in this strange fashion manœuvred so close along the windward side of Bird Rock that one could almost touch it. As a great wave approached, the little launch would rise up and up very agreeably, but then, when the wave had passed on, we would sink, and apparently for minutes would never stop descending into a fearsome void. As the next wave advanced the boat would tip over towards the rock at such an angle that it seemed impossible for it to escape sliding down the slope and being engulfed. Actually reason said there was not the slightest danger even if the motor were to fail, but instinct did not enjoy the impression.

To the west of Bird Rock there was a submerged shelf, shallow enough to cause the exceptional waves of the August (winter) storms to break. It was one of Francis's favourite places for fishing, and on one occasion we were there when the sea was about as bad as it could be at that time of year. We were drifting and wallowing broadside in the trough of the waves when a series of them arrived which surpassed any of the others. First came a huge one, then a bigger, and then the biggest. This last seemed the height of a four-storey building, and looked as if about to curl.

When Francis saw it, he remarked in his amusing New Zealand drawl: " Well, I propose we get out of here before one of these waves rolls over on us."

He then put the launch in motion, and I, for my part, was quite ready to second the motion!

During all this period of big seas[1] I had not had a single strike, and indeed had been perhaps not looking forward to playing a giant fish under such a handicap. At last the sea abated, and after a few days of real sport everything had quieted down so much that the little fleet of Swordfish

---

[1] I was lunching with White-Wickham recently, and asked him what he thought would be the height of the big waves in bad weather. He said that he had seen them dashing against Piercy Rock to a height of sixty or eighty feet, and that he considered sixty feet would be a moderate estimate.

launches had scattered widely over the ocean in a vague hope of finding something. In my own launch, *Alma G.*, we were quite discouraged. We had spent the morning trolling without a sign of fish, and had then run out seven miles to the Tide Rip, where all we saw were some stormy petrels, those charming little sea swallows which, I am informed, appear frequently on the menu of the greater black-backed gull – surely an unconsidered prevision of Mother Nature.

That afternoon Francis thought possibly to divert me with something new, and took the launch inshore to about twenty fathoms. I will say at once that this was the only interval of relaxation he afforded me in five weeks of fishing. As a task-master he was as relentless as any guide I have ever encountered. The launch was stopped, and, unwinding some hand-line, he let it down with a piece of bait and showed me the art of pot-fishing. In an extraordinarily adroit manner, and in a few minutes, he brought up all kinds of astounding fish. Some of them, the Snappers, were brilliant scarlet; Blue Cod were sapphire blue; Parrot Fish were vivid green; and there were many others of peculiar shape and strange colour; in fact he seemed to be able to haul in fish to suit anyone's fancy. He said that in New Zealand they could never tell what they were going to catch, and that the varieties appeared endless. Tui Brooker, my spare man, brought Francis back from this unwonted interlude by remarking that he thought he could see a Swordfish fin. In a moment he had pulled in the hand-lines, and we were away on business. At twelve knots we raced over the placid sea looking for the sickle tail-fin of the Swordie. After a search, however, we concluded that the fish had moved off, and that he might be lingering in the vicinity of Piercy Rock. We accordingly went there and put out the usual deep and shallow baits for a drift. Piercy Rock is a miniature Gibraltar which lifts

out of considerable depths to a height of two hundred feet.
Once it must have formed part of a small peninsula, as
between it and the mainland there is a pass of shallower
water. In this pass and on the sheltered north side of the
rock itself is a good place to find bait fish called Kahawai and
Trevalli. By watching these fish it is frequently possible to
judge whether any game fish are in the vicinity, as under
these circumstances they flare in a great splash and disappear into the depths.

Our drift had brought us within thirty yards of Piercy
Rock. It was five o'clock in the afternoon of the 17th
February, 1930, and the sun was shining full on the bait,
which extended in a long phalanx near the base of the rock.
The bait were feeding placidly, all pointed towards the
east. It is entertaining to observe so many nice-sized fish
together within such a small compass, and I was watching
them with vague interest. Suddenly in the very midst of
them a great form surged out of the water. It appeared
about five feet wide, and I saw some ten feet of its length.
It was a sickly pink in colour; forward there seemed to be
an immense eye; behind it looked as if the creature was
divided in two parts. It dived and then once more foamed
out of the sea, exposing about a foot of its body, while
through the pellucid water a gigantic shape was outlined
below. It was a curious circumstance that the bait, usually
so nervous that the shadow of the non-dangerous Sunfish
will send them off in a panic, at this juncture failed to show
the slightest alarm. In fact this monster had come up in
their midst and must have pushed many aside without
frightening them.

I called out, " What was that ? " and then added, " I
want to catch that." One gets big ideas in New Zealand,
for the creature may well have been the size of the launch.
Francis had not seen it, but Tui Brooker had. I questioned
him closely, and he agreed with every detail that I saw,

except that he thought the creature was grey and not pink. I continued to cross-examine him, but he confessed that, though he had lived and fished all his life in that neighbourhood, he had never seen or heard of anything like it. We described what we had seen to Francis, but he could form no opinion.

We chugged over to the probable line which this thing had taken, and trolled and drifted about with baited hooks for an hour, but without getting another sight of the monster. What was it? Russell, the nearest town to my fishing camp, used to be a whaling centre, and this creature might have been an enormous squid, the favourite food of the Sperm Whale. Whatever it was, Tui and I are ready to bear witness that we both saw it, and, until someone can prove it to the contrary, I am going to maintain that I have seen the sea serpent – or something.

MY WITNESS TUI, AND FRANCIS

26

SLIGHTLY TECHNICAL,
AND MOSTLY FOR THE TROUTER

TACKLE (RODS)

IT is perhaps regrettable that the real angler has only
two topics of conversation: the first is fishing, and the
second is fishing tackle. Under the circumstances it
would be an omission if in a book on fishing no mention
were made of the second most important thing in life, and
I am therefore giving, for the benefit of confirmed anglers,
a few details concerning my equipment.

Recently I re-united in Austria my complete collection
of gear and was myself impressed with its variety and bulk.

There were thirty-two rods, including fourteen for Trout.
That sounds ridiculous, and yet last summer every one of
them was in service at some time or other. It is, indeed,
very useful to have a number of Trout rods to choose from
when there are friends to be outfitted and children to be
taught the principles of casting. There were seven Leonard
rods, two Hardys, and one each by Payne, Goodwin, Goodwin-Granger, Hamlin and Ogden Smiths. No two of them
were alike.

My first rod was a Goodwin ($9\frac{1}{4}$ ft., $5\frac{1}{2}$ oz.). It was a
moderately priced weapon of three pieces, with a moderately
stiff action. In fact, if one were to seek a long time one
could scarcely find a more average rod; it was an ideal
purchase for a beginner. It is still unblemished in spite of
much hard usage. It is with this one that I instruct novices

wishing to learn to cast, and it is the one I lend when uncertain of the capabilities of the borrower. It can be used for either wet- or dry-fly fishing, and is perhaps the best kind of rod for Black Bass, where the lures exert too great a strain on a fine stiff rod and slow up altogether too much the action of a soft rod.

A six-foot bait rod which I bought at the same time has disappeared; fortunately it was of no value. It was intended for Black Bass and Muskellunge fishing. Like the average bait rod sold in America, it could only be used for trolling as it lacked all resilience for casting. One sometimes finds the same type of rod sold as an " American bait rod " in English tackle shops, but it is no use for any kind of genuine angling. I have described elsewhere what a fine art Black Bass plug casting can become, and will not further insist on it. Some time later I bought a set of three plug rods, of which details have been given, and these were the first rods I obtained of which I am still proud.

About that time I contracted a bad attack of angling fever and started to do some reading on fishing. I was carried away, as many novices must have been, by the idea that it is more sporting to fish with very light tackle. Particularly the rod seemed the correct handicap. At the same time I began to hear about Leonard rods, and I invested in three beauties. Two of them were nine-foot rods weighing $4\frac{1}{2}$ and $3\frac{1}{2}$ oz. respectively. The $4\frac{1}{2}$-ouncer, owing to heavy reel fittings, should have been labelled a 4 oz. rod. The Leonard rod is made by William Mills & Sons of New York, and these two were splendid examples of their manufacture. I have yet to see English rods of their length brought to so fine a taper and still possessing such wonderful backbone for their weight. I used them a good deal for Black Bass, a criminal proceeding really, but still they held up. The third rod was only seven feet long, but it weighed $1\frac{5}{8}$ oz. It is the most delicate weapon I have ever used, though this firm also makes a six-foot rod weighing $\frac{15}{16}$ oz.! My rod puts out a level " H " line in a remarkable manner, and one could scarcely find a more charming weapon for small brooks and small fish.

The following summer I visited England and decided I must get a Hardy rod. The one I chose was a "*de luxe.*" The finish of it, as of all English rods, was exquisite, but after my stiff American rods I was disappointed in its performance. I do not know what I was expecting, but the action of the rod was so much slower than that of my others that I could not handle it successfully. So I put it aside for some years and only brought it out from time to time to display it to envious friends. Since then I have discovered that it is an altogether admirable rod when fast action is not required, and it has thus returned to active service.

After this there was a pause until I was preparing to go round the world, when I bought three rods. The first of these, a $9\frac{1}{2}$ ft., 6 oz. Goodwin-Granger, was a mistake, and I have never had much use for it. It felt very powerful in the shop but the weight was in the wrong place. A $9\frac{1}{2}$ ft., $6\frac{1}{8}$ oz. Leonard, though slightly heavier, gave a lighter feel, due to its fine balance, and I used it often during my tour with great pleasure. The third rod, a 9 ft., $4\frac{7}{8}$ oz. Leonard, I never took out of its case throughout my travels, but of that anon.

Before going to England with the intention of fishing on the Test, I went to Mills and had them make up for me two nine-foot rods, specially for the dry-fly. Without ever having tried my $4\frac{7}{8}$ oz. Leonard, I had decided that I wanted something either lighter or heavier for this fishing. But I was, somehow or other, rather disappointed with the $4\frac{3}{4}$ oz. rod with which they supplied me; it seemed to me light in the tip and lacking power there, while a $5\frac{1}{8}$ oz. rod, though excellent, appeared rather heavy for a long day's fishing. By this time I had collected nine Trout rods, and though I was fishing regularly on the Test it was difficult to give them all exercise. I did not like the shape of the handle of my $4\frac{7}{8}$ oz. rod, but one day decided to take it out. To my astonishment I discovered with the first cast that I had a gem. I think all rod makers (in spite of their vigorous denials) occasionally " fluke " a great rod which surpasses their normally fine productions through some innate quality. This rod was such a one, nor have I ever found a friend to claim he had a better. Its balance is perfect, its power extraordinary, and it can be fished all day without the slightest strain. Several of my angling acquaintances have tried it in comparison with their own rods, and have invariably found, to their surprise, that they could get extra yardage with it.

The Trout rods I have purchased since then have been extravagances. I bought a Hardy " Marvel " ($7\frac{1}{2}$ ft., $2\frac{3}{4}$ oz.) because I wanted a short rod, and I found it a marvel for strength and lightness. Then I got a Payne ($7\frac{1}{2}$ ft., $3\frac{3}{4}$ oz.) of the same size, but slightly heavier and not quite so delicate. A Hamlin ($8\frac{3}{4}$ ft., 6 oz.) I bought from R. D. Hughes, the professional casting instructor. It seemed to work so perfectly for him that I thought it must be the rod which was accountable, *le mauvais ouvrier blâme*. . . . It is a wonderful weapon which almost forces that desideratum, a slow cast; but there is much more to Hughes's superb casting (the most beautiful I have ever seen) than the rod he employs. He still holds at least one world record.

As for an Ogden Smiths ($8\frac{1}{2}$ ft., $4\frac{7}{8}$ oz.) rod, it took me a year to wheedle it away from my friend Bunny. He had come to fish with me on one occasion, and I picked it up to try it. I was amazed to discover that it was an extraordinary rod which, for its length and weight, put out a tremendous line. Whenever I saw my friend after this I teased him to make up his mind when he would sell it to me. I had no expectation of ever getting it, but one day he said that if I would buy him a rod of another length and weight which he had chosen, I could have his rod. Needless to say I jumped at the opportunity, and still think it is another of those " fluke " rods.

Generally speaking, there is an obvious difference between English and American rods. The English rod has a more gradual taper, and one that rarely attains the extreme fineness of the American. The English rods are better finished and are probably more wrapped than the Americans, and also seem to be coated with much more varnish. These divergencies combine to make the English rod slower and the drive much lower towards the handle, with a consequence that one has the impression of greater power and better suitability for wet-fly work. On the other hand, the quicker action and greater delicacy of the American point makes them superior for dry-fly casting. It is strange that in America, where dry-fly fishing is the exception, the dry-fly rod has been brought to such perfection, while in England, the home of the dry-fly, the wet-fly rod has reached its highest development.

Of my rods for big game fish there is much less to say; big game fishing lacks one of the delights of small fish angling in that one cannot really get so much pleasure out of the weapons. When I have said, for instance, that I possess a sixteen-foot Ogden Smiths greenheart, " vibration " rod, weighing $36\frac{3}{4}$ ozs. there is not much more to be remarked on the subject. The finesse, the delicacy, is gone with the small fish, though this does not by any means imply that all vibration rods are the same; far from it. A sixteen-foot rod is, however, such a vast affair that to criticise it without being also a rod maker and an expert Salmon angler is an impertinence.

I have two other Salmon fly rods. They are both

Leonards of built cane. One is a fifteen-footer weighing 29½ oz., in three pieces. It is an extremely powerful tournament rod which can handle a very long line. The other is fourteen feet, weighing 22½ oz. It is a delightful rod, and is the one with which I got my Tarpon at Panama. I have, besides these fly rods, a Hardy " Murdoch " Salmon spinning rod (10⅔ ft., 20½ oz.) which is a standard affair and quite perfect for its purpose.

Then there are six ocean rods for Tarpon or other strong sea fish, five of them made by Murphy, of Converse, Indiana; the sixth is a Leonard. They vary in weight. The most important is the so-called 3–6 rod. This rod is prescribed by various clubs in America for obtaining certain fish. It is too light, I think, and I cannot see the point in making it so delicate, as the hooking thus becomes a fluky business, depending a great deal on how the barb has happened to turn in the fish's mouth. This rod consists, like all of these sea rods, of a butt and top. The rod, complete, weighs 6 oz., and the top is 4 oz. The length of the top is five feet and the butt one foot. The others mentioned are of different weights and lengths, the tops ranging from 6 oz. to 10 oz. in weight, and the overall lengths from 6 ft. 3½ in. to 7 ft. These rods are very useful for general sea angling purposes, and are made of split cane.

Murphy also made me my two big game rods of hickory. They were 6 ft. 10 in. long, with a top 5 ft. 1 in. long, and weighed 41 oz. I only have one of them left. As it so happened, the other was responsible for most of my big fish in New Zealand and it eventually acquired such a set that it was not worth bringing back from the antipodes.

My Bonefish rod was made by E. Vom Hofe. It has a 5 ft. 3 in. top and is 6½ ft. overall. The weight of the top is 4⅜ oz.

I have two surf casting rods. One made by the Westrod Co. is 10 ft. 10 in. long, with a top 7 ft. 7 in., and weighs

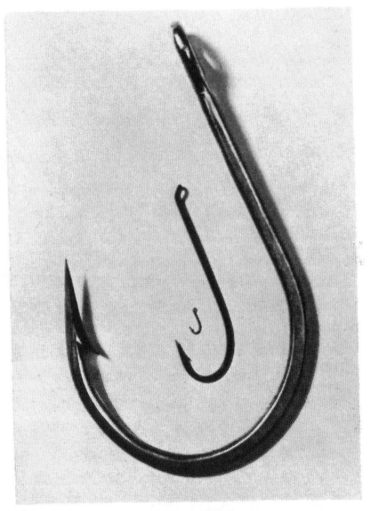

ANGLER'S TOOLS
SWORDFISH, SALMON, AND TROUT HOOKS : ACTUAL SIZE

33⅝ oz., the top weighing 17 oz. This one is a copy of the rod with which A. Livenais made his world record distance cast of 632 ft. at Belmar, U.S.A., on July 2nd, 1933. The other was made by Leonard, and is 8¾ ft. long, the top being 6 ft. 5 in. and the weight complete 15¼ oz. It is one of my favourite rods and the one with which I did a good deal of my fishing for Dorado and Tigerfish.

My last rod was made for me specially by Hardy Bros. It is a very heavy surf rod 10¼ ft. long, with a 7¼ ft. top. It weighs 47 oz. I had intended to use this rod in South Africa for the Sharks of Hermanus Bay, but I never had the opportunity of trying it.

TACKLE (LINES)

Of lines there is not much to be said. Most of the reliable firms sell excellent ones, but I prefer " Ashaway " Cuttyhunk for Tarpon and other salt-water fishing, and I fancy the white lines more than the green. The line mentioned is obtained in America, and compared with English lines appears slightly finer in diameter in proportion to its strength. It is made in different thicknesses according to the number of threads of which it is composed, the tensile resistance running about two pounds to each thread.

The Trout line which I prefer was brought to my attention in an amusing manner. I was flying to London from Paris some time ago on a day when the wind was high. I happened to be carrying with me two or three rods in their cases, and as I was entering the plane I noticed a fellow passenger regarding my rods with great interest. He was an American, I thought, and he sat down opposite to me. From time to time I could not help observing that he seemed on the point of addressing me. But I had a good book to read, and it was not till we approached the shores of

England that I laid it down. The American seized the opportunity to remark:

" You're a fisherman, aren't you ? "

I admitted that I was, and he then asked me:

" Do you know which is the best Trout line in the world ? "

I said I had no idea; and he went on:

" It's the yellow ' Mayfair ' line, sold by Carter of London."[1]

I thanked him for the excellent tip, but further conversation was interrupted by bad wind currents which we encountered at that moment. In fact my informant was much occupied with a brown paper bag until we reached Croydon. It was only when we were in the bus on the way to London that he was able to resume talking, and for the rest of the journey he continued to give me advice as to where to go for different kinds of tackle. Visiting Carter's a few days later, I found this line was indeed excellent. It is very stiff, and has a very hard external surface. It is thus easy to " shoot," while its light colour seems to be also an advantage, making it discernible to the angler at night while it is less obviously visible to the Trout in daylight. Another valuable quality is its resistance to changes of temperature. On my world tour I found that whereas all my other dressed Trout lines perished in the heat of the tropics this yellow line was not affected at all; and, in fact, I am still using the Carter line which I purchased at that time, thanks to my altruistic aeroplane companion.

Tackle (Reels)

In regard to reels I have again very little to say. In Trout reels, almost everybody seems to prefer the narrowly contracted drum which avoids the necessity of guiding the

---

[1] I believe this type of line can now be obtained from other dealers.

line on to the spool when retrieving. I do not know why the others are bought. I have described the M. J. Meek reels for Black Bass. There is a brotherhood of anglers (to which I belong) which refuses to have anything to do with those bait reels which have various mechanical devices to prevent over-runs, backlashes, kinking, tangles and careless spooling. I notice, however, that these complicated affairs sell well. I don't like them and I think the angler should learn to cast without these aids. He will get more fun out of fishing if he does.

I use a " Silex " for Salmon spinning, but next time I try for Salmon I intend to take my heaviest Bass casting rod along, and a Meek reel. I hope to have wonderful sport with that outfit.

Salmon fly reels are not of great interest; there are many good ones on the market. My reels for big game fish are made by either E. or J. Vom Hofe, rival firms of New York. They are quite perfect mechanically and I have six different sizes of them, ranging from a tiny Bonefish reel (without automatic brake) to the size 12/0 for Swordfish. Hardy Bros. make a fine reel for Swordfish called the " White-Wickham " and also the " Zane Grey." Besides these I have several reels for surf casting without automatic brakes, but they are not remarkable.

CASTING

The average sportsman frequently refuses to take pains about the things that interest him most. And unless he has superlative genius he will fail to surpass less gifted persons who have gone to the trouble of learning the correct technique of their chosen speciality. The art of casting a fly for Trout illustrates the point very well. I have only had the opportunity of watching four great anglers, and only one of them was an expert caster. There are, of course, many really great casters, but I have not had the pleasure of observing their methods. My experiences with the other three mentioned were amusing and interesting.

The first one I encountered during the first season that I had a piece of the Test. A friend had invited me to fish the Itchen with him, and when I suggested in return that he should come and try my water, he asked if he might bring along with him a famous angler. I was delighted, as I had already heard tell of his exploits. He had, it appeared, secured four- and six-pounders all up and down the Test where such monsters had not even been suspected before. The day they arrived was dull, with a difficult wind blowing, but after rigging our rods we hurried down together to an open stretch of the main river. After a while we came to a hungry fish and the expert suggested my friend should have a go at him. He tried, but after several attempts was ready to give up without really having put the fly over the fish. My turn came next, and I also failed. It was not really difficult, but I was perhaps overawed by the presence of the great angler; at any rate, I was longing to see him perform, and quickly begged him to show us how.

He astonished me. He got his line out at extraordinary speed, waving his rod back and forth at a dazzling rate; then there was a sharp crack behind and the fly was off. The second fly was also lost; it was caught up in the long grass on the back cast and could not be found. The third fly got to the fish and, in spite of the fearful velocity with which it had seemed to travel, fell like thistledown right on the Trout's nose. Nobody could blame the Trout for making a mistake in such circumstances, and a nice pounder came to net in short order. After this demonstration of how to catch fish, my friend and I left the expert and went off to other waters. It was not till late that evening that we met again at my house. The expert had caught a very fair two and a half brace, while my friend and I had to content ourselves with our whiskies and soda.

My next experience was equally peculiar. I had met a very famous authority on several branches of sport. The conversation had somehow turned to fishing, and I had *bêtement* given my views on the subject of the stiff wrist in casting. To my surprise he took my remark seriously and said he would like to see the theory in practice. I protested that I had only expounded an idea, but nothing would satisfy him except that I should show him what I had described. A few days later I was, accordingly, at his house, where I found three rods set up on the lawn. After tea I was offered my choice of them. One appeared to be a grilse rod, the second was equally cumbrous, while the third, which he explained belonged to his wife, was so old that its varnish had crackled like a fine Chinese porcelain. I got out some line on this one, and, though much embarrassed, still managed to demonstrate the principle in question. Nobody could have been more open-minded than this gentleman who had been catching Trout before I was born. When he had essayed some casting himself, he was prepared to admit that my system was superior. But, as he observed, he was too old to learn to cast all over again, and besides he could catch enough fish to satisfy himself with his own methods. His casting, I should explain, was, like that of the other expert's, far too quick, requiring much too much exertion; but in spite of this he could get out a good straight line.

My last experience was less striking. I had met a very celebrated angler and asked him over to fish my water. He arrived in due course and I escorted him down to one of the beats, which he looked over with flattering expressions of approval. I left him at once but remained in the background to observe his art. Once more I was surprised at his casting method, which was not at all impressive for one so famous. It was noticeable, however, that he brought back seven fish in his creel that evening; and they compared favourably with the brace I had to show.

Here are three examples of the casting of famous anglers, and I should be constrained to admit that my judgment of correct casting must be wrong if I had not seen the fourth expert putting out a line with such extremely lazy beauty. As I have heard him described at the Fly Fishers' Club as one of the greatest anglers in England, Scotland, Ireland, or Wales, I can only conclude that there are many great fishermen who are also poor casters. Perhaps it is well for the rest of us, as otherwise we would surely find our rivers completely denuded of fish. It is useless for me to try and describe correct casting, nor as a very average rod would I have the presumption to do so. I prefer instead to watch others from the comfortable standpoint of critic. It is thus possible for me to aver that really great casting has the same quality which one can observe in all games performed by their champions. The superlative master in every case seems to have so much more *time* at his disposal. One can see the same thing in ping-pong, polo or partridge shooting; though each of these, in a different manner, requires the utmost speed. Great casting exhibits clearly this slow quality. Without wave or tremor the line is made to eat into the wind resistlessly. It must be very pleasant to be able to do it.[1]

FLIES

I ran into my friend H. R. in Piccadilly the other day, and the little incident which then occurred was typical of scores of similar encounters. After exchanging news as to what fishing we had been having lately, he went on to tell me of a remarkable fly he had invented. It had apparently

[1] The secret of putting out a line against the wind is to obtain a "narrow entry" as it goes forward. I would refer those interested to R. D. Hughes's book.

caught fish when there were none to be captured, and, in fact, was responsible for a whole series of minor miracles. I thanked him for his information, and at once took a taxi to Farlow's. A few minutes later I emerged from the shop with four of these precious flies in my pocket. Why had I thus expended 3*s*. 4*d*.? There is no answer to this question, except that I always react to such conversations in this manner. Let the psycho-analysts make what they can out of it, but I will further add that I had no faith in the fly, nor did I expect then or now that it will bring me any greater success than some hundreds of others which already clutter my fly boxes.

What is more, I trust I shall continue to purchase flies in which I have no confidence, for the buying of flies (or the tying of them, if one is so industrious) is one of the major amenities of Trout fishing, without which it would lose a large part of its charm. Since I have got so far, I may as well admit the whole truth that I do not believe in ANY of this fly worship. I am aware that in making this confession I am going against the accepted convictions of almost every writer and angler since the time of Dame Julyan Barnes, but still I must hold stubbornly to my heresy.

When I first took up dry-fly fishing, I did indeed follow the formulæ recommended. I carried with me a little net with which I dipped up the flies on the water, and then carefully matched them with the contents of my fly case. If there did not seem to be any satisfactory imitation of the real insect, I sought advice from friends or from the water-keeper. This appeared to work well, and the Trout came with sufficient avidity to my offerings. Later I became lazy; I forgot to bring out the net with me; and my mentors were often absent. Under these circumstances I would put on any fly in the box which happened to strike my fancy. It might be a medium olive, an iron blue, a B.W.O. or almost any other.

Did my random choice make any difference? The answer is: None that I could observe. Sometimes the fish would pay no attention to my fly; and then I changed it. I would select another fly very different from the first in form and colour. If the Trout was still reluctant another change was indicated, always on the same principle.

I am now wedded to this system, and, on occasions when a fish I particularly want has taken a good look at the fly and let it go by, I make the change at once and do not allow him to see it again. I have so often noticed that a Trout will evince considerable interest in a fly the first time it goes over; the second time he shows less interest; and so on, until finally he will not take an interest in any fly at all. If one changes the fly immediately, he does not get used to rejecting something which he has already in the first instance decided is not quite right.

Of course, there are fish which give the impression that they will take the fly one has on, and, if one continues casting, they do take it eventually. It seems rather foolish to say that one can read a Trout's thoughts and it is difficult to explain, but much can be deduced from the manner in which he approaches the fly and how he turns away from it. Four examples will perhaps demonstrate the theory. First: the Trout may come quickly to the fly and as quickly turn away. He has only taken a cursory glance; he is hungry, and he is busy feeding; the fly may be kept on, as the Trout is in such a hurry that he may make a mistake the next time or several casts later. Second: he comes slowly to the fly, looks at it, and then lets it float past him in a negative manner; the fly may be shown to him once more; he is not frightened and may decide he wants it next time. Third: he comes to the fly, looks at it, and backs down with it or follows it down, and then turns away slowly; the fly should be changed; for the fish, though not alarmed, has concluded he does not want that fly. Fourth: he comes to the fly slowly, looks at it carefully, and turns away quickly; he has realised that the fly is dangerous; it should be changed and the fish rested. There are many other indications which a Trout gives to show how he feels about a fly: the movement of his fins, the turn of his body, the closeness of his approach before refusing – such small hints can inform the angler quite clearly of the Trout's intentions.

If the fish is not visible, it is naturally more difficult to judge when to change the fly; but one may obtain some evidence of his mood by the character and frequency of the rise. If he is only rising periodically in slow water, it seems best to change the fly as soon as one is certain that it has passed over him twice. One might imagine that such a system would mean changing flies so continuously that there would be no time left for catching fish; but in practice I find the first or second fly often proves tempting enough if I have not ruined my chances through some error in performance. I think it is exactly in this last respect that the purist sometimes defeats other anglers; his performance is apt to be more accurate. Thus when, as has often happened, my basket is less replete at the end of the day than a companion's, I have usually put it down to faulty technique, and not to the use of the wrong fly *ab initio*.

Yet books upon books have been written about flies. Minute differences in tying and colour have been discussed apparently without end, and I cannot help feeling that even to question this flood of words lays me open to charges of the most abysmal obtuseness. It is not necessary for me to illustrate with many quotations, but perhaps a well-known one will suffice to show the immense importance placed on the correct fly in most Trout literature. In a famous book by one of the greatest of angling authors, occurs the following: " The difference between landrail and starling dyed to landrail colour is not very obvious . . . but I have known a trout reject the sedge fly winged with dyed starling and greedily accept an exactly similar pattern winged with landrail." A continuation of the discussion of this phenomenon, either by the same or another observer, appeared in a sporting periodical; and the explanation was offered that it was due to the landrail's feathers causing the fluorescence or transfiltration of some kind of light rays which are visible and noticeable to the fish but invisible to man, while the dyed starling feathers did not produce similar effects. This may, indeed, be the reason which correctly solves the mystery. It must, however, be noted that the celebrated ichthyologist, Professeur Roule, claims that the constituent organs of a fish's eye lack several mechanical essentials necessary to provide either a clear vision or one capable of accurate focusing. He insists that the retina, the membrane which contains the microscopic parts for the reception of light (together with the nerve cells employed to receive the sensation), possesses only an elementary structure; thus making it incapable of any delicacy, and giving the resultant vision only a confused and coarse perception.[1] It may indeed be that a Trout's eye is extremely sensitive to rays invisible to man, but from the above it would appear probable that it is unable to distinguish outlines with any exactitude. How often, indeed, must anglers have observed a Trout take a floating vegetable fragment into its mouth and immediately reject it. Obviously the Trout has mistaken the fragment for some kind of insect. Nor would these fragments have deceived any man with normal eyesight in such conditions. If the Trout can make such errors in regard to shape, it may be concluded, even without Professeur Roule's anatomical analysis, that, as far as exact outline is concerned, a Trout may try to be particular but has not the power necessary for fine discrimination.

I do not believe that Trout are able to distinguish minute

[1] See Appendix Note for complete quotation, p. 289.

differences between flies, and I could bring many arguments
to support my contention, but will offer only three. To
repeat again: my usual procedure for some time has been to
choose a fly haphazard from my fly box without troubling
to observe what is on the river. Usually, in very bright
weather, I take a small fly, and in dull weather a larger one.
It is but rarely under these circumstances that it has been
necessary to change this chance fly as long as it has remained
intact. Now I would claim that the odds are very great
that the flies thus selected do not correspond to the flies
actually on the water, and yet the Trout do take them with
reasonable frequency. So much for a general observation.
Here is a case from a different angle:

During my first season on the Test, I one day netted
a fly which did not seem to have any counterpart among
my artificials. I observed it very exactly with a view
to having some flies tied to represent it. The fly had pale
blue-grey wings and pale, dirty-yellow-coloured legs. It
was medium to small in size and I concluded a single o
hook would be about right for it. A few days later I went
to one of the leading tackle firms and gave specifications for
a dozen such flies to be made up for me. When they arrived
I was disappointed to find that they were not at all what I
had expected. The wings were a vivid royal blue with no
grey about them, while the hackles had been made a brilliant
yellow; in fact they reminded me of the parrots one sees in
zoos, and I promptly named the pattern the " McCormick
Macaw." I put the flies aside, as it occurred to me that
such exotic splendour was hardly suitable for England. It
was not till my last season on the Test that I came across
them again, and sentimentally added two or three of them
to the jumble in my fly box. Not long after, I went out in
the morning on the number one beat, and to my astonishment discovered an immense fish lying in the open stream.
As I already knew all the really big fish by sight, I realised

that this one must have dropped down from some higher water, and that I must catch him at once or, perhaps, never see him again. Hastily examining my point, I put out the fly I had on, a ooo dark olive. The fish looked at it, but let it go by. Such a fish was worthy of great pains, and I changed my fly at once to a large variant. This time he was distinctly interested, and turning sidewise as it went past him exposed a depth of flank which shook me. Since I had now tried him with a small and a large fly, it seemed that a medium size was next indicated; but the first one I put my fingers on was a " McCormick Macaw." I had a moment of misgiving, and then impulsively tied it on. When the fly came to the fish, he examined it closely and then took it so deliberately that I could not miss him. He turned out to be the biggest fish I have ever had on the Test, and if in good condition would have gone to three and a half pounds. This wise old Trout had rejected two standard imitations of living insects, and had then taken, confidently enough, an artificial representing no fly that has ever existed. Since then I have used up the rest of my " Macaws " and have found that when a single o hook was required they seemed to be as successful as any other of the regular patterns. Let me recommend them to my readers!

My last argument is also from another angle. The iron blue dun is a well-known Ephemerida, and its artificial imitation must often be found among the flies of most anglers. One would think, then, that the pattern would not vary much, and that if one were to go to any fly maker and ask for a ooo iron blue, quill body, one would obtain a similar fly in every shop; but such is very far from the case. To illustrate my point I submit herewith a little analysis in tabular form showing some of the differences between these flies as obtained from the stock of four leading tackle dealers in London:

	Carter	Farlow	Hardy Bros.	Ogden Smiths
Shape of wings	Long, broad, upright	Short, broad, rounded ends	Long, narrow, close together	Short, tapering, well spread apart
Colour of wings	Dark, neutral tint	Darkish, purple-blue	Medium, steely-blue	Pale, greenish-blue
Colour of hackles	Dark, neutral tint	Dark, burnt sienna	Dark, raw sienna	Medium, purplish-grey

I have taken above three characteristics, and, as can be seen, not one of the flies from the different shops agrees in any one particular with the fly from any other shop. Yet I have no doubt that all these flies secure their quota of fish annually when the iron blue dun is on the water. I should think, however, that so many distinct varieties of iron blues must prove quite bewildering to the Trout.

I have spoken of the haphazard method of selecting a fly, and have said that I limited the pure luck of the draw to the extent that I do consider the size of the fly. Thus I usually begin on a bright warm day with a small fly, while if the weather is dull I prefer a larger one, and at night I generally make use of one of the sedges. I once, however, experimented on the Test with a fly which has proved successful in other lands. This fly was called a " Hair Basser," and was made of buck-tail hairs dyed to various colours and arranged in a peculiarly flattened manner on a No. 6 hook. With this fly I had obtained some fine Rainbows and Brown Trout in Chile, and it had also proved deadly for Bass in America. The fly had the splendid quality of swimming beautifully in fast water. On the occasion in question the weather was bright and hot, and I found myself at a slow and deepish part of the river in which I could see many fine fish lying still and far down. Not one of them was making the slightest attempt to feed, and the thought occurred to me to stir them up a bit with a Hair Basser. I put it on and, wetting it well so that it would sink, cast it far up and across so that I could retrieve it within range of several fish. My intention was to let the fly submerge deeply enough to pass the fish at about their level. As far as stirring up the Trout was concerned the result went far beyond my most sanguine expectations. When the fly hit the water, all the Trout turned instantly and rushed downstream past me with the speed of greyhounds. I have related this little incident to explain why, since that day, though my method of selecting flies may appear unusual my choice still remains rather more conservative than revolutionary.

27

WHAT IS A GAME FISH?

THE question as to what constitutes a " game fish "
has been debated for generations by anglers, and
there is no doubt that many definitions have been proposed
with due gravity after proper argument and exposition.
But new ideas permit a new approach to the question, and
in recent times there have been sufficient developments in
the art of angling to warrant further controversy.

To look back at what has been decided hitherto on the
subject: the *Oxford Dictionary* says: " Game fish: a fish
which affords sport to the angler in its capture." Holder
says that typical game fish are " edible and hard fighters on
rod and reel." A famous editor of a sporting magazine
says, " Many anglers and old writers used to include
Salmon, Trout, Grayling and Pike as game fish . . . but,
I think, to-day in this country [England] are inclined to
reserve the term ' game fish ' for Salmon and Trout only."
My friend Pelham says, " A game fish is a fish that is fun
to catch." There is also another definition that a game fish
must have an adipose fin – why, I don't know.

From the above dicta, which I have obtained without
too much labour, six concepts emerge: (1) sport to the
angler, (2) edibility, (3) hard fighters on rod and reel, (4)
only Salmon and Trout are game fish, (5) fun to catch, (6)
the adipose fin complex. I have heard a seventh, that a
game fish must be a predatory fish; and presumably many
other qualities have been proposed as necessary attributes
of game fish.

Without trying to split hairs, it is obvious that most of these definitions fail because they either restrict insufficiently or too much. To take the first, for instance, " A game fish is one which affords sport to the angler in its capture." One may well ask what is " sport," and then one may further ask how much sport the fish must afford to qualify as a game fish.

Almost any fish I can think of would afford me " sport " in varying degree. The same observation would negative the quality of being " hard fighters " or Pelham's " fun " concept. The necessity of being edible cannot be a test or Tarpon would fail at once, and the Sailfish, being neither Trout nor Salmon and yet an undoubted game fish, rules out the strict interpretation of English anglers. The adipose fin requirement would, strangely enough, admit the Dorado and Tigerfish but would disqualify Mako Sharks. It is a fact, however, that many of the great game fish do possess either an adipose fin or a small second dorsal fin in its place. Finally, the Bonefish disposes of the predatory essentiality unless it is considered predatory to eat hermit crabs and molluscs. In this connection it must be noted that there are comparatively few fish in the world which are not predatory within the strict interpretation that the eating of any living creature makes the fish predatory. Carp, for instance, eat worms readily enough. I have thus in one paragraph disposed of the seven different qualifications which I have gleaned for defining what is a game fish, and it is probable that no short definition can be evolved, nor one which does not also require standards of comparison.

In a general way one might say that a game fish differs from a non-game fish as a thoroughbred horse differs from one that is not thoroughbred. But the unrelated shapes of various game fish make a selection by simple observation impossible until the " rod test " has been applied.[1] I would now offer a new definition: A game fish is one which

---

[1] See Appendix Note, p. 300.

by swimming or artifice defends itself adequately, when hooked, against the skill of an angler using appropriate tackle. I have introduced several new elements into the definition, but whether these additions are of any value is problematical. I will take the additions in order.

Swimming. Fish which rely for defence solely on swimming are, for instance, the giant Tuna and the Wahoo. There is no artifice about these fish in their defence. The Tuna goes down and uses its weight, plugging away and trying to get rid of the hook by sheer strength. The Wahoo tries speed instead, and essays, sometimes with success, to defeat the angler by its sheer mobility. A fish which has no artifice except swimming in its defence enters with more difficulty into the class of game fish, and its swimming must be exceptional for it to qualify.

Artifice comes into the fight of most game fish. Whether of intention or not, the circular run of the Bonefish is admirably adapted for cutting the line of the angler on coral projections. The Black Bass entangles the line round stumps and branches, the Trout makes its flight through weeds, the Tarpon jumps and appears to try to fall on the line, the Dorado shakes its head to get rid of the hook, and the Salmon goes over rocks and into fast waters to circumvent the angler. Most disconcerting of all artifices, the Mako bites off the line.

The *adequacy of the defence* of the above-mentioned fish is hardly in question. Since all anglers who have tried for them must frequently have been defeated by their various tactics, it is difficult to judge the adequacy of defence of fish except by using standards of comparison. These standards will follow later in this chapter.

Skill. Obviously if the angler requires little or no skill to circumvent the fish's defences, then the defences are not adequate. For instance, a Perch has so little strength for its size and so little artifice in its fight that even on very light

tackle its resistance is too feeble to necessitate the employment of much skill by the angler. Be it noted I am not
seeking to minimise the joys of Perch fishing, which provided me with my first ambition to become an angler;
indeed, I am eternally grateful to Perch for that initial fillip
which added so much to the amenity of my life. One may
say superficially that skill is required in the capture of a
particular kind of fish when it is an unlikely eventuality
than an angler can capture the fish without having had
similar previous experience or coaching from a person who
has already had such experience.

When hooked. I have included this qualification chiefly
because there are many fish which, before they are hooked,
require the employment of considerable skill by the angler,
owing to the difficulty of inducing them to take the lure;
and yet these fish cannot be considered game fish because
of their lack of strength and guile on the hook. I would
mention in this connection from my own experience the
Chub, which is quite a wary fish to tempt with a dry-fly
and yet has no adequate subsequent defence considering
its size. Besides this fish, there are a great number of
coarse fish which similarly afford sport before the hooking,
but for which I have not yet had the pleasure of fishing —
for instance, the Roach, of which it has been written in an
authoritative book, " Several decades of intensive angling
and of ever-increasing persecution have evolved a strain of
Roach so shy, so cautious and such crafty feeders, that one
must devote time and thought, without stint, to achieve
anything like consistent success."[1] Into this category of
fish which are on occasion difficult to hook enter, as well,
Pike or Muskellunge, and other biggish predatory fish.
Their fight is, however, incommensurate with their size
and the strength they would appear to possess.

Fair tackle means, for an angler, rod, hook and line.

[1] Lonsdale Library.

There are many fish which afford sport and require skill to secure them by spearing, graining or shooting with bow and arrow. I can recall several amusing days spent in Florida graining Gar Pike. It is difficult and exciting, but it is not angling. The hook, line and rod are the only correct weapons for an angler, and these must be, according to the different methods employed for putting the lure to the fish, of a just and reasonable power to give the fish a fair chance to escape.

There are some obvious handicaps which the sportsman can impose voluntarily on himself to equalise what will otherwise prove a foregone conclusion against his gallant adversary, the fish. He may employ a very light (1) rod, (2) line, (3) cast, or (4) he may eschew the multiple hook. To take the last of these first: obviously the angler cannot, to handicap himself, use a hook which is wanting in strength, as there is no satisfactory manner of calculating the strength of a hook. It would be too exasperating to be considered equitable that the hook should not have sufficient strength to hold a fish once it has taken hold. The angler can, however, use a single hook instead of a double or treble one, and the self-abnegation of a single hook offers the game fish an opportunity, perhaps, to twist itself out of the death hold which a double or treble hook frequently exerts. The single hook is obviously more sporting and humane. The other handicaps which an angler can employ are dictated and limited by the various exigencies of the technique required to obtain the fish. Thus where casting is necessary the rod must be of sufficient strength to put out the fly or bait. In such conditions the angler may use a light line with a strong cast, or a heavy line with a light cast. Where no casting is required, the handicap may be either a light rod, line, or cast. The light rod offers a severe handicap to the angler who is fishing (without casting) for big fish, as it will frequently prevent his sinking the hook with sufficient force to hold the fish. The light line is also a good handicap against strong fish. In my opinion, however, it is the least satisfactory handicap, as a light line can fray or part through no fault of the angler, and without his being able to observe that it has not its proper minimum strength. The light cast is the best handicap an angler can impose on himself where the quarry has no teeth to sever the cast. It is an ideal handicap in such conditions, for a cast can easily be scrutinised and, if there is a defect, it can be at once replaced by a new one.

To sum up in regard to fair tackle: (1) the triple hook should rarely, if ever, be used; (2) the rod, where casting does not require a mandatory power, should be commensurate with the expected quarry; (3) the line should be adequate for the purpose in view; (4) the cast (trace) should be only just adequate in the case of toothless fish, but in other cases must be able to resist against all probable contingencies. I have reviewed the various conditions which govern the use of " fair " tackle, and which in the same connotation cover to a certain extent the term " appropriate " tackle. It is difficult for us humans to limit ourselves to a just appreciation of the fact that unless we give the fish a chance we shall destroy what we love the best. To show how difficult it is for man to avoid falling into error, I would remark that each year the tackle dealers, urged on by their customers, are bringing out new and more complicated mechanical devices to make the taking of fish simpler, whereas it is the tackle which should be simpler. Selkirk caught his 2,176 lb. fish with his thumb. Recently I have read of a new kind of cast made of tungsten so fine that the fish cannot see it, so strong that the fish cannot break it. I have myself considered, for a moment, the possibility of making a hook out of some not-yet-invented, resilient, unbreakable glass which would be invisible to the Trout. On second thoughts one asks: To what purpose these modern miracles? Fishing would be too easy, and with facility would come the end of fishing skill and pleasure. We should eventually, with such advantages, discover that netting fish was more interesting and more difficult.

I have digressed a little from my argument in this exposition of different methods of handicapping the angler so as to obtain " fair " tackle. It is obvious that if the tackle is not " fair," then it is impossible for a fish to prove its game qualities, and all fish would thus be relegated to the Perch class. For instance, it would not be impossible to catch giant Tuna on an immensely strong trace attached to the steam winch of a trawler, so that the Tuna could simply be hoisted on board without being able to offer any resistance or display its gameness.

I have now explained and amplified my definition, except for a complete covering of the word " appropriate " when applied to tackle. It is evident that " appropriate," being a word of indefinite significance, cannot be given an exact meaning without examples to illustrate it. For this reason I have made a list of great game fish of the world which will serve as standards of comparison in judging other fish. It must be understood that in making this list I have attempted to select the highest type of game fish in its respective field, having regard to the size and weight of the fish, and the conditions under which it is to be captured. It is obvious that as this is a list of some of the greatest of all game fish, there will be few other varieties which can exactly equal them from a sporting point of view. To the extent, however, to which other fish do approximate those I have selected, to that extent do such fish attain the designation of *game fish*. I shall not attempt to describe the *appropriate* tackle employed for the capture of these standard game fish, as such a description enters more properly into the catalogues of tackle dealers, but to illustrate my point I will give one example. Presuming that a rod with an eight-ounce top, a line of eighteen-thread Cuttyhunk, a No. 4–0 Vom Hofe reel, a piano-wire trace of six-foot length and a single No. 12–0 hook is considered *appropriate tackle* for a hundred-pound Tarpon, then other fish of such a weight should be properly fished for with such tackle. If one were, however, to try for a hundred-pound Nile Perch, for instance, with this tackle, one would find that the Nile Perch would not offer anything approaching the Tarpon's resistance, and for that reason Nile Perch could not be considered a game fish.

Passing to the standard game fish list, I will say that the occasion for the making of this list occurred in the following manner: I had the opportunity to make a world tour some years ago, and, as if this were not interesting enough, I decided to combine with my travels the pursuit of whatever famous game fish I might find *en route*. I had already done some fishing, and had served my apprenticeship in this most fascinating of sports, but in order to prepare for what might be encountered I had to lay in a stock of rods and tackle sufficient in quantity and variety for the purpose in hand. Before doing so, however, I realised that it would be necessary to make a preliminary list of my proposed victims, so as to be able to judge what paraphernalia was required. In ten minutes my roster was ready, and on numbering it I found there were twenty-one varieties, as follows:

1. Barracuda
2. Black Bass
3. Black Marlin
4. Bonefish
5. Broadbill Swordfish
6. Channel Bass
7. Dorado
8. Grayling
9. Kingfish
10. Mahseer
11. Mako Shark
12. Muskellunge
13. Nile Perch
14. Sailfish
15. Salmon
16. Striped Bass
17. Striped Marlin
18. Tarpon
19. Trout
20. Tuna
21. Wahoo

I can well imagine that there will be few readers of these lines who will not be considerably indignant at my failure to include his own favourite fish, nor do I expect to find anyone to agree with the list; as a matter of fact, I no longer agree with it myself!

When I began my outfitting, it seemed highly probable that I would become a victim of the sports salesman who was to help to supply me, but I did not make many mistakes, and indeed have scarcely had to alter or renew in subsequent years the purchases I made at that time. When everything had been got together, I packed the gear in three tackle boxes: one for reels alone; one for hooks, spoons, spare lines and such items; and one for small fish necessities and general purposes. I also had two rod cases made for me which were to contain sixteen rods of various potentialities. In reviewing my list of fish, I found I had already obtained numbers 1, 2, 6, 9, 12, 15, 16, 18 and 19, so that there only remained twelve more to try for, and I was expecting to take these all in during my itinerary.

My start was from New York, and I went south after one of the most unusual fish, Dorado. This splendid fish I obtained in Paraguay. Then I went west to New Zealand and captured two more: Mako Shark and Striped Marlin. Continuing ever west, I reached India, and there occurred my first disappointment. I had intended to try for Mahseer, but when I got to India I found I had made a serious miscalculation. It was the month of July, and the heat was appalling. Not only this, but India was seething with half-prepared insurrection. Never since the Mutiny had there been such an offensive spirit abroad in that vast Empire. In the streets great mobs in Gandhi caps hindered and made disagreeable the progress of visitors. As a result, after some hesitation, I decided I must postpone Mahseer. I was influenced strongly in my decision by a maxim which I

have laid down privately for myself — that unless a pleasure
can be had pleasurably it is not a pleasure.

Next I was intending to try for Nile Perch in Africa,
crossing from Bombay to Mombasa. Again I realised that
the weather was far from favourable, and that it would mean
fishing under the equator in midsummer. Furthermore,
the ship on which I had booked a passage had been cancelled and a very small ship substituted. Finally the trip
itself involved ten days' bucking into the monsoon. Therefore, acting again on my maxim, I postponed Nile Perch
and continued on to England, where I caught Grayling and
then, returning to America, I had completed the tour with
only four new fish added to my list. Many interests cropped
up to prevent the accomplishment of my plans, but the
following spring I obtained Sailfish, Bonefish and Wahoo.
Then I took a trip to Africa and at last captured Nile Perch,
which were not worth while, and that is as far as I have got.

Of the remaining four not accounted for, Black Marlin
I had on for forty-five minutes in New Zealand; Broadbill
Swordfish requires infinite patience and fortune to obtain
either at Block Island or Catalina; Mahseer I think has an
exaggerated reputation; and giant Tuna I can get off the
English coast when I have summoned up enough energy.
I have caught many other varieties of fish beside these
seventeen, and, having well scanned my list, would revise it
and remove some of the candidates. My opinion is based
on my own experience with the fish mentioned, and other
anglers have, no doubt, had far greater opportunities to
decide on the merits of particular fish and to have formed a
more exact judgment than I have, but for the purpose of
making a new list I will now go through the old one in
detail.

1. BARRACUDA. Comes off the list. The Barracuda is a
    ferocious brute, and is more feared by naked natives,
    I am told, than any other fish, but it has not got a

fighting heart, and gives up much too soon considering its size, speed and build.

2. Black Bass. Retained on the list.

3. Black Marlin. Also retained.

4. Bonefish. O.K.

5. Broadbill Swordfish I have not fished for, but it must be retained. White-Wickham tells me that Broadbill swim even faster than the Marlins and their fight is spectacular.

6. Channel Bass. A good, honest fish, but not good enough for the list.

7. Dorado. O.K.

8. Grayling. Despised and treated as vermin in many Trout rivers, Grayling is difficult to hook, takes a fly with great delicacy and makes an excellent fight. It swims faster than a Trout, but does not jump. It should remain on the list.

9. Kingfish. An excellent fighter, very strong, but unfortunately does not jump. The Kingfish is one of a type of sea fish to which I shall refer later.

10. Mahseer. I have never fished for, but have caught a relative, *Barbus radclyffei*, in Africa. Unless Mahseer is a very much greater fighter than its African cousin, it does not deserve a place on the list. This fish has probably obtained its reputation owing to its size and not to its qualities regardless of size. It does not jump on the hook.

11. Mako Shark. O.K.

12. Muskellunge. To the annoyance of its many admirers, I must remove this fish from the list. It suffers from the same lack of qualities as the Barracuda, which it greatly resembles. With Muskellunge are included its brothers Great Northern Pike and European Pike.

13. Nile Perch. Certainly not worth a place. This fish has gained a false reputation on account of its size.

14. Sailfish. O.K.

15. Salmon. O.K. I would remark that I have not distinguished between the different kinds of Salmon and include with them Salmon Trout. All varieties are excellent.

16. Striped Bass. A fine fish with a good heart, but not quite good enough.

17. Striped Marlin. O.K.

18. Tarpon. O.K.

19. Trout. O.K. Again I have not distinguished between different varieties of Trout and Char, they are all good.

20. Tuna. O.K. When I put this fish on the list I had the giant Tuna in mind, but all Tuna are very strong plugging fish. They do not jump on the hook.

21. Wahoo. An extremely powerful fish, and one of the world's fastest. Well worth its place on the list, though it does not jump.

Since my list has now lost numbers 1, 6, 12, 13 and 16, the question arises, have I got any fish to add to it? Yes, decidedly. I would add Tigerfish, one of the world's greatest. Huchen is of the Trout family, and so it does not get a separate place. Are there any others? Yes, of course, there are hundreds of different varieties of fish which " pull their weight " and will give the angler all the sport he could possibly want. There is, for instance, a vast number of different sea fish which resemble, from an angling angle, the Kingfish and small Tuna. To give but a few: Spanish Mackerel and the rest of the Mackerels, Spanish Pompano, Yellow Tail, Dolphin (*Coryphæna*), Amber Jack, Bonito, Albacore, Bayad, Dorăq, and many others. Their distinguishing feature is that they do not jump on the hook,

THE PIKE IS A FEROCIOUS BRUTE, BUT LACKS A FIGHTING HEART

or only rarely. It is curious, however, that some of them are great jumpers without the hook, such as Kingfish and small Tuna. Besides these sea fish there is the class of fish of the family Black Bass. There is also the Tucunaré and a great number of fish of the Dorado tribe which are worth their place on light tackle.

In addition to these fish, which obviously cannot be kept out if we leave the door only slightly ajar, there are hundreds of fish in remote regions of the earth which only require a little publicity to be at once recognised as deserving all praise. I read recently, for instance, of a medium-sized fish in Africa rejoicing in the native name of " Bellie "[1] which it was claimed fights better than a Tigerfish. (I don't believe this, by the way.) There is also a small fish in Borneo which takes a fly and fights like Black Bass – it does not appear to have a discoverable name. Then there are numbers of game Sharks such as the Mackerel Shark, not to speak of the Thresher Shark. Finally, if one wishes to go into the cetaceans, there are the Dolphins and Porpoises. I was told, in this connection, by my guide in New Zealand, that it is impossible to catch the large Porpoises, as they are too strong and run too fast and straight. There seems, however, to be no limit to man's angling audacity. Recently even Whales have been captured with rod and line. These, I am informed, were specimens of the Dwarf Cachalot (*Kogia breviceps*); but one may soon expect to find large Whales brought in with Trout tackle if modern angling technique continues at its present pace.

With such an immense variety – say, sixteen thousand – of well-known and little-known fish to try for, it is obvious that a young man could go about the world fishing continuously for different kinds of fish, and at the end of his life there would still remain many which he would have had

---

[1] Bellie (*Heterotis niloticus*), is, curiously enough, related fairly closely to the Arapaima of the Amazon. They are both of the same family, Osteoglossidæ, and do quite distinctly resemble each other in general form.

to leave unmolested. No man could sort out the best sporting fish from such a vast array, but I will now whittle down the list already offered to the bare essentials. In the original list it will be noticed that the Swordfish occupied three places. They were thus shown in view of the different kinds of fights which the three varieties provide, but if Trout and Salmon have been pared down, we must do the same for Swordfish. We must eliminate Kingfish, and let Wahoo represent this great family of sea fighters which do not jump. If it were not for the giant Tuna I would eliminate Tuna as well, but will keep them in out of deference for the big ones. Our list now reads:

1.	Black Bass	8.	Swordfish
2.	Bonefish	9.	Tarpon
3.	Dorado	10.	Tigerfish
4.	Grayling	11.	Trout
5.	Mako Shark	12.	Tuna
6.	Sailfish	13.	Wahoo
7.	Salmon		

We have got down to a round baker's dozen, consisting of what I call the standard representative game fish of the world, and I am not going to try to compress or enlarge it, as I believe that this list covers well, for size and variety of combat, all the best types of fish the world over.

I have spoken, so far, of game fish, and must appear to have been very severe in condemning some fish which provide fine sport for a great number of anglers. It is, however, far from my intention to give the impression that I consider non-game fish to be not worth the catching. On the contrary, I disapprove very much of the ennobling of certain species, when others, not quite so famous, are relegated to an apparently non-existent status. The joy of fishing is what each angler gets out of it and, besides, to a great extent, the man-on-the-water can, if he so chooses, elevate his own particular quarry to a very high position in the fish world by reducing the holding qualities of his tackle. For, indeed, even the feeblest fish will prove a formidable opponent on 6x gut. Then, too, there are hardships and difficulties endured by the modest angler for lesser fish which do sublimate very much his recreation. It is to be regretted, but it adds much to the glory of his sportsmanship, that the coarse fish angler finds too often, alas, in his barren waters a dearth of fish which would quite defeat or send off in a huff the arrogant pursuers of more renowned species. My admiration is unbounded for those numerous fishermen one sees lining the banks of so many unpropitious rivers. With long rods and all the paraphernalia of their chosen pastime, they remain motionless for hours until at last night brings to an end a day which may have been completely void of success. And yet they have enjoyed their experience. Perhaps a friend has pulled in some minuscule fish which has confirmed their opinion that there is actually something to be caught in the river. To them, too, arrives at last a day when fortune and skill have vindicated their much-studied wiles, and they too can boast a full creel which they will remember all their lives.

I am convinced that in its modern development coarse fishing embraces all the highest elements of game fish angling, all the finesse, all the science and all the delights. Some day, I hope not distant, it is my earnest desire to be instructed in its varied arts and have the good fortune to enjoy its many pleasures.

To return to the subject of game fish. With few exceptions, I have had the opportunity to judge the sporting qualities of most of the famous fish. It would be surprising, therefore, if in the course of my angling I had not been asked the same question which would be bromidic did it not occur in varied circumstances.

The water-keeper on the Test, the Scotch ghillie, and my

guides in different seas have each enquired whether there was any angling the world over to compare with what they respectively had to offer. I must say that my response has ever been the same, and, out of the sincerity of my heart, I have always confessed that theirs was the only fishing of any worth. Such was my honest opinion at the time, but then I am easily carried away by the enthusiasms of the moment.

It is only on reflecting over a longish interval that one can estimate values with considered calm. I would further assert that to choose out the greatest game fish in the world entails first a decision as to what are the qualities one seeks in game fishing. To my mind its seems that three kinds of emotion are offered by the sport to its devotees, and these may be concerned with physical force, with external factors, or with intellectual considerations. It also appears obvious that no single fish can provide all the delights which one might envisage in this the most fascinating of pastimes.

If an angler, wishing to enjoy the varied amenities of the angle, is in search of primitive physical thrills, I recommend that he try a combat with Striped Marlin. There is no fish, I believe, which can provide, in its strength, speed, resource and glorious heroism, the wonderful fight of a Striped Marlin of New Zealand.

If the angler seeks a fish which, considering its size and numbers, is more difficult to hook, more difficult to land and more difficult to come by, then let him pursue Tigerfish in Africa, where the external hardships of environment provide such handicaps and where the fish can be so fierce and impossibly exasperating to hook that success requires not only good fortune but also victory against odds unrelated to fishing.

If, however, the angler desires less robust sport, and prefers the pleasures of intellectual and technical triumphs, then let him be satisfied with essaying the capture of sophisticated Trout in the chalk streams of England.

APPENDIX

Note to Chapter 2, p. 22

I have not been able to identify this fish exactly. The commonest variety is called locally Bagre Amarillo, which would signify that it is of a yellow colour, but these appeared purple to me. If they were this fish, then the name is *Arius spixii.*

It must appear strange that such a large and important fish cannot be identified. The fact is that there are possibly twenty varieties of Siluroidea in this river, and no exhaustive work on the subject of Paraná fishes is available in English, nor does any catalogue appear to have been undertaken in Spanish. In this connection G. S. Myers, Curator of Zoology at Stanford University, California, has written me : " Among the vertebrates, fishes are by far the least known, and in fishes, the least known area outside the deep seas is South America."

Note to Chapter 2, p. 31

I am inclined to think that this small fish was the most peculiar of all those we caught. Unfortunately, I did not examine it carefully enough before releasing it in surprise at its audacity. I did not fail, however, to weigh it on a small spring-balance, nor to notice the immensely long teeth which seemed out of all proportion to the fish. I also perceived that its jaws were opened to such an extensive gape that they were almost at right angles to its body ; an arrangement which was, of course, necessary in order to seize my spoon. I can remember wondering at the time how the fish could shut its mouth with such teeth, but now that I have identified it as a Needletooth (*Rhaphiodon vulpinus*), the matter is explained. This fish is remarkable for two excessively long teeth in the lower jaw which, unlike the big teeth of other creatures, are so placed that they cannot be sheathed either outside the gums or the lips. It would thus seem that the fish cannot close its mouth without puncturing the palate of the upper jaw. *R. vulpinus* has solved this apparently insoluble problem very simply by letting the two teeth pass through funnels in the bones and flesh of the snout from which the points emerge on the far side in two short, but effective, spears.

Though the snout-bones of crocodiles are also provided with foramina into which fit the canines of the lower jaw, this original and fantastic arrangement of *R. vulpinus* has no counterpart in all nature except for a similar and even more extreme development which is found in its fierce cousin the Pirá Andirá of the Amazon system.

R. vulpinus, like the Dorado of South America and the Tigerfish of Africa, belongs to the Characinidæ family. This same dispersion is discovered in the family Cichlidæ, to which the Ngege of Africa and many fish of the Amazon basin belong. From these facts, among others, scientists have concluded that at some remote period Africa and South America were connected together.

Note to Chapter 6, p. 66

Strong-swimming pelagic fish, such as the Swordfish, travel great distances and are sometimes found far removed from their usual range. Thus, during the 1935–6 season a Blue Marlin weighing 706 pounds was obtained at Bimini, and a lady angler, Mrs. Sanborn, also captured one of 510 pounds in the same waters, though these fish should normally be found much further south.

One would think that such distinctive fish could be easily classified, and that the Swordfish of New Zealand and Florida would be the same species, as indeed they appear to be on cursory inspection ; but this is far from being so. The Black Marlin alone has been separated into sixteen varieties by one noted authority. Dr. Philips, of the American Museum of Natural History in New York, has, however, been content, pending further research, to distinguish three main species : *Makaira albida*, the White Marlin which is common in Florida ; *M. mazara*, the Black Marlin of New Zealand, and three other sub-species including the Blue Marlin (*M. ampla*) of Bimini ; and, thirdly, *M. mitsukurii*, the Striped Marlin of New Zealand.

When one considers the record Swordfish of Zane Grey, weighing more than a thousand pounds, which he caught in Tahitian waters, and the Striped Marlin taken off Chile and Peru by Stokes and Tuker, which do not seem to correspond to any of the usual species, one begins to realise that it will be years before these various species can be exactly determined. The difficulty consists in the large size of the fish and the obstacles in transporting them to some place where they can be properly compared.

In Florida, besides Marlin, anglers are securing giant Tuna up to 700 pounds, though at the time of my last stay there, such big fish were quite unknown. In these waters there are also great numbers of Sharks of many varieties. The Mako is probably rare, and is replaced by a closely related species *Isurus oxyrhynchus*. Fishing for these Sharks has not yet been widely exploited.

In London recently, while my friend Howard and I were trying to decide how much sherry would be good for us, he described to me the difficulties of catching Tuna in these Shark-infested waters. It appears that the moment the Tuna is dead the Sharks attack. He said that a friend, having caught a Tuna estimated to weigh 650 pounds, could not lift it into the launch. It was at that instant that the Sharks arrived. Swimming up at speed so as to use their momentum, they ploughed great furrows along the Tuna's body with their teeth, the flesh rolling up in coils as if it were being planed away by some huge machine tool. In twenty minutes, he was told, nothing remained of the Tuna except the head and backbone.

There is an interesting new development in technique which may solve this Shark plague. My friend John Wentworth tells me that experiments are now being made with a firecracker called " cherry bomb " which can be detonated under water by a delayed waterproof fuse. It is said that the resultant explosion will drive away the Sharks when the Tuna is ready for the gaff, and thus permit landing the Tuna intact.

Note to Chapter 7, p. 75

The Bonefish (*Albula vulpes*) has proved a mysterious fish for other reasons besides the difficulties once experienced in trying to capture it. It has been confused since early days with the Ladyfish (*Elops saurus*), and the two fish have constantly interchanged a number of names which are applied in common to both of them to such an extent that, unless their scientific name is also given, nobody quite understands to which of them the name " Bonefish " refers.

Another curious fact is the statement of Dr. Henshall in one of his books, that *Albula vulpes* jumps so much during its fight that it is half the time out of water. Yet none of our fish showed its nose once until it was in the net. Furthermore, a friend of mine told me recently that he had caught at least fifty Bonefish in his life and that he does not remember ever seeing one jump.

Note to Chapter 12, p. 117

There are five varieties of Tigerfish : *H. forskalii*, *H. lineatus*, *H. brevis*, *H. vittiger* and *H. goliath*. Those I caught on the Zambesi were *lineatus*, and in Lake Albert they were *forskalii*. I am not sure about the others, but they were not *H. goliath*. This last variety is described by Boulenger as growing to six feet in length. It resembles the others in form but is considerably larger. Recently one was reported to have been captured by Dr. H. Gillet in the River Kasai, Belgian Congo, which weighed 83¾ pounds and measured 77¾ ins. in length. Dr. Gillet continues in his account of the capture (which was published in the *Fishing Gazette*) as follows : " . . . But, although very large, it is not an exceptional specimen. I have hooked – and lost – a much larger Tigerfish in Matshi Lake (on Loange River) two years ago. It raced on the surface and leaped three times high in the air, giving me the opportunity to appreciate its size. I believe its weight to be at least a hundred and fifty pounds."

All I can say to this is that if *H. goliath* approximates in fighting qualities and hooking difficulties to its smaller relatives, then it must be by all odds the fiercest, most dangerous and most thrilling fresh-water fish to catch in the world ; nor indeed do I believe that in any angling respect it will yield to any salt-water fish.

Note to Chapter 15, p. 156

There is but one strictly fresh-water Shark in the world. It is called *Carcharinus nicaraguensis* and is only found in Lake Nicaragua and in the Rio San Juan which connects that lake with the Atlantic. This species, known locally as " Tigrone," has never been observed in salt water. It attains a length of about seven feet and is undoubtedly a survivor of an ancestral Shark which was left behind, probably in Eocene times, when the lake was cut off from the sea by an uplifting of intervening land.

There are Sharks which frequent the brackish waters of the Ganges and similar Eastern rivers, but they can scarcely be considered fresh-water Sharks.

Note to Chapter 23, p. 228

C. H. Dunford's 873-pound Mako, caught at Matangi, New Zealand, on September 9th, 1926, was reported to *The Field* by W. W. Dunsterville. There appears to be some question about the record, however, as F. E. Thornton, editor of the *New Zealand Fishing and Shooting Gazette*, has never heard of it, though for the last two years the staff of the magazine has been occupied in compiling an authoritative list of the angling records of that country. The world record generally recognised is the Mako of White-Wickham, weighing 798 pounds, which was caught at Bay of Islands on January 23rd, 1931.

Recently a Shark, described as a Mako, was caught by Norton Conway in the Gulf Stream near Bimini which weighed, by a strange coincidence, exactly the same as White-Wickham's fish. It is possible that this was the other species of Mako (*Isurus oxyrhynchus*) and not the true Mako, *I. glaucus* ; from photographs, however, it would appear that a great record has been precisely duplicated a hemisphere away.

There is actually but little difference between the two species of Mako, the main variation having to do with the position of the dorsal fins, which in *I. oxyrhynchus* are set rather more forward than in *I. glaucus*. From illustrations it would also appear that *I. oxyrhynchus* possesses larger fins. If this is the case, it is probably a less active fish than *I. glaucus*; though it is possible that, when opportunities are had for the comparison of actual specimens, it will be found that the two fish are identical.

Note to Chapter 26, p. 274

The full quotation from Professeur Louis Roule's *La Vie des Rivières* follows :

" . . . Tout pêcheur en est persuadé ; et, souvent, les techniques de la pêche basent leurs méthodes sur cette capacité visuelle qu'elles accordent volontiers aux poissons.

" Pourtant, à l'étude, on doit convenir que la structure de cet œil ne s'accorde point avec celle qu'il devrait avoir pour posséder une vision aussi complète. Son état est de plusiers degrés inférieur au nôtre, comme à celui de la plupart des animaux terrestres. Son cristallin sphérique, rond comme une boule transparente, ne peut jouer le rôle d'une lentille projetant avec netteté les images des objets extérieurs. Sa rétine, membrane principale où se trouvent les pièces microscopiques de la réception lumineuse, avec les cellules nerveuses chargées de percevoir la sensation, n'a qu'une structure élémentaire, la rendant incapable de toute délicatesse, et ne lui procurant qu'une perception confuse, grossière. La constitution de l'organe entier peut se comparer à celle des appareils photographiques d'autrefois, où, par rapport à ceux de maintenant, l'objectif et la plaque donnaient des images diffuses et brouillées. De même l'œil du poisson, bien que possédant le nécessaire, n'a pas l'agencement, ni le perfectionnement, qui lui permettraient de tirer bon parti des pièces lui appartenant."

Note to Chapter 27, p. 280

It is possible to judge somewhat of the sporting qualities of fish from the conformation of their fins, though even this gives no sure indication.

All the greatest game fish have lunate or forked caudal fins except Dorado, Black Bass, Salmon, and Trout. Of these four, the tails of the first two are of the emarginate type which is dynamically the next best development. The caudals of Salmon and Trout are truncate or subtruncate ; but the fine streamline of their bodies compensates them, to a certain extent, for this serious defect in functional design.

Though fish which do not have tails at any rate tending towards a fork are sometimes capable of negative defence, they generally cannot swim fast, even for a short distance, and thus fail to show sport to the angler despite adjuvant conditions.

The same considerations apply in respect to the size of fins. If a fish has a large dorsal fin, for example, its speed is compromised unless it has methods of overcoming this handicap. Thus the Sailfish folds its huge dorsal into a slot for rapid swimming, and the humble Perch collapses the spines of that fin when it is in a hurry. One may say that the larger the fins the slower the fish. It is particularly noticeable that the fins of the Wahoo, perhaps the fastest of all fish for its size, are reduced to minimum proportions.

I would add that the large caudal and pectoral fins of some Sharks cause them to be slow swimmers and easy victims for a man with a dagger, if the distraction of pursuing them in that manner appeals to anyone.

INDEX OF NAMES OF FISH

SUPPLEMENTARY INDEX